LEGAL ASPECTS OF SPORTS MEDICINE

– SECOND EDITION –

by
David L. Herbert, J.D.
Partner, Herbert, Benson & Scott, Attorneys at Law
The Belpar Law Center • Canton, Ohio 44718-3629
Co-Editor, *The Sports Medicine Standards and Malpractice Reporter*
Co-Editor, *The Exercise Standards and Malpractice Reporter*

ISBN # 0-9441-83-18-2
Library of Congress Catalog Card Number # 94-92196

Published by:
PRC Publishing, Inc.
4418 Belden Village St., N.W.
Canton, Ohio 44718-2516
(216) 492-6063
1-800-336-0083

Cover design by:
Laurance C. Herbert

TABLE OF CONTENTS

PUBLISHER'S NOTICE

This publication is written and published to provide accurate and authoritative information relevant to the subject matter presented. It is published and sold with the understanding that the authors and publisher are not engaged in rendering legal, medical, or other professional services by reason of their authorship or publication of this work. If legal, medical or other expert assistance is required, the services of competent professional persons should be sought. Moreover, in the field of sports medicine, the services of such competent professionals must be obtained.

Adapted from a Declaration of Principles of the American Bar Association and a Committee of Publishers and Associations.

DEDICATION

This edition of this book, as with the first, is dedicated to my wife, Lynda J. Herbert.

PREFACE

Medico-legal developments in the sports medicine field have quickened with each passing year. In fact, since the first edition of this work was published in 1990, many new developments have occurred which have great medico-legal significance to sports medicine practitioners. Members of the sports medicine team now face a variety of problems as well as a number of opportunities which were not even defined but a few short years ago. The duties and responsibilities of the team are changing, while also constantly developing and in large part expanding. Questions are being raised in the professional and legal arenas as to who can do what within the delivery mechanisms for sports medicine services. Professional associations are promulgating and publishing sports medicine standards and guidelines which in some respects are having a rather dramatic impact upon practitioners, some of whom are not even familiar with the potential impact of these standards upon their individual practices. Since the first edition of this book was published, many new standards statements have been developed and published. All of these to one degree or another have had and will continue to have a dramatic impact upon the practice of sports medicine. The "face" of sports medicine is changing and practitioners are being asked to become more involved with a variety of services, many of which are not even purely "medical" in nature.

Given this background, coupled with the proliferation of sports medicine litigation which has occurred, along with and as part of the general litigation epidemic, as well as the rapid development and publication of practice standards which has occurred in the last several years, the publishers of this work introduced *The Sports Medicine Standards and Malpractice Reporter* in 1989. This quarterly newsletter was well received and served a need to identify and analyze current and developing sports medicine issues. However, it was felt that another document was needed to serve as a foundation for the examination of a variety of basic, important and often reoccurring sports medicine topics. Consequently the first edition of this book was developed and written in 1989 and 1990 to meet this perceived need. However, in but a few years that work too needed to be rewritten and updated to meet the informational needs of sports medicine providers. As a result, the first edition of this work was revised in 1993 for publication in early 1994.

The publication of this second edition comes at a time when the author of this work is in the midst of making numerous presentations across the country on a variety of legal issues associated with exercise, recreational activity, sport, sports medicine, malpractice and other similar topics. Many practitioners in attendance at these seminars are becoming increasingly frustrated and admittedly distraught at the proliferation of claims and litigation in these areas. Sports medicine practitioners are also distressed at their inability in many situations to meet published standards of practice due to certain organizational or financial shortcomings of the programs with which they are associated. At the same time, many practitioners are being asked to become involved in ever expanding roles, in an ever broadening scope of practice duties and responsibilities dealing with conditioning, training, equipment, counselling, drug testing, infection control, and numerous other developing topics aside from standard, and somewhat "everyday" delivery of care issues. All of these and many other concerns have a number of legal and practical overtones which need thorough initial examination as well as ongoing analysis. This is why this updated work should act as a natural foundation for other periodical publications including *The Sports Medicine Standards and Malpractice Reporter* and *The Exercise Standards and Malpractice Reporter,* produced by the publisher of this work.

The goal of this publication has been to provide comprehensive, current, practical and useful information to sports medicine practitioners. However, despite the discussion and the citation of numerous authorities herein, it is absolutely essential for programs to have the benefit of individualized legal counsel and assistance. No discussion presented herein should be considered for implementation without such advice and assistance.

David L. Herbert, 1994

iv

1 INTRODUCTION

Standards of practice for the provision of sports medicine services are changing very rapidly and expanding with the publication of new standards statements each year.[1] New techniques, methods and modalities of treatment and care are being introduced with some frequency.[2] Varied and diverse professionals are becoming involved in the delivery of a wide spectrum of sports medicine services. Some of these practitioners are licensed and/or certified but many are not. Some have limited backgrounds and some are not even professionally trained. In addition, many providers such as athletic trainers, are expanding into non-traditional sports medicine settings such as the industrial and clinical setting.[3]

Many different provider groups are becoming involved in sports medicine. These providers include general and family physicians, orthopedic surgeons, internal medicine specialists, rehabilitative physicians, chiropractors, psychiatrists and psychologists, dentists, podiatrists, nutritionists, dieticians, athletic trainers, fitness specialists, physiologists, and a whole host of other licensed and non-licensed individuals including physician assistants, nurses, EMTs and others. The diverse interest in this area has also resulted in the proliferation of a number of written documents aimed at defining the practice, setting minimal or optimal standards of care and a whole host of other matters. The development of such guidelines from so many different groups has created some overlap in these recommendations, as well as some inconsistency and confusion as to who can do what within the sports medicine team. Moreover, the development of numerous standards statements has in some respects, "clouded" clear definitions of some segments of the standard of care and created some question surrounding who can do what in the provision of service.

Sports medicine "teams" may typically consist of physicians, either specialists or non-specialists, a physician assistant or therapist, a trainer, some students helping the trainer or an assistant trainer, and sometimes an EMT or a paramedic who will be present for some athletic contests, not to mention coaches who often serve on the "front line" to deal with a whole host of sports medicine problems. Not every member of this team will be available for conditioning, practice, counseling, injury prevention, game or match situations, rehabilitation or other aspects of care. As a result, some segments or components of care delivery will often be delegated to others on the team who are likely to be present when service or care is needed – most particularly, coaches.

Members of the sports medicine team are being called upon more and more frequently to become involved in such non-traditional areas as drug and substance abuse testing and counseling, the development of rules of play or conduct designed to make participation safer and fairer and a whole host of other matters. Emerging health concerns for the population as a whole are making their way into sports medicine areas with ever increasing and complex demands being placed upon practitioners.

While sports medicine services have been growing in the last twenty years, there has also been an unprecedented growth in the number of claims and lawsuits arising out of the practice area. Some of these cases have been noteworthy from several perspectives and some have involved nationally recognized college and professional athletes and practitioners. The stakes are often high with demands for judgments exceeding several million dollars. For example, one recently settled sports medicine suit involving the death of a well-known college athlete sought an award of $32.5 million.[4] Such requests and sometimes resultant jury awards or settlements are not infrequent. Talented college and professional athletes can command and realize astronomical salaries pursuing their athletic careers. Interference with those careers, due to the negligent provision of sports medicine services can be extremely damaging to the athlete and to the erring provider in the event of settlement or recovery for injuries related to sports medicine care.

Coupled with all of the foregoing, there seems to be a growing tendency in this nation to resolve an ever growing number of conflicts and disputes in the court system. There also seems to be a growing trend to place blame upon others for anything that goes wrong despite evidence of personal responsibility. In addition, the public expects cure and treatment from health care providers in the absence of which patients often seek compensation for malpractice. These three concerns along with many others, create an extremely serious setting within an area that was for many years considered to be outside of the litigation and malpractice problem in this country.

Many of the foregoing sports medicine topics as well as others of a more traditional nature (preparticipation physicals, re-entry to play decisions, informed consent) are beginning to weigh heavily upon practitioners who need timely and complete discussion of these complex issues and topics. While individualized legal and other appropriate professional advice is absolutely essential to assist these practitioners in individualized problem solving, what follows can hopefully serve to focus the issues and to provide useful, adjunct information to individualized professional advice.

FINAL THOUGHT

The ever changing nature of sports medicine and the rapid expansion of sports medicine services makes any discussion of this subject complex and multifaceted. Moreover, given the rather fast paced development of guidelines and standards for sports medicine practitioners, it behooves all practitioners to become familiar with their potential legal and professional liabilities and the ever changing and developing standard of care.

CHAPTER 1 FOOTNOTES:

1. *See* Herbert, THE SPORTS MEDICINE STANDARDS BOOK (PRC Publishing, Inc., Canton, OH 1992, supplemented 1993).

2. *See e.g.,* American Academy of Family Physicians (AAP) American Academy of Pediatrics (AAP), American Medical Society for Sports Medicine (AMSSM), American Osteopathic Academy of Sports Medicine (AOASM), PREPARTICI-PATION PHYSICAL EVALUATION (AOASM, Middleton, WI 1993).

3. Herbert, "The Use of Athletic Trainers Outside of Sports Medicine Settings," *The Sports, Parks and Recreation Law Reporter* 7(2):23-24, 1993.

4. Herbert, "The Death of Hank Gathers: An Examination of The Legal Issues," *The Sports Medicine Standards and Malpractice Reporter* 2(3):45-47, 1990.

2   SPORTS MEDICINE DEFINED

A rather interesting and amusing cartoon was published several years ago by The Tribune Media Services which depicted a sports medicine practitioner's office filled with individuals holding various items of sporting goods equipment in need of repair. The implication of the cartoon was that these goods, as opposed to the individuals holding them, were the ones in need of treatment. The cartoon focused rather poignantly upon the potential confusion inherent in the phrase "Sports Medicine," *i.e.,* is it the treatment and diagnosis of various maladies associated with sport, repair of items of equipment, rehabilitation of individuals who participate in sport or exercise, the provision of educational services or what? While some may consider this discussion to be needless, it must be clear that the phrase "Sports Medicine" is subject to ambiguity, confusion and even misuse in certain settings.

Many consider the phrase to be topic specific, applying to health care providers who render professional service to those who participate in sport type activities. However, it must also be abundantly clear that service of this nature while involving a great many athletes, also involves recreational activity participants, exercisers, dancers, and even workers who may be in need of such services.[1] Notwithstanding this initial and somewhat obvious conclusion, it must also be remembered that the term is also used in relation to the provision of exercise and sporting equipment, exercise or activity routines and other products and services. The term is also used to describe college graduate degree programs which do not lead to the right to practice medicine at all, but rather to pursue other supportive provider roles or some sports business professions. The term is also used to make reference to services which are not even medical in nature, nor rendered by or through those who might be traditionally viewed as health care providers. (One may well then wonder why the term "medicine" for this group is used at all?) Aside from the foregoing, it must also be remembered that there are charlatans of sort also rendering service under the label of "sports medicine" who do not fit within any particular service mold.

When one superimposes the network of innumerable state and federal laws, regulations, licensing requirements and penal laws, along with professional association standards, recommendations, guidelines and statements over the broad spectrum of those who provide service under the label of "sports medicine," a clear grasp of the term as used in actual practice may become even more difficult.

Sports medicine is now an established and recognized medical subspecialty of the American Board of Medical Specialties (ABMS).[2] Notwithstanding the creation of the new subspecialties for sports medicine within the specialty certifications for family practice, emergency medicine, internal medicine and pediatrics,[3] some sports medicine provider groups have turned to certification as a means of recognizing the attainment of a certain degree of proficiency by providers in a particular practice area. These certifying groups include among others the American Osteopathic Academy of Sports Medicine (AOASM), the American Academy of Podiatric Sports Medicine (AAPSM), and the American Academy of Sports Physicians (AASP). While certification of some providers may provide presumptive evidence of competency, it is also important to remember that such efforts can impact the definitional process for sports medicine and may thus have implication to the way the topic should be addressed and examined as well as to the way the public may perceive those practicing under the term or providing goods or services related to the phrase. It should also be remembered that those who attain subspecialization or certification may well be held to a higher standard of care than those who are but general practitioners.[4]

The American Osteopathic Academy of Sports Medicine has defined sports medicine as: *"Sports Medicine is that branch of the healing arts profession that utilizes an wholistic, comprehensive team approach to the prevention, diagnosis and adequate man-*

agement (including medical, surgical and rehabilitative techniques) of sports and exercise-related injuries, disorders, dysfunctions and exercise-related disease processes."

Implicit in the definition as offered by the AOASM is the concept that the physician must be the leader of the sports medicine team. Such an implication as we shall later examine hereinafter, appears to be in conformity with certain legal obligations that would likely be imposed upon those providing services.

While the definition offered by the AOASM is comprehensive, it does not and cannot bring all of the various factions involved in the area under one definitional "roof" or within one grouping. If anything, however, such definitional references will certainly affect the way the legal system will deal with matters within the topic area and with the way jurors may examine conduct within the context of judging various aspects of sports medicine care in the event of litigation and trial.

In all likelihood, given the definitional terms which have been put forth for this subject to date, as well as the notion that it is, despite some inconsistencies, perceived as a branch or part of the practice of medicine, a legal analysis of the topic must direct its examination within the context of medicine and allied health care provider law. Consequently, it will be necessary to examine negligence and malpractice concerns along with a whole host of other matters within this work from such a perspective. Moreover, given the fact that various sports medicine products and devices are involved in this practice area, the concepts of negligence, products liability, including strict liability in tort and even breach of warranty may also have to be mentioned.

Due to the breadth of services provided under the label of sports medicine, it will also be necessary to examine certain medical practices, therapy, nursing, rehabilitation, athletic training, first aid, cardiopulmonary resuscitation, nutritional counseling, drug screening and counseling, medical and prescriptive drug dispensing and a whole host of other emerging areas. The encompassing nature of the practice area as well as the wide and diverse array of services and products which are provided under the label should make the discussion of benefit to a wide range of practitioners.

In the final analysis, the term "sports medicine" must be defined by reference to the provision of service from one person to another. While most of these services must necessarily be viewed as medical or supportive thereto, any definition must also take into account (despite obvious problems with the use of the term "medicine" when used for non-medical practices), the fact that non-medical and non-allied health care providers are also rendering services or providing products under this general label.

For the purposes of this work, sports medicine shall be defined as: *"The provision, primarily, of medical or allied health care to athletes, exercisers, recreational enthusiasts and others and the delivery of preventive, primary or rehabilitative care related to the prevention, treatment or rehabilitation of injuries and conditions related to sport, exercise or recreational activity, as well as the rendition of service and advice for fitness and training purposes to individuals who desire to engage in the aforementioned activities, and secondarily, the provision of medically or non-medically related services or products to those who are interested or involved in sport, exercise or recreation even though in this latter sense, the use of the term 'medicine' may be inherently inappropriate."*

While this definitional reference takes into account the realities of life associated with the use of the term, it may be that many professionals, especially those within the healing arts, will object to the use of the word "medicine," for the provision of non-medical services or products or as to those providing services or products who are not properly licensed.[5] Except for this one area, the word "medicine" is not used to describe anything outside the confines of health care provider practices.

Some professionals are beginning to express concerns in regard to the use of the term "medicine" for non-medically related services, which concerns center principally upon one or more of the following:

1. Public misconception as to the use of the term "medicine" by those not so licensed;

2. The potential or actual unauthorized practice of medicine by those non-licensed practitioners using the term; and,

3. A lowering of respect and esteem for those physicians and other licensed or certified providers actually rendering medical or related service to those seeking same in light of public misconception as to non-licensed practitioners involved in the area.

One incident occurring in 1992 perhaps illustrates what problems can arise in this area. Apparently a Georgia "sports psychologist" provided "sports psychology" services to a professional baseball player in that state. Since the sports psychologist was not licensed as a "psychologist," the matter was referred to the Georgia Board of Examiners of Psychologists for determination as to whether or not such services could be provided by one not licensed by them. In this regard the Board ruled that Georgia law *"protects the title 'psychologist'. The Board does not license a 'sports psychologist' ...[However] the Board would prefer that such individuals not refer to themselves as any type of psychologist, because doing so may lead the public to think that the person is licensed."*[6] Consequently, that Board ruled that there was no violation of the state licensing law. However, other analogous instances can lead to directly opposite results.[7]

Many of these concerns as well as others have and will continue to have potentially adverse consequences for those licensed as well as non-licensed professionals practicing these services. While we shall address the legal consequences associated with these concerns, debate beyond the scope of this work is undoubtedly needed to resolve these and other issues related to the use of the term "sports medicine." The issues examined herein may help to focus certain aspects of the debate including those issues dealing with the unauthorized practice of medicine or allied health care as well as those issues centering upon licensure and certification, the standard of care, appropriate delegation of care, the provision of prescriptive medications and appliances and a myriad of other issues which we shall examine in the forthcoming chapters.

FINAL THOUGHT

While the term "sports medicine" is not easy to define, and while the phrase to some extent may be inappropriately used for some practices, the practice of sports medicine is subject to a variety of legal concerns. Definitional references for the practice must take an objective and far reaching view to cover all areas of concern; otherwise important and significant practice areas might be overlooked.

CHAPTER 2 FOOTNOTES:

1. *See* Herbert, "Just Who Is A Sports Medicine Practitioner?," *The Sports Medicine Standards and Malpractice Reporter* 4(4):56-57, 1993.

2. "New Subspecialties Created," *The Sports Medicine Standards and Malpractice Reporter* 5(3):37, 1993.

3. *Id.*

4. *Id.*

5. *See, supra* footnote 1.

6. "Georgia Sports Psychologist Not a Psychologist," *The Sports, Parks and Recreation Law Reporter* 5(4):63, 1992.

7. *See e.g.,* "Nutritional Counselor Enjoined From Practicing Without a License," *The Exercise Standards and Malpractice Reporter* 7(5):75, 1993, analyzing the case of Ohio Board of Dietetics vs. Brown, 83 Ohio App.3d 242 (1993) which held that a nutritional counselor could be enjoined from providing relevant services without a license.

3   THE SPORTS MEDICINE TEAM

Typically and appropriately, the sports medicine team is and should ideally be composed of a number of members. These members should include the physician, a physician's assistant, nurse, therapist or trainer as well as various other personnel such as assistant or student trainers. In some larger or more sophisticated programs, this list will expand somewhat to include sport psychologists, chiropractors, podiatrists, dentists, nutritionists or dieticians, fitness or weight/strength training personnel, personal fitness trainers and behavioral type motivators. Given the broad range of potential personnel involved in many sports medicine programs it is important for several reasons to develop a structure for the delivery of services to those within a particular program.

In most programs, the care provided will be medically related. As a consequence, any legal examination of the activity must be viewed from such a perspective and with reference to the statutes and regulations governing the practice of medicine. Given the breath of those providing services within this professional domain, it appears appropriate to examine the scope of typical legislative authority for these professionals.

The practice of medicine is always state regulated even though it is also governed to some degree by various federal enactments. The former provisions define who may practice the profession and under what circumstances while the latter statutes typically affect a variety of aspects related to the profession or its business practices which include for example, the dispensing of particular drugs, the reporting of malpractice claims or settlements, self-referrals and a whole host of other matters dealing with payment of medical bills pursuant to Medicare or Medicaid requirements, the delivery of care in accordance with specific guidelines, the provision of laboratory services within the physician's office, etc. To say that the practice of medicine is laced with regulation would seem to be a rather gross understatement to say the least.

State regulations which define the practice of medicine typically provide definitional references like the following:

CALIFORNIA (ACC §2052)

Any person who practices or attempts to practice, or who advertises himself or herself out as practicing, any system or mode of treating the sick or afflicted in this state, or who diagnoses, treats, operates for, or prescribes for any ailment, blemish, deformity, disease, disfigurement, disorder, injury, or other physical or mental condition of any person, without having at the time of so doing a valid, unrevoked, or unsuspended certificate as provided in this chapter, or without being authorized to perform such act pursuant to a certificate obtained in accordance with some other provision of law...

FLORIDA (FSA §458.305(3))

Practice of Medicine means the diagnosis, treatment, operation, or prescription for any human disease, pain, injury, deformity, or other physical or mental condition.

MICHIGAN (MCLA §333.17001(c))

Practice of Medicine means the diagnosis, treatment, prevention, cure, or relieving of a human disease, ailment, defect, complaint, or other physical or mental condition, by attendance, advice, device, diagnostic test, or other means, or offering, undertaking, attempting to do, or holding oneself out as able to do, any of these acts.

NEW JERSEY (NJSA §45:9-5.1)

The practice of medicine or surgery and the phrase the practice of medicine and surgery shall include the practice of any branch of medicine and/or surgery, and any method of treatment of human ailment, disease, pain, injury, deformity, mental or physical condition, and the term physician and surgeon or physician or surgeon shall be deemed to include practitioners in any branch of medicine and/or surgery practi-

tioners in any branch of medicine and/or surgery or method of treatment of human ailment, disease, pain, injury, deformity, mental or physical condition...the practice of medicine and/or surgery shall be deemed to include, inter alia, the practice of osteopathy, and nothing herein contained shall be construed to exempt the holder of a license issued under or validated by the provisions contained in section 45:9-14.10, (osteopath and chiropractor licensing) to 45:9-14.10, inclusive, from the operation of the provisions contained in section 45:9-16 (suspension, revocation) of this title.

NEW YORK (NYA §6521)

The practice of the profession of medicine is defined as diagnosing, treating, operating or prescribing for any human disease, pain, injury, deformity or physical condition.

NORTH CAROLINA (GSNC §90-18) effective until 1/1/95

Any person shall be regarded as practicing medicine or surgery within the meaning of this Article who shall diagnose or attempt to diagnose, treat or attempt to treat, operate or attempt to operate on, or prescribe for or administer to, or profess to treat any human ailment, physical or mental, or any physical injury to or deformity of another person. [Exceptions to the definition include domestic remedies, licensed dentists, pharmacists, military medical personnel, optometrists, chiropractors, physicians, surgeons, radiologists, faith healers – all within prescribed limits].

OHIO (Rev. Code §4731.34)

A person shall be regarded as practicing medicine... who examines or diagnoses for compensation of any kind, or prescribes, advises or recommends, administers or dispenses for compensation of any kind, direct or indirect, a drug or medicine, appliance, mold or cast, application, operation or treatment, of whatever nature, for the cure or relief of a wound, fracture or bodily injury, infirmity or disease...

TEXAS (RCST §4495(b))

Any person shall be regarded as practicing medicine within the meaning of this law: (1) who shall publicly profess to be a physician or surgeon and shall diagnose, treat, or offer to treat, any disease or disorder, mental or physical, or any physical deformity or injury, by any system or method, or to effect cures thereof; (2) or who shall diagnose, treat, or offer to treat any disease or disorder, mental or physical, or any physical deformity or injury by any system or method and to effect cures thereof and charge therefor, directly or indirectly, money or other compensation; provided, however, that the provisions of this Article shall be construed with and in view of Article 740 (licensing, Penal Code of Texas, and Article 4505, Revised Civil Statutes of Texas as contained in this Act. [Exemptions for duly licensed dentists, physicians, surgeons, pharmacists, optometrists, chiropractors, military personnel, faith healers as provided – all within prescribed limits].

Likewise, statutory enactments also generally proscribe and prohibit non-licensed individuals from practicing medicine without proper state licensure. These enactments usually contain prohibitions which are criminal in nature prohibiting those who are not properly licensed from practicing medicine. Generally, these statutes are rather broadly interpreted and all encompassing. Courts interpreting such statutes which are generally enacted for the benefit of the public, apply the statutes broadly (except in criminal prosecutions) so as to serve the legislative purpose and the public good.

For example, in 1975, in the case of <u>Mirsa vs. State Medical Board</u>,[1] the Ohio Supreme Court in examining the status of a commercial blood plasma donor bank held as follows: *"[The plasma donor bank's] procedures include the initial in depth medical history and...[an] examination consisting of a series of tests outlined in the above statement of facts [the taking of blood pressure, pulse, temperature, weight and hematocrit]. From the medical history and these tests [the bank]...must evaluate whether the prospective donor is acceptable. This determination necessarily involves a diagnosis of the donor's current health on the basis of the medical examination...From all of the above, we conclude that [the bank]...engages in the practice of medicine [as defined by Ohio law]."* [*See,* statute *supra.*]

Upon the basis of this decision, the plasma bank undoubtedly was faced with terminating its operations as then constituted or incorporating into its procedures the services of a licensed physician. Prior to the decision, the bank's association with a physician consisted only of one on call for emergencies. In addition, a procedural manual was developed providing in part for instructions in the event of donor medical emergencies. The factual parallels between some sports medicine programs and the rendition of some sports medicine services and the plasma bank and its procedures may be frightening to some in light of the Ohio Supreme Court's pronouncement. It may be that more direct, and more personal physician involvement is needed for a good many programs which may operate with only loose physician contact, supervision or involvement.

Other decisions relating to the unauthorized practice of medicine should also be of some concern as to certain procedures. For example, in an earlier Ohio case,[2] the defendant, a licensed chiropractor, and electro-mechanical therapist, was criminally charged with the unauthorized practice of medicine. The State contended that she prescribed, dispensed or recommended certain minerals, foods and fluids to cure and relieve certain infirmities and thereby engaged in the unlawful practice of medicine. Although a jury initially found her guilty, the conviction was reversed on appeal with the court finding that there was no proof that the foods or other items were intended for use in the cure, mitigation or treatment of disease. However, the court did note that food items could be deemed to be drugs if given for *"care, mitigation, treatment or prevention of disease."*[3]

In a more recent case from the state of Indiana,[4] a state investigator posed as a person seeking certain advice from a nutritionist defendant as to the investigator's physical condition. The nutritionist obtained information from the investigator and examined the investigator's eyes. Based upon the information and examination, the nutritionist determined that the investigator had certain nutritional problems, poor circulation and other conditions. To correct these conditions, the nutritionist suggested among other things, mineral water, kelp, raw food and certain other substances.

Based upon these facts, the State Medical Licensing Authority sought a permanent injunction preventing the nutritionist from engaging in the unauthorized practice of medicine. Relying upon earlier cases, the trial court ultimately granted the state's request but determined that the nutritionist was not enjoined from lecturing or educating members of the public as to nutrition nor from selling products so long as she did not examine, diagnose, treat or sell products based upon an assessment of an individual's needs or problems. The court also implied that advice such as "take a rest" or "take a walk" which was given to treat might indeed amount to the unauthorized practice of medicine.

In examining this decision in light of the Ohio court's prior pronouncement as to the unauthorized practice of medicine, practices which include recommendations or treatments given to prevent disease, or even the prescription of exercise, *i.e.,* "take a walk," as well as a variety of other recommendations might well be deemed to be the unauthorized practice of medicine. When considering the activities and modes of care and rehabilitation which are prescribed by countless non-physician sports medicine practitioners to prevent, treat or rehabilitate, there is room for concern. A number of other recent cases in this area have also been reported which may have application to this discussion. These include decisions from the states of Georgia,[5] California,[6] North Carolina,[7] Michigan,[8] Mississippi,[9] and Washington.[10]

Aside from the foregoing, many states, moreover, have enacted criminal statutes proscribing the unauthorized practice of medicine. Often, such statutes make the unauthorized practice of medicine a misdemeanor, subjecting violators to fine and imprisonment not to exceed one year. These enactments usually contain prohibitions such as the following: *"No person shall practice medicine or surgery, or any of its branches without a certificate from the State Medical Board; no person shall advertise or announce themselves as a practitioner of medicine or surgery, or any of its branches, without a certificate from the Board...,"* Ohio Revised Code §4731.41. (Comment: Contained within this definition is a prohibition against advertising oneself as being a practitioner of medicine. Question: One must wonder whether or not advertisement of the term "sports medicine" by a non-physician would be sufficient so as to permit the imposition of criminal sanctions or injunctive relief?)

Very serious criminal charges are also a possible consequence to the non-physician sports medicine care provider who renders service under circumstances where a patient dies, and the procedures involved are deemed to be medical in nature. Based upon such a factual finding in connection with a death, charges of manslaughter or even murder to one degree or another might be possible,[11] wherein a self-styled "healer" providing, *inter alia,* deep abdominal massage for a leukemia patient was initially convicted of felony murder as a result of the patient's death, who did not, in apparent reliance upon the healer's efforts, obtain other treatment. The felony murder conviction was reversed on appeal by the California Supreme Court which held, however, that the defendant, in the absence of proof of malice, was susceptible to the charge of involuntary manslaughter only. Although this particular case involved a "charlatan" of sorts, the same principles of law could conceivably be applied to the non-physician or non-licensed sports medicine service provider should he or she be deemed to be practicing medicine or some other licensed or regulated provider profession without a license or authorization where such practice causes a patient death.

It is important to note that these possibilities are not necessarily probabilities or even "likelihoods." They are matters of concern which should be evaluated by the program and its legal counsel according to state statutes, local medical customs and program practices so that every effort might be made to reduce the risks of civil as well as criminal exposure to the non-physician sports medicine staff members. A medical director's active association with a program can go a long way in reducing the possibilities of legal entanglements relative to these concerns as we shall hereafter examine. However, there is clear precedence, as we have seen, for the leveling of charges against non-licensed individuals based upon these and similar state statutes where such providers exceed their authority.

Aside from the foregoing statutory forms of physician regulation and licensure, state statutes also regulate and license other related but separate limited practitioners, some of whom are involved in the provision of sports medicine services. These typically include nutritionists or dieticians, chiropractors, podiatrists and psychologists. Generally, these professionals are licensed or authorized to provide limited care under particular circumstances. For example, podiatry may be defined as: *"the medical, mechanical and surgical treatment of ailments of the foot, muscles and tendons of the leg governing the functions of the foot; and superficial lesions of the hand other than those associated with trauma. Podiatrists are permitted the use of such preparations, medicines and drugs as may be necessary for the treatment of such ailments. The podiatrist may treat the local manifestations and systemic diseases as they appear on the hand and foot, but the patient shall be concurrently referred to a doctor of medicine or a doctor of osteopathic medicine and surgery for the treatment of systemic disease itself...,"* Ohio Revised Code §4731.51.

Sometimes issues arise as to whether or not such licensed individuals exceed their limited areas of statutory authorization in particular cases. Under certain circumstances, allegations can arise that these limited practitioners were engaged in actuality, in the practice of medicine and therefore would be subject to the prohibitions of the unauthorized practice of medicine statutes which were just examined herein.

Aside from these limited practitioners, other allied health care providers are certainly involved in the delivery of services to patients in the sports medicine setting. While these professionals generally derive their authority to act from state statutes, they are generally subject to the supervision and control of the physician. Such individuals include physician assistants, nurses, paramedics, therapists, athletic trainers and sometimes emergency response personnel. These statutes typically provide a "patchwork" of legislative authorization to these professionals. For example, a physician's assistant is sometimes defined as *"a skilled person qualified by academic and clinical training to provide services to patients under the supervision and direction of a licensed physician or group of physicians who are responsible for his performance,"* Ohio Revised Code §4730.01.

Sometimes these allied health care providers must obtain certification or licensure from a state authorizing board and govern their practice pursuant to and under the direction of a licensed physician. Other practitioners such as nurses are often similarly regulated although some of the newer definitions for the practice of nursing are somewhat broad in scope. For example, pursuant to the provisions of Ohio Revised Code §4723.02, the practice of registered nursing is defined as *"providing to individuals and groups nursing care requiring specialized knowledge, judgment and skill derived from the principles of biological, physical, behavioral, social and nursing sciences. Such nursing care includes: (1) identifying patterns of human responses to actual or potential health problems amenable to nursing regimens; (2) executing a nursing regimen through the selection, performance, management and evaluation of nursing actions; (3) assessing health status for the purposes of providing nursing care; (4) providing health counseling and health teaching; (5) administering medications, treatments and executing regimens prescribed by licensed physicians, dentists and podiatrists; (6) teaching, administering, supervising, delegating and evaluating nursing practice."* Under this statute, the term nursing regimen is defined as including *"preventative, restorative and health promotion activities."* Licensed practical nurses are similarly defined and granted certain similar but somewhat more limited authorization. Prior definitions of nursing practices were much more restrictive. For example, prior Ohio Revised Code §4723.06 defined the practice of professional nursing as *"The performance for compensation of acts requiring substantial judgment and specialized skills based on knowledge and application of scientific principles learned in an approved school of professional nursing. Acts of medical diagnosis or prescription of medical, therapeutic or corrective medical measures by a nurse are prohibited."*

Like other allied health care providers, therapists are also typically licensed and their authorization is defined by state statute. The practice of physical therapy for example is sometimes defined as follows: *"Physical therapy means the evaluation and treatment of a person by physical measures and the use of therapeutic exercises and rehabilitative procedures, with or without assistive devices, for the purpose of preventing, correcting or alleviating any disability. Physical therapy includes the establishment and modification of physical therapy programs, treatment, planning, instruction and consultive services. Physical measures include massage, heat, cold, air, light, water, electricity, sound, and the performance of tests of neuro-muscular function as an aid to such treatment. Physical therapy does not include the diagnosis of a patient's disability, the use of rotegen rays or radium for diagnostic or therapeutic purposes or the use of electricity...,"* Ohio Revised Code §4755.40(A).

In some states (approximately half of all states as of the time of this writing), athletic trainers are also subject to legislative definition, licensure and regulation. For example, in the state of

Georgia, an athletic trainer is defined as: *"A person with specific qualifications, as set forth in [another code section]...who, upon the advice and consent of his team physician, carries out the practice of prevention or physical rehabilitation, or both, of injuries incurred by athletes on the team by which the athletic trainer is employed; and, in carrying out these functions, the athletic trainer is authorized to use physical modalities such as heat, light, sound, cold, electricity, or mechanical devices related to rehabilitation and treatment,"* Ga. Code Ann. §43-5-1.

In New Jersey contrawise, an athletic trainer is defined as: *"A person who practices athletic training as an employee of a school, college, university or professional team,"* N.J. Rev. Stat. §45:9 - 37:36(c).

The practice of athletic training in New Jersey is defined as: *"The practice of physical conditioning and reconditioning of athletes and the prevention of injuries incurred by athletes. Athletic training shall also include, at the direction of a physician licensed in this state, the application of physical treatment modalities, as recommended by the advisory committee and defined in regulations by the board, to athletes,"* N.J. Rev. Stat. §45:9 - 37:36(d).

Some of these statutes are very broadly written as to what duties may be performed by a trainer and by what means, *i.e.,* Ky. Rev. Stat. §311.900: *"'Athletic Trainer' means a person [with the advice and consent of a team physician][who] carries out the practice of prevention or physical rehabilitation, or both, of injuries incurred by participating athletes...[by] whatever physical modalities...are deemed necessary by a team physician."*

Other statutes are very specific. For example S.D. Codified Laws Ann. §36-29-1 provides in its legislation defining an athletic trainer and the practice of athletic training as follows: *"'Athletic trainer' [means] a person with specific qualifications set forth in [another statute]...whose responsibility is the prevention, evalu-*

ation, emergency care, treatment and reconditioning of athletic injuries under the direction of the team or treating physician. The athletic trainer may use cryotherapy, which includes cold packs, ice packs, cold water immersion and spray coolants; thermotherapy, which includes topical analgesics, moist hot packs, heating pads, infrared lamp and paraffin bath; hydrotherapy, which includes whirlpool; and therapeutic exercise common to athletic training which includes stretching and those exercises needed to maintain condition; in accordance with a physician's written protocol. Any rehabilitative procedures recommended by a physician for the rehabilitation of athletic injuries which have been referred and all other physical modalities may be administered only following the prescription of the team or referring physician...".

Pursuant to many of these statutes, the athletic trainer must carry out his/her duties only upon written prescription (*e.g.,* N.M. Stat. Ann. §61-14 D-2(A)), or only upon prescription or protocol by a team or consulting physician (*e.g.,* LA. Rev. Stat. Ann. 37 §3302) or upon the direction of such a professional (*e.g.,* MO. Rev. Stat. §334.702(3)). In some states, athletic training is limited to the physical conditioning or reconditioning of athletes or the prevention of athletic injuries unless physical treatment modalities are prescribed by a physician, *see,* N.J. Rev. Stat. *supra.* Other states require the advice and consent of a physician before prevention or rehabilitative activities may be carried out (S.C. Code Ann. §44-75-20(a)). In many states, the practice of athletic training in violation of state statutory enactments, is criminal in nature, *see e.g.,* N.D. Cent. Code §43-39-04. Likewise in most states, the unauthorized practice of any regulated health care profession, is also criminal, subject to fine and imprisonment upon violation.

A significant problem can occur for many trainers in carrying out their professional practices within the literal terms of these statutory enactments. For example, if a written prescription or authorization is not obtained in advance of treatment, or if insufficient direction or supervision is provided, trainers may be found to have overstepped their bounds in reference to the athletes whom they serve. In the event of such unauthorized activities and participant injury, the standard of care owed by these individuals may be judged by reference to that owed by a physician or some other health care provider (*e.g.,* therapist), in relation to the injured party. In those states where no athletic trainer licensing statutes exist, such a result may in fact be more likely to occur where trainer conduct would be judged by reference to other statutory legislation for licensed professionals.

The result of such a comparison could be devastating to the trainer facing claim and/or suit if an injured athlete claims improper practices or substandard treatment. First, if a trainer was found to be engaged in the unauthorized practice of medicine or some other licensed professional practice, his conduct and the duty of care owed to the participant may be judged by reference to the presumed conduct of a physician or other licensed health care provider acting under similar circumstances. Obviously, and particularly as to a comparison with a physician, the trainer could not withstand such a comparative analysis. Secondly, if the facts justify a finding of the unauthorized practice of some statutorily defined and licensed profession, criminal prosecution under many state statutes is possible. Thus a trainer could be faced with adverse civil and criminal consequences due to statutorily defined unauthorized activities. While such findings are less likely to occur in those states which have licensing statutes for trainers, and such trainers do not overstep their authority, they are not beyond the realm of possibility. In states without these trainer enactments, such results may be somewhat more likely to occur. It would seem that uniform and perhaps model athletic trainer statutes enacted in all of the states could clear up these potential problems.

Currently, there is also a movement to expand the roles of some athletic trainers beyond the traditional sports medicine framework and to utilize them in the industrial, clinical or corporate wellness, health promotion or similar setting.[12] The use of athletic trainers within these settings may well be beyond the state authorization granted to such providers which statutes often limit the scope of their practice to athletics, or to athletes[13] except in those states with broad provider delegation statutes[14] allowing the delivery of services to those non-physicians acting under the supervision of a physician.[15]

While there has been an attempt within these various definitional references to develop a consistent pattern of authorization and delegation to particular professionals within the provider population, there are overlapping areas of care, even entire gaps in some cases where state regulation is absent. In those states for example where athletic trainers are not licensed, the question obviously arises as to whether or not these individuals may carry out duties which might under some circumstances be judged to be limited to, for example, physical therapists. In those states where regulation and licensure is not in existence, certification of such individuals may provide some evidence of presumptive qualification; however, certification does not provide the "safe harbor" of licensure to trainers who may be subject to particular charges related to the unauthorized practice of medicine or some other allied health profession.

In some settings, the options available to sports medicine team physicians seeking to delegate care delivery to other members of the team might be limited by reason of state regulation. For example, in other instances, certain treatment modalities that a physician wishes to prescribe may not be appropriately delegated to an athletic trainer by reason of the authorization granted to others such as physical therapists.

Standing orders may be used in some circumstances where there can be a proper delegation to act to authorized individuals. While variously defined, standing orders are simply orders which have been pre-determined by a physician but carried out under certain circumstances by other health care providers in the physician's absence or as a matter of routine protocol. A number of legal concerns can arise with the use of standing orders.

Frequently, the question can become whether or not the order is "legally sanctioned" – that is – is the order properly delegable to the provider.[16]

The use of standing orders to provide care delivery has been "legally" approved by a number of states.[17] The question becomes even more significant when the person carrying out the order is a non-nurse or even a non-licensed provider. Since in a majority of programs athletic trainers rather than nurses will be the one member of the sports medicine team most frequently available during athletic contests and practice sessions, the question often arises as to whether or not certain aspects of care may be delegated by the physician to the trainer particularly in situations where the trainer has no state licensure legislation defining duties and responsibilities under law.

As previously stated, the practice of athletic training is not regulated by state law in about half of the states.[18] However, athletic trainers have worked closely with team physicians in the care of athletes for many years – *"Athletic trainers were working as 'physician's assistants' long before the terms were coined. They still assume this role within the limits of their competence and the confidence of their physician associate."*[19] Despite this close relationship, the appropriate delegation of care is often determined by reference to state law. *"[M]any states have chosen to exclude athletic trainers from the list of health-care professionals whose duties are specifically regulated by state law. In many cases, this places the athletic trainer, even one who possesses extensive advanced professional education and national certification, in a very precarious position. To provide even the most basic of sports medicine care for an athlete in a state where such care is specifically limited by law to physicians, nurses and physical therapists is to perform outside the apparent authority (and perhaps in violation of many medicine/allied health statutes) of the law."*[20]

When an inappropriate or legally impermissible delegation of authority is attempted by one physician to another, the provider as well as the physician may face a number of legal consequences – including the possibility of criminal sanctions. This may be particularly true in the prescription and dispensing of medication to athletes which shall be examined in more detail in Chapter 10.

To date, the legal system has not focused in the course of litigation, on the scope of practice of athletic training within the health care provider population.[21] The issue of the appropriate management of care by various members of the sports medicine team, including athletic trainers, needs to be addressed,[22] and at some point this will undoubtedly occur.

Aside from these issues which are clearly applicable to the rendition of service in sports medicine settings, new practice areas have also arisen which need to be mentioned as they are governed by the same statutory morass which has just been reviewed. Many sports medicine providers have begun to enter into new areas: exercise testing, evaluation, analysis, prescription or supervision of activity; weight loss or gain; the provision of sports massage; the provision of exercise equipment and related services or products. Each of these areas gives rise to similar practice concerns such as those which have been discussed in this chapter. A brief examination of one of the more important of these areas should be of benefit to the sports medicine team – especially in deciding who is authorized to provide services within certain of these practice areas.

EXERCISE TESTING AND PRESCRIPTION AS MEDICAL PROCEDURES

The use of exercise and graded exercise stress testing (GXT) and other similar procedures has increased substantially in recent years. Test protocols involving various types of controlled exercise stress with physiological assessments, *e.g.,* exercise ECG, thallium perfusion scanning and radionuclide cineangiography are now widely utilized by physicians to diagnose coronary artery disease, measure changes in disease status, forecast outcomes (prognosis), and support decisions on treatment selection. According to the results of a recently published study,[23] cardiologists are ordering significantly more diagnostic tests for acute MI patients than they did a decade ago. The use of exercise stress testing procedures has increased dramatically rising from .1% of all acute MI patients in 1975 to 40.3% in 1984.

Findings such as these may also be reflective of increased physician efforts to engage in careful and deliberate diagnostic evaluation of patients to minimize the likelihood of malpractice claims due to alleged omissions in diagnostic procedures. Such testing methods however are not without legal risk in the event of an untoward event.[24] Further increases in the use of such tests may be predicted especially in light of a 1988 Los Angeles, California, arbitration award.[25] In this case, the plaintiff's family was awarded $500,000.00 as a result of the plaintiff's death due to a myocardial infarction at the age of 40 after having undergone a physical examination without stress testing which examination reportedly failed to reveal the presence of silent ischemia. As a result of this award, some attorneys are contending that graded exercise testing procedures are now necessary to screen all individuals over 40 years of age to determine the presence of silent ischemia before such individuals embark upon a program of vigorous physical activity or participation in sport.[26]

Prescriptive and therapeutic applications of exercise have also gained wide acceptance for management of selected patients with ischemic heart disease, intermittent claudication, cardiac pacemakers, diabetes myelitis, chronic obstructive pulmonary disease, obesity, arthritic disorders, renal disease and even psychological difficulties (*e.g.*, depression). Also, many physicians, after concluding a patient's treatment in a therapeutic cardiopulmonary exercise program, will want that individual to continue physical activity in a cardiovascular maintenance program. Decisions to advance patients to programs of this type, although based upon substantial medical and physiological criteria, simply show that the individual's disease is temporarily stable. New and life-threatening manifestations may present at any time. The inclusion of such "stable" patients as well as those highly predisposed to CHD pose exceptional legal risks for exercise programs that have substandard medical support on site. Essentially, if a program admits individuals with overt or covert CHD, the staff may also in fact be accepting the legal obligation to render the same care as would be provided by a physician relative to proper exercise monitoring, supervision and especially contingency emergency cardiac care. Taking a defensive position after the fact that the purpose of a given program was to develop fitness or provide healthful and enjoyable physical recreation may not be sufficient legally to preclude the judgment that acceptance of individuals with stable disease or significant risk for disease also carries with it the responsibility to provide the type of exercise and the degree of supervision appropriate to the patient's health status.

Even though state statutes and regulations may clearly address the exercise specialist's relationship to medical practice, other statements or standards may impact a professional engaged in exercise testing, prescription or supervision. Standards of practice promulgated by respected associations should be examined even though the standards do not totally resolve all problems facing the sports medicine program engaged in providing exercise activities.

STANDARDS OF THE AMERICAN HEART ASSOCIATION

The American Heart Association (AHA), in its 1972 EXERCISE TESTING AND TRAINING OF APPARENTLY HEALTHY INDIVIDUALS: A HANDBOOK FOR PHYSICIANS, published the first guidelines for exercise testing and training. In 1975 the AHA also published the HANDBOOK FOR PHYSICIANS: EXERCISE TESTING AND TRAINING OF INDIVIDUALS WITH HEART DISEASE OR AT HIGH-RISK FOR ITS DEVELOPMENT, which was one of the first attempts to specifically define the exercise circumstances that constitute medical practice. This work defined therapeutic exercise and equated it with other beneficial clinical agents.

These works of the AHA were subsequently revised in 1979/1980,[27] 1986,[28] and most recently in 1990.[29] The publications, while recognizing the role of non-medical providers engaged in certain exercise related activities, emphasize the role of the physician in the performance of these tasks.[30]

STANDARDS OF THE AMERICAN COLLEGE OF SPORTS MEDICINE

The 1980 edition of the American College of Sports Medicine's (ACSM) GUIDELINES FOR GRADED EXERCISE TESTING AND EXERCISE PRESCRIPTION (Second Edition) addressed in some respects the same matters discussed by the AHA. In 1975, the American College of Sports Medicine (ACSM) also began to address the same issues as the AHA with the publication by ACSM of GUIDELINES FOR GRADED EXERCISE TESTING AND EXERCISE PRESCRIPTION (Lea & Febiger, Philadelphia, PA 1975). The work, which has been revised three times since, is now in its fourth edition.[31] This work from the ACSM provides for a team approach to exercise testing, prescription and training among various health care providers.

The foregoing guidelines coupled with similar standards statements from among others the American College of Cardiology, the American College of Physicians, the American Medical Association, the American Association of Cardiovascular and Pulmonary Rehabilitation and several others[32] provide the professionally stated framework for most exercise testing, prescription and training modalities, especially for diseased or at risk populations or for diagnostic purposes.

WEIGHT LOSS/GAIN COUNSELING

A number of weight loss and other dietary programs are now "under the gun." Some lawyers are beginning to focus their energies on such programs on behalf of weight loss customers who claim to have been injured or adversely affected by some of these programs and/or related diet products. Many of these suits focus upon gallbladder ailments and other similar conditions. Hundreds of these lawsuits may be filed against programs due to claimed injuries arising from these dieting regimens. Some of these suits may well involve allegations of the unauthorized practice of medicine or other similar claims.[33] While most of these threatened or filed suits have yet to be tried, program sponsors and product manufacturers have promised a vigorous defense.[34] Given the financial remuneration associated with some of these programs and products, extensive litigation efforts will be likely. An examination of a very recently reported decision in one dieting product case may well point out the issues to be litigated in such cases, as well as the areas of disagreement and likely focus of judge/jury attention.

In the case of Riley vs. Physicians Weight Loss Centers, Inc.,[35] the plaintiff went to the defendant's place of business in September of 1984. At that time she was 42 years of age and weighed 251 pounds. She had previously been on other diet programs achieving mixed results. After a physician performed a simple physical, the plaintiff started on the Center's diet program which was based upon a reduced-calorie, limited-carbohydrate, ketogenic diet designed to induce a state of ketosis in the dieter causing stored body fat to be metabolized, thus hopefully resulting in weight loss.

Although contract documents were signed by the plaintiff with the Center on at least two occasions, there *"was no discussion between the Center's personnel and plaintiff about any health risks connected with the ketogenic diet...the diet was promoted...as being completely safe."*[36] The plaintiff lost more than 70 pounds on the diet but by December of 1984 she was suffering from severe pain to her mid-epigastric area which was eventually diagnosed as gallstones requiring the removal of her gallbladder in mid-March 1985. She was told that her gallbladder problems were due to the diet. She later underwent further tests, examinations and two other surgical procedures in connection with reoccurring stomach problems.

She later brought suit contending that the Center failed *"to warn her...[of the] known possible consequences and hazards of the ketogenic diet...[including] gallstones, kidney stones, anorexia, death, and other serious health problems."* [37] She also contended that the Center failed to adequately monitor her while on the diet, and otherwise was negligent, engaging in willful and wanton conduct and false advertising. While the last claim was stricken from the case by the trial court, the court also granted a summary judgment in favor of the Center on all of the plaintiff's allegations. The plaintiff appealed.

On appeal, the appellate court examined the facts and evidence which had been submitted to the trial court as to the plaintiff's two main allegations (failure to disclose risks and failure to monitor) and held that a material question of fact existed as to whether or not the plaintiff would have undertaken the diet if she had been warned of the known possible health risks. As to the second issue, the court determined that any *"alleged breach of...[the Center's] duty to monitor plaintiff was not the proximate cause of her injury."* [38] Consequently the case was returned to the lower court for jury determination of the risk disclosure issue.

Cases like this one will invariably revolve around expert witness testimony and disputed factual scenarios which will require jury or judge determination. At issue along with many other matters is the question, as the Riley court noted, of whether or not *"the standard of care applicable to physicians applied to [the Center]..."* [39] Such issues will invariably be explored in this and other similar cases which may take many years to complete.

Programs which offer dieting advice, regimens or diet products would be well advised to undergo an audit of their practices by risk management personnel as well as legal and medical advisors. Program offerings, as well as policies and procedures, should be examined and adjusted as the case may be to minimize the potential legal consequences associated with these activities.

THE PROVISION OF EXERCISE/TRAINING FACILITIES AND EQUIPMENT

Some program activities might require special services and precautions. For example, certain flexibility and muscular toning exercises might require floor mats of a particular minimum thickness or resilience, so that friction burns of the skin or possible trauma to soft tissue and bone may be avoided. Failures to provide such mats, or insistence upon exercise without such equipment, could clearly result in litigation, and in appropriate cases, liability.[40]

Other serious problems can occur in special exercise testing and training facilities. The design of the physical plant and instructions to participants about facility use and monitoring practices by staff will affect the likelihood of mishaps and consequently, the likelihood of litigation.[41] For instance, when activity areas require electrical power, the facilities must be properly equipped with grounded electrical outlets and, in areas where wet or perspiring participants will come in contact with electrically powered devices, such devices must be equipped with ground-fault circuit interrupters that will automatically shut down power in the event that deteriorated insulation or other incident allow potentially dangerous current leakage to ground wires (e.g., treadmills and ECG systems).[42] Likewise, exclusive use of electrically powered equipment fitted with heavily insulated and grounded power cords and larger plugs must also be standard for all programs.

Many other examples of risk could be cited in relation to program facilities, including those associated with locker rooms, shower areas, steam rooms, saunas, hot tubs, and swimming pools.[43] Inappropriate and harmful conditions in these areas may increase the risk of lacerations related to sharp objects that protrude into participant pathways or access ways. Hyperthermic injury can occur when water temperature control devices do not function properly, when instructions on proper use are not clearly written nor appropriately posted or when safe egress is not possible (*e.g.,* sauna doorways). Substantial claims have already been brought forth as to these conditions. For example, in the case of <u>Lennen vs. Rutgers Ocean Beach Lodge Hotel</u>[44] the plaintiff, a pregnant (19 weeks) guest at the defendant resort, entered a resort owned hot tub which she alleged reached a temperature of as high as 110 degrees Fahrenheit. Although she indicated that she left the tub when it seemed too hot, she contended that her unborn child was detrimentally affected. The child was later born with cerebral palsy which she contended was related to the hot tub exposure. After the third or fourth day of trial the case was settled for $560,000.[45] Other similar cases have also been filed including, <u>Simon vs. Eaton Corp., et al.,</u>[46] and <u>Tirella vs. American Properties Team, Inc.</u>[47] Individuals with cardiac or circulatory problems, and those who have other adverse health conditions should seek expert advice and clearance prior to using hot tubs, saunas, steam rooms or similar devices. Sports medicine programs offering these amenities would be well advised to appropriately clear these individuals prior to allowing use.

Physiologically stressful levels of heat, humidity and air pollutants coupled with poor air circulation or other conditions represent additional risks for exercisers which must be addressed and which can contribute to exercise injury or death.[48] Failures of participants or program staff to properly consider such factors may contribute to serious injury or death as well as claim and suit.[49]

In general, facilities must be properly designed, equipped and maintained in all program areas if liability is to be controlled at manageable levels. All areas must be regularly checked and kept free of defects and nuisances so as to minimize the chances of participant injury, illness or death.

INJURIES FROM EXERCISE DEVICES

The equipment used in exercise testing and training is integrally related to the physical plant. Such devices may include bicycle ergometers, treadmills, elevated stairs or other climbing units, rowing machines, mini-trampolines, body inversion systems, strength-power training units (*e.g.,* Nautilus® or Universal® equipment), isometric racks, free weight sets for use with bars and dumbbells, exercise boards and a host of items principally controlled by electrical power. The courtroom presentation of personal injury claims involving such equipment is not unusual. In fact, injuries associated with exercise devices are somewhat common occurrences although the extent of most injuries is frequently minor. However, pinched, partially crushed, or even amputated fingers or toes can be quite common in these instances,[50] although much more serious injuries can and do occur. In this latter category, the legal system has been called upon to resolve cases where a teenaged girl was impaled upon a bicycled ergometer seat alleged to be defectively designed and maintained,[51] where a man fell while using gravity inversion boots and became a quadriplegic,[52] and where an out of condition man suffered an MI following prescribed and "supervised" use of exercise equipment.[53] Litigation in these cases is frequently accompanied by claims of defective design, assembly, maintenance or similar allegations also sometimes related to allegations of improper instruction in equipment use or inadequate supervision by the staff.[54] Potential liability arising from these allegations is likely to be more prevalent in the years to come, with increasing participation levels and the growing variety of conditioning devices available for use in fitness centers and in the home.[55]

The provision of facilities and equipment is now the subject of standards and guidelines from among others the American College of Sports Medicine (ACSM).[56] These pronouncements will likely affect the delivery of care and the provision of equipment for participant utilization. These standards will probably become the benchmark of care in this area.[57] Providers should keep abreast of such developments in order to meet the expected standard of care.

Sports medicine practitioners are entering new and ever broadening activity areas. The provision of exercise equipment and activities is but one of those areas where many practitioners are investing their time and financial resources. Reference should be made to topic specific resources for this practice area.[58]

FINAL THOUGHT

The sports medicine team as a unit is really the sum of its individual providers. It is clear that a properly composed, formed and authorized unit can provide appropriate care to sports medicine patients. When individual state legislative authorizations are unclear, overlapping or non-existent, however, the delivery of care and service must be carefully thought out and preplanned. The assistance of knowledgeable legal counsel for these purposes is absolutely essential. The appropriate development of program position descriptions along with clear program policies and procedures delineating who does what, for whom and under what circumstances will address these concerns. The use of written protocols and standing orders as well as a clear line of supervision by the team physician will minimize the team's legal risks related to the appropriate delivery of services to patients.

CHAPTER 3 FOOTNOTES:

1.   42 Ohio St.2d 399, 402.

2.   State vs. Winterich, 157 Ohio St. 414 (1952).

3.   *Id.*

4.   Stetina vs. State Medical Licensing Board, 513 N.E.2d 1234 (Ind. App.2d Dist. 1987).

5.   Foster vs. Board of Chiropractic Examiners, 359 S.E.2d 877 (1987).

6.   King vs. Board of Medical Examiners, 65 Cal. App.2d 644 (1944).

7.   State vs. Baker, 229 N.C. 73 (1948).

8.   People vs. Bovee, 92 Mich. App. 42 (1979); Attorney General vs. Beno, 422 Mich. 293 (1985).

9. Norville vs. Mississippi State Medical Association, 364 So.2d 1084 (Miss. 1978).

10. State vs. Wilson, 528 P.2d 279 (Washington 1974).

11. Cf. Peoples vs. Burroughs, Supreme Court of California, Crim. Case No. 23151 (April 19, 1984).

12. See Zimmerman, "Industrial Medicine and Athletic Training: Cost Effectiveness in the Non-Traditional Setting," Journal of Athletic Trainers 28(2):131-136, 1993.

13. See Herbert, "The Use of Athletic Trainers in The Clinical, Industrial and Corporate Setting," The Sports, Parks and Recreation Law Reporter 7(2):23-24, 1993.

14. Michigan Statutes, Article 1 and 15 of Act 268 of 1978.

15. See, supra footnote 12.

16. AAP, SCHOOL HEALTH: A GUIDE FOR HEALTH PROFESSIONALS, at page 175 (AAP, Elk Grove Village, IL 1987).

17. See e.g., Armchief vs. Gonzales, 660 S.W.2d 683 (Mo. 1983), analyzed in Brent, "Risk Management in Home Health Care: Focus on Patient Care Liability," Loyola University Law Journal 20:775-795, 1989.

18. See Herbert, "Should Athletic Trainers Be Held To The Standard Of Care Of Physicians," The Sports, Parks and Recreation Law Reporter 1(4):56-58, 1988.

19. AAP, SPORTS MEDICINE: HEALTH CARE FOR YOUNG ATHLETES, at page 225 (AAP, Evanston, IL 1983).

20. Hawkins, "The Legal Status of Athletic Trainers," The Sports, Parks and Recreation Law Reporter 2(1):6-9, 1988.

21. Leverenz and Helms, "Suing Athletic Trainers: Part I, A Review of the Case Law Involving Athletic Trainers," ATHLETIC TRAINING 212-216, Fall 1990.

22. Leverenz and Helms, "Suing Athletic Trainers: Part II, Implications for the NATA Competencies," analyzing Sorey vs. Kellett, 849 F.2d 429 (5th Cir. 1988).

23. ARCHIVES OF INTERNAL MEDICINE 147:1729-1732, (1987).

24. See e.g., Harvey vs. Stanley, 803 S.W.2d 721 (Tex. App. - Fort Worth 1990) analyzed in "Stress Test Results in Death and Million Dollar Verdict," The Exercise Standards and Malpractice Reporter 6(2):22, 1992.

25. See, Arbitration Case of Ricardo Camerena, analyzed in Herbert, "Exercise Prescription Without Testing Results in A Plaintiff's Award," The Exercise Standards and Malpractice Reporter 6(1):5-6, 1992.

26. See, "Are GXTs required for screening of all men over 40?," The Exercise Standards and Malpractice Reporter 2(2):18 (1988).

27. AHA, THE EXERCISE STANDARDS BOOK (reprinted from Circulation 59:421A, 1979; Circulation 59:849A, 1979; Circulation 59:1084A, 1979; Circulation 62:699A, 1980) (AHA, Dallas, TX 1980).

28. AHA, "Guidelines For Exercise Testing," JACC 8:72538, 1986.

29. AHA, "Exercise Standards," *Circulation* 82(6):2286-2322, 1990.

30. *See,* Herbert and Herbert, LEGAL ASPECTS OF PREVENTIVE, REHABILITA-TION AND RECREATIONAL EXERCISE PROGRAMS, THIRD EDITION, at 169-180 (PRC Publishing, Inc., Canton, OH 1993).

31. ACSM, GUIDELINES FOR EXERCISE TESTING AND PRESCRIPTION, 4th Edition (Lea & Febiger, Philadelphia, PA 1991).

32. *See,* Herbert & Herbert, *supra* footnote 30 at 184-205.

33. *See* Shermon, "Suits Mounting: Diet Plan's Maker Maps Response," *The National Law Journal* 3, Monday, April 23, 1990.

34. *Id.*

35. 548 N.E.2d 811 (Appellate Court, Il. 1989).

36. *Id.* at page 813.

37. *Id.* at page 814.

38. *Id.* at page 821.

39. *Id.*

40. *See* Richie, "Medical-Legal Implications of Dance Exercise Leadership: The Aerobic Dance Floor Surface," *The Exercise Standards and Malpractice Reporter* 2(6):87-88, 1988.

41. *Id.*

42. *See* Herbert, "Equipment Deficiencies and Improper Instruction," *Fitness Management* 12-19, January, 1989; Herbert & Herbert, "Frequent Claims and Suits in Equipment Related Injuries," *Fitness Management* 22, July, 1988; Rabinoff, "An Examination of Four Recent Cases Against Fitness Instructors," *The Exercise Standards and Malpractice Reporter* 2(3):43-47, 1988.

43. *See* Herbert, "Legal Aspects of Water Based Fitness Activities," *Fitness Management* 37, March 1988.

44. Case No. 87-10004-CIV, U.S. District Court, Southern District of Florida, Miami Division, some issues reported in 662 F. Supp. 240, *analyzed in* "Superheated Hot Tub Leads to Significant Claim and Suit," *The Exercise Standards and Malpractice Reporter* 2(1):11-12, January, 1988.

45. Herbert, "Superheated Hot Tub Case Resolved for Substantial Settlement," *The Exercise Standards and Malpractice Reporter* 3(2):23-25, 1989.

46. Case No. 88-CV-1835, El Paso County District Court, El Paso, TX.

47. 535 N.Y.S.2d 252 (A.D.3, Sept. 19, 1988).

48. *See,* "Two Corporate Challenge Series Participants Die," *The Exercise Standards and Malpractice Reporter* 2(6):94, 1988; *see also,* Kenney, "Considerations for Preventive and Rehabilitative Exercise Programs During Periods of High Heat and Humidity," *The Exercise Standards and Malpractice Reporter* 3(1):1-7, 1989.

49. Gehling, Admx. vs. St. George's University School of Medicine, 698 F. Supp. 419 (E.D. N.Y. 1988).

50. CPSC, Consumer Product Safety Alert, "Prevent Finger Amputations to Children From Exercise Bikes," August, 1990.

51. Brown vs. Sperry L. Hutchinson Company, Case No. 82-245, U.S. District Court, E.D. Ky. 1984;

52. Thompson vs. Gravity Guidance, Inc., Case No. K84-50 CA8, U.S. District Court, E.D. Mich., 1984;

53. DeRouen vs. Holiday Spa Health Clubs of California, Case No. C346987, Super. Court, Los Angeles, CA 1983.

54. Rabinoff, "Weight Room Litigation: What's It All About?," *The Exercise Standards and Malpractice Reporter* 7(4):49, 52-55, 1993; Rabinoff, "An Examination of Four Recent Cases Against Fitness Instructors," *The Exercise Standards and Malpractice Reporter* 2(3):43-47, 1988.

55. Herbert and Herbert, "Frequent Claims and Suits in Equipment-Related Injuries," *Fitness Management* 22, February 1988.

56. ACSM, HEALTH/FITNESS FACILITY STANDARDS AND GUIDELINES (Human Kinetics, Champaign, IL 1992).

57. Herbert, "An Examination of The New ACSM Standards and Guidelines for Health/Fitness Facilities," *The Exercise Standards and Malpractice Reporter* 6(2):17, 20, 1992.

58. Herbert and Herbert, *supra* footnote 30.

4 SPORTS MEDICINE TEAM DUTIES AND RESPONSIBILITIES

The sports medicine team has an ever-growing list of duties and responsibilities covering a wide variety of areas beyond just practice and game situations. The American Academy of Pediatricians (AAP), for example, defines the role of a team physician rather broadly to include duties related to preparticipation evaluations presence at athletic activities, evaluation and treatment of athletic injuries, counseling in nutrition and substance use and abuse, and a whole host of other matters.[1]

Similar statements of the AAP[2] provide that: *"The team physician, in conjunction with school health personnel, teachers, and administration, should be responsible for developing policies regarding (1) medical eligibility of athletes for participation in various sports; (2) medical eligibility of athletes to resume activity after illness or injury; (3) availability of medical services (e.g., first aid procedures, arrangements for transportation to hospitals) at athletic events; (4) supervision of personnel providing health services to athletes; (5) selection of training practices with health implications, including diets, conditioning, physical therapy, training room facilities, protective equipment, and drug use; (6) protection against legal liability.*

The team physician must have final authority to determine the physical and mental fitness of athletes participating in school programs. This authority should be understood by trainers, emergency medical technicians, athletic directors, coaches, and school administrators. Although an athlete's pediatrician must first approve the resumption of physical activity after a serious injury or illness, the team physician is responsible for the final decision to return a student to competition.

The team physician should be responsible for assuring that only safe, well-fitting, and reliable equipment is used in athletic programs; however, the responsibility for purchasing, fitting, and maintaining equipment belongs to the school's athletic department. The team physician should evaluate the health of all team candidates and review examinations done by athletes' physicians before the beginning of the season."

Even the NCAA SPORTS MEDICINE HANDBOOK[3] contemplates a rather broad range of responsibilities for the sports medicine physician and team. It would seem that the provider's roles are beyond simple practice and game duties and responsibilities and may extend far beyond any given sports season. Given the nature and extent of sports medicine responsibilities, a team approach to the provision of service may be the only viable method for the delivery of care.[4]

The broad and somewhat all encompassing role which many expressed statements forge for the sports medicine physician and team could conceivably create a myriad of problems for them if injury results to a patient as a proximate result of a negligent omission or act. In many programs, especially with part-time or volunteer providers or as to some younger age sports groups, the expectation of some of the expressed standards may be somewhat unrealistic and beyond the budgets of many programs. Nevertheless, such documents will in all likelihood be used in the event of litigation as benchmarks of behavior for comparison with provider acts or omissions. Such comparisons are almost always provided by expert witnesses. Expert witnesses are often allowed to express opinions during their testimony as to various matters which lay witnesses would be prohibited from expressing. Experts are allowed to opine on such matters because of their education, background, training and professional qualification. Prior to expressing such opinions during testimony, however, the witness' relevant qualification as an expert must be established through questioning. Once the proper qualification testimony is established, however, the witness, through responses to the examining lawyer's questions, must lay a proper foundation or set of facts upon which the witness will express opinions.

In the event of claim and litigation involving someone in the sports medicine setting, expert testimony will often be focused upon the issues of: 1) whether or not the practitioner adhered to the proper professional standards of practice in rendering service and/or in providing advice to individuals engaged in sports, athletics or various exercise activities; and, 2) whether or not the provider in rendering the service or providing the advice or supervision fell below the accepted and appropriate standard of care thereby negligently and proximately causing injury to the individual in question. Based upon even a cursory review of the possible standards of practice applicable to the sports medicine area, and given the wide range of individuals providing service to a diverse patient population, it is quite clear that a variety of standards promulgated by a number of professionals might be utilized in an effort to judge a sports medicine practitioner's conduct in court.[5]

While there has been a proliferation of written standards type statements by a variety of groups, not everyone has been convinced as to the benefits of such statements. Some fear that the development of these standards will hurt professional freedoms and may lead to near automatic findings of negligence when provider conduct deviates from written expressions as to the standard of care. While such fears may impact the subject to some extent (at least arguably), this aspect of concern can be minimized through appropriate drafting of such statements and proper legal analysis.[6] Until these issues are fully determined, some groups, including the American Academy of Orthopaedic Surgeons, for example, are still debating whether or not standards should be developed.[7]

Given the fact that there is a high likelihood of judicial adoption of association standards of care through expert witnesses in the event of claim and suit, it is extremely important for sports medicine providers to understand areas of likely concern that could impact their procedures and practices. Some of these standards also create greater potential exposure for members of the sports medicine team in the event of injury than do other such statements. An examination of several of these areas of concern in reference to the expressed duties and responsibilities of the sports medicine team would seem to be of importance.

A. SPORTS MEDICINE PRESENCE AT BOTH PRACTICE AND GAME SETTINGS

While many sports medicine physicians are only present for game or match situations, a good many injuries or other instances requiring advice or care arise in the course of practice situations. Often trainers or other members of the sports medicine team (including coaches) must deal with practice injuries or provide post-practice first aid, "treatment" or rehabilitative type activities. Notwithstanding this scenario which may be all too common at high school and lower levels of athletic competition, there is at least an expectation if not a rather strong recommendation within the existing standards statements for physician presence at game and practice situations.[8]

Given the realities of many sports medicine programs, the expectation of physician presence at all practice and game situations is probably beyond the grasp of many programs. However, appropriately prepared and trained individuals including physician assistants, nurses, therapists, trainers and other such providers, including coaches, should be in a position under the broad general supervision of the physician (even in his or her absence), to meet the intent of the expressed association statements or other expressed guidelines which could be construed as part of the standard of care. Since the intent of these standards dealing with competent provider presence at game and practice situations is to deal with instances of injury and emergency, appropriate and lawful delegation of authority to certain non-physician members of the sports medicine team would seem to be appropriate in the absence of the physician. Standing orders, written protocols and/or on call and available physicians should all be utilized to meet the intent of this expected standard of care, (*see,* discussion on standing orders, Chapter 10).

B. SELECTION AND FITTING OF EQUIPMENT

One of the most potentially troublesome expectations for the sports medicine physician and the sports medicine team relates to those written expressions dealing with the selection and fitting of equipment, especially for contact sports. Negligent acts or omissions in this area can expose providers to very large claims arising out of very serious injuries due to equipment related injuries. Some of the expressed standards provide that program equipment "should be the best available."[9] Other similar statements require physician assurance as to the provision of "safe" equipment.[10] The use of the term "safe" may have special and precise legal connotation. In many circumstances, individuals may imply that the term "safe" means that no injury or harm can occur from participation with the use of such designated equipment. However, there is no completely safe activity and no completely safe item of protective athletic equipment.[11]

Over the years, a variety of products and activities have been advertised as safe. When individuals are injured while using these products or participating in the advertised activity, suit and liability sometimes resulted.[12] The trend of such cases seems to be to hold those who advertise a safe activity or product actionable for injuries which occur to individuals while using such products or participating in such activities.

When a standard requires the provision of "safe" equipment under circumstances where safe equipment is really not available, liability could potentially attach inasmuch as "safe equipment" cannot readily be provided. Even where standards require the provision of the "safest available equipment," that is subject to a matter of interpretation and may additionally expose providers to situations of liability in the event of injury related to equipment failures or deficiencies. Standards like the one previously cited should perhaps be couched in terms of "appropriate, well-designed and well-constructed equipment," or "equipment constructed in accordance with established industry standards," rather than using the term "safe" or "safest" available.

Aside from the duty to assist in the equipment selection and provision process, sports medicine personnel may be expected by some of the relevant standards to be involved in the fitting of equipment, instruction as to its use and even education as to its maintenance. Since ill-fitting or poorly maintained equipment may lead to injury, aggravation of injury or even enhancement of injury, it would seem prudent for providers to set up and oversee a system whereby equipment will be properly fitted to participants, followed by periodic equipment inspection and maintenance. Providers, it would seem, should also be engaged in delivering information on product care and use so that this aspect of the duty of care will be fulfilled.

C. THE PROVISION OF EXERCISE OR TRAINING PRESCRIPTIONS, INSTRUCTION IN THE USE OF FACILITIES OR EQUIPMENT AND THE SUPERVISION OF THE USE OF SAME

Many sports medicine providers are venturing into health club-like operations for their patients providing a wide range of services and equipment for their use and enjoyment. The provision of such equipment and facilities is not without legal significance in that injuries arising out of equipment usage including injuries due to the provision of defective or improperly maintained equipment, or the lack of appropriate instruction or supervision related thereto is a frequent source of claim and suit.

Although it appears, based upon recent U.S. CONSUMER PRODUCT SAFETY COMMISSION REPORTS, that the estimated number of injuries related to the use of various forms of exercise devices has decreased from the 1985 Reports, it also appears that claims and litigation related to such devices may be on the increase.[13]

A number of cases dealing with exercise equipment related injuries have either recently resulted in verdicts or are presently awaiting trial. An examination of the issues and results in a few of these cases will surely be of value and importance to the discussion of this topic area. The first of these cases Heher vs. Strafford Racquetball Club,[14] dealt with certain questions as to instructor qualifications in reference to participant use of particular exercise machinery. The plaintiff's counsel claimed that the professional staff of the facility was insufficient and improperly trained and that the negligence of the facility caused an injury to his client while he was using the exercise equipment. The case was resolved prior to trial.

In another case, Sosa vs. Jack LaLane,[15] the plaintiff claimed that instructors caused him to aggravate a pre-existing condition in reference to his use of certain exercise devices and exercises at the defendant's facility. The plaintiffs in this case concentrated their discovery effort on obtaining information as to the "qualifications" of those individuals working at the facility.

In another case, Battaglia vs. Holiday Health Club, Inc.,[16] a young woman was injured while using an exercise device at the defendant's facility in Colorado. Again the qualifications of the facility's instructors were a major issue in the discovery effort put forth in the case.

In still another case, <u>Jacobsen vs. Holiday Health Club</u>,[17] a weight machine fell upon the plaintiff during her use of the device causing certain injuries. The plaintiff brought suit contending that the weight equipment was not properly adjusted which created a present and foreseeable danger to her and that the conduct of the health club (which the plaintiff claimed had prior knowledge of similar incidents) amounted to wanton and reckless disregard for her rights and safety. Based upon these allegations, a jury returned a verdict finding willful and wanton negligence in the sum of $84,500.[18]

It is important to emphasize that it seems that the trend as to exercise equipment injuries appears to not only center upon defects in the maintenance and operation of various devices but also as to the instruction, supervision and monitoring of the use of such devices by facility staff members.[19] It may well be that a good many future claims that relate to exercise equipment injuries will focus upon an instructor's or supervisor's training and experience in an effort to demonstrate inadequate experience, training or qualification as to instruction or supervision of clients using such equipment.[20] It seems clear that the emerging standard of care[21] requires proper instruction and supervision in the use of equipment rather than just the mere provision of same.[22]

D. GRADED EXERCISE STRESS TESTING PROCEDURES

Graded exercise tests (GXTs), commonly performed on motor-powered treadmills or bicycle ergometers are fast becoming popular fitness assessment tools. At the same time, the use of diagnostic exercise stress testing procedures in medical practice has grown dramatically and is now used for almost half of all acute MI patients, compared to less than .1 percent in 1975.[23]

Along with the dramatic increase in the use of such procedures in both the medical and fitness professions, a number of rather significant legal issues have also arisen. These issues center upon: 1) the relative safety of stress testing; 2) the propriety of non-physician personnel carrying out such procedures; and 3) the legal risks associated with the performance of the tests.

In 1971, the results of a large-scale study of exercise stress testing procedures were reported by Rochmis and Blackburn.[24] An analysis of the results of this study, as well as other studies that have been conducted since, indicate a rather low incidence of serious risk associated with GXT procedures.

Most within the medical community consider GXTs to be relatively safe, especially when supervised by a physician. However, many believe that GXTs should not be carried out or supervised by anyone other than physicians.[25]

The State of North Carolina Medical Examiners issued a statement in June, 1987 declaring: *"When a non-physician administers a graded exercise test, the standard of care in North Carolina is that a physician is in the room or immediate area."*[26] Expressed concerns like these can raise significant legal issues as to who can properly carry out GXTs, and under what circumstances. These concerns have obvious relation to sports medicine practitioners who use such procedures in their practices. These problems relate to the unauthorized practice of medicine which were discussed in Chapter 3, and have clear application to these professional practices.

Putting aside any further discussion of the unauthorized practice of medicine issues associated with who can perform those procedures, a number of cases dealing with GXTs have arisen during the last several years. Although most of these cases deal with medically conducted procedures, at least one health club facility case centered upon injuries related to treadmill use.[27]

One of these cases, <u>Tart vs. McGahn</u>,[28] although resulting in a defendant's verdict, was settled for $50,000 pursuant to a pre-jury verdict agreement. The plaintiff in this case suffered a post-test MI. The case centered upon the physicians' supervision of the test and their alleged failure to terminate the test in light of the patient's facial and other non-verbal expressions of fatigue.

In the case of <u>Hedgecorth vs. United States</u>,[29] (which we will review in more detail hereinafter) a verdict in favor of the plaintiffs was returned for $825,000. The case dealt with the defendant's alleged failure to disclose certain risks during the informed consent process preceding the GXT (possibility of stroke). The plaintiff suffered a stroke and resultant blindness as a result of the procedure and a finding of liability resulted due to a deficiency in the informed consent process.

GXTs can be very valuable fitness assessments or medically-based diagnostic procedures. When carried out with properly selected and pre-screened subjects and by appropriately trained or licensed personnel, the procedure may be an appropriate venture for some members of the sports medicine team. However, proper medical and legal consultation should be obtained before implementation of any of these testing procedures, to ensure compliance with state law and minimal legal exposure to the program.

(Portions of this section have been reprinted with permission from Herbert, Law Notes: "Know Your Legal Responsibilities in Administering Stress Testing," Fitness Management 16:67, July/August, 1988, Copyright 1988 by Leisure Publications, Inc.)

E. CONDITIONING AND TRAINING

Athletes and others seeking advice on activity, weight lifting, weight gain or loss, training and conditioning, rehabilitation, injury prevention or fitness assessment are turning in ever-increasing numbers to the sports medicine team for advice and guidance.[30] Despite this occurrence, there are certain legal risks associated with these activities. Aside from the question related to who can do what within the sports medicine setting, it must be remembered that participation in these activities is not without risk of injury, claim and suit.[31]

Given the fact that some studies have indicated that training, conditioning and fitness may indeed help to prevent injuries,[32] it seems only logical to presume that the sports medicine team would be under a duty to provide appropriate and proper advice on such issues. Findings such as these can have a rather dramatic impact upon potential claims such as those that were raised in the case of Benitez vs. New York City Board of Education,[33] (reviewed in detail hereinafter) where the plaintiff claimed that his injuries were attributable to fatigue and mismatch.[34] Sports medicine personnel as well as coaches can have a rather dramatic impact upon the development of fitness and conditioning programs for athletes to help reduce the risk of certain injuries. A failure to do so could well be challenged based upon findings like the one reported in the foregoing study. While the findings of this study may seem obvious to many providers, the issuance of the article and results adds yet another bit of information available for citation in reference to standards of practice in court proceedings where there has been an alleged deviation from the standard of care.

The AAP has in fact promulgated statements as to the need for sports medicine personnel to become involved in training and the recommendation or prescription of activity.[35] Others have similarly expressed the same or similar recommendations as to the need for sports medicine professionals to become involved in these activities.[36] In order to comply with such statements as to the standard of care, sports medicine personnel must become knowledgeable as to safe exercise and conditioning activities.[37] Since this area is developing and changing, there is also a need to stay current so that recommendations might be provided as to appropriate conditioning and training practices. Failures in this regard related to improper recommendations or negligent prescriptions are clearly actionable.[38] Activities related to conditioning and training advice, including nutritional advice and counseling have legal ramifications which must be considered.[39]

F. MISMATCHES

A recent case from New York rather poignantly demonstrates the legal concerns associated with mismatched competitions. Sports medicine personnel have clear duties to avoid matching immature players or participants with more mature participants due to the potential for injury in the event of contact.[40]

Mismatching of personnel can be actionable. For example, in the case of Tepper vs. City of New Rochelle School District,[41] a high school junior was injured during lacrosse practice. He brought suit for his injuries contending that the sponsoring school district by and through the lacrosse coach was responsible for his injuries and resultant damages.

The plaintiff in this case was a 130 pound, inexperienced player who had only 30 days of organized lacrosse team experience. The team of which he was a member was divided into three squads: varsity, junior varsity and a smaller group in between the two. The practice field area was limited which caused the squads to sometimes practice together. The JV team had a no cut policy. Seniors could not however play on the JV team. Although the coach routinely warned smaller players against going head to head with larger athletes, he apparently was willing to permit *"anyone with sufficient skill and physical prowess to play on the varsity."* [42]

On the day of the plaintiff's injuries, the plaintiff was matched against a 260 pound senior with three years experience during a one on one ground ball drill. During the drill (which was obviously capable of producing injuries) the senior player used an advanced checking technique (and apparently his size and weight) to subdue the plaintiff causing him to break his arm. Based upon these facts the court concluded: *"[T]he plaintiff has raised an issue of fact as to whether the coach was negligent in permitting the plaintiff, a player of slight build and very limited experience, to go head to head with a 260 pound senior varsity member, a player possessing substantially greater experience."* [43]

In considering the school board defendant's arguments that the plaintiff assumed the risk of injury by reason of his participation and that the claim was barred by reason of parental execution of a consent form, the court stated: *"[I]n light of this peculiar factual setting, it cannot be said as a matter of law that the plaintiff assumed the risk of injury...or [that] the plaintiff comprehended the true nature of the risk when he opted to join the team."*[44] As a consequence of these conclusions, the issues in this case were scheduled for jury determination.

Although the Tepper case was directed at a coach as opposed to another provider member of a sports medicine team, the ruling has clear implication to the physician/trainer responsible for care of such athletes according to expressed standards of practice. Unless there is adherence to the appropriate standard of care as to these issues, it is likely that more cases like this will be filed with potentially far-reaching consequences.[45]

G. CLIMATIC CONDITIONS
Participants in sport, exercise or other recreational activities can be affected by a number of factors including climatic conditions. Such conditions can adversely impact participants and contribute to unnecessary injury or even death.[46] To illustrate the various medico-legal considerations involved in these issues, (although other significant issues are at stake as well) consider the case of Gehling, Admx. vs. St. George's University School of Medicine, Ltd., et al.[47] The facts of this case which were in part reported in Gehling vs. St. George University School of Medicine[48] might be briefly summarized as follows: Earl Gehling, the decedent, was a 25 year old male medical student at the St. George's University School of Medicine on the island of Grenada. He was approximately 75 pounds overweight and suffered from hypertension as well as an enlarged left ventricle of his heart. Although he was "athletic" and had apparently practiced jogging before participating in the race in question, it appears from the record that he may not have been properly prepared for racing. The student however entered a race, a 2.5 mile "fun run" conducted on the

West Indies Island on public roads between two campuses. On the late afternoon of the race, the temperature was approximately 80 to 85 degrees and the humidity was high. Approximately half way through the race, water was available to runners at a roadside spigot and oxygen followed all of the approximate 100 racers in a school vehicle. No doctors or other providers were made available during the race but water, towels soaked in cold water and ice were available. Medical students who had been trained as physician assistants were located at the race's termination point. The decedent died following the race. His estate brought suit against the medical school among others alleging negligence.

In examining the relevant issues surrounding the conduct of the race, the court stated: *"In a short race of 2.5 miles run in tropical environmental conditions some type of assistance should be provided for the runners at the end of the race, in this instance, primarily by the students of SGU. The availability of water, ice, oxygen and wet towels at the finish line, coupled with the stationing there of medical students with some emergency training, was sufficient to satisfy this duty of care. In view of the short distance of the race it was not necessary to have a doctor and special provisions for emergency, such as intravenous capability..."* (one wonders whether or not these conclusions are in fact supported by the literature, consensus statements, position statements and other documentation applicable to the activity?)

The court also went on to note that even if SGU was determined to have a duty to control, monitor or supervise the race, any failure on its part to do so could not have been the cause of the student's death. The court in fact found that the student had taken Ephedrine, (an amphetamine-like substance which speeds the heart rate) prior to the race. The court found that the decedent who was an advanced medical student knew or should have known *"of the potential consequences of ingesting amphetamine-like drugs and that he had borderline hypertension."* The court also noted that *"overweight persons are more susceptible to heat exhaustion and heat stroke; accordingly his obesity was a contributing factor in his suffering from exposure to heat."* Based upon these facts the court went on to determine that even if SGU had been determined to have a duty to control, monitor or supervise the race any failure on its part to do so could not have been the cause of the student's death.

The court, based upon all the foregoing, determined that the cause of the student's death was *"his physical condition – his being overweight, having hypertension, taking Ephedrine and his hypertrophied left ventricle – and the circumstances under which the race was run."*

The court also lastly concluded that the decedent had assumed the risks of his participation. Specifically the court stated: *"The decedent being a sixth semester medical student, is charged with knowledge of his own condition and of the tropical conditions of the Island, and by entering the race he assumed the risk of thermal injury under the circumstances including the risks of suffering heat prostration and/or heat stroke."*

Although it appears that the American College of Sports Medicine Position Stand On The Prevention Of Thermal Injuries During Distance Running was presented to the court, the court determined: *"These guidelines apply only to races of at least ten kilometers (2.6 miles) (sic) and therefore not to this race."* The court therefore placed little if any reliance upon the position stand because the race at hand was only 2.5 miles (approximately). Based upon all of the foregoing, the court entered judgment for the defendants and denied the plaintiff's various causes of actions.

The court's failure to place emphasis upon the American College of Sports Medicine Position Stand based upon the statement that the guidelines applied only to races of at least 2.6 miles appears to be misquoted. Aside from the Court's failure to recognize the fact that 10 kilometers is approximately 6.2 miles, not 2.6 miles, the guidelines and statements as contained within the Position Statement are designed to provide safeguards during instances of participation in distance running. A failure to place emphasis upon the standard of care as provided in the Position Statement appears to be unfounded.

Regardless of the court's failure to fully consider the ACSM Position Stand, the facts of this particular case may have dictated the result in that the decedent was an advanced and trained medical student who should have known the various complications associated with his conditions (especially under the applicable climatic conditions) (not to mention his ingestion of an amphetamine-like substance prior to the race). In a situation where another individual would have participated under like circumstances, one wonders if the result as found in this case might have been different. Moreover, based upon findings as published elsewhere, noting that runners who collapse are primarily undertrained and not acclimated to heat, the result in this case may well have been different under slightly different circumstances especially with someone other than an advanced medical student. In any case, the various issues involved in screening, allowing participation, allowing a race to proceed under extremes of heat and/or humidity and in providing various safeguards during such activities have been addressed in this case which may have some precedent to other situations. However, the court's blanket conclusions as to the sufficiency of the precautions which were taken during the race may not be in accordance with the appropriate standard of practice for conducting such events. The court's conclusion that the availability of certain aids such as ice, oxygen and wet towels at the finish line, together with the stationing of medical students with "some" emergency training at the end of the race was tantamount to adherence to the appropriate standard of care does not seem to be in accordance with the accepted standard of practice.

While there are a variety of factors which can lead to the collapse, injury and even death of runners or other sports participants,[49] activity or sport may need to be scheduled around adverse climatic conditions if necessary to avoid needless injuries[50] and/or other safeguards may need to be put into place. In fact, according to W. Larry Kenney, Ph.D., even though there may be no promulgated standards applicable to conducting exercise or sport programs during periods of high heat and humidity, there is an accepted basis for heat stress evaluation based upon a document proposed by NIOSH under the Occupational Safety & Health Act of 1970 (Public Law 91-596): *"While written for industrial application, this document contains information on heat stress evaluation, control of heat stress, biologic effects of heat, education, and record-keeping suitable for exercise programs as well. [Pursuant to]...the NIOSH approach to heat stress evaluation, three distinct limits are presented which are based on exercise intensity (expressed here as VO2) and ambient WBGT. First, a 'ceiling limit' is proposed above which no one should exercise without special clothing or equipment. Secondly, two other limits are proposed – one for acclimatized persons (Recommended Exposure Limit, REL) and one for unacclimatized persons (Recommended Alert Limit, RAL). Healthy exercisers should not aerobically exercise above these representive combinations of intensity and environment without special precautions.*

For environments below the ceiling limit but above the RAL or REL (whichever applies), the following actions are recommended:

1. *Change the environment. If adequate cooling by means of fans or air conditioning is not available or practical, move the site to an environment meeting the WBGT requirements;*

2. *Change the exercise. Lower overall VO2 requirements to an acceptable level by any of several methods. These include slowing the pace of exercise appropriately, adding rest cycles to a routine, intermittent exercise, etc. Typically, within most training zones, heart rate is increased about 1 bpm for every degree Centigrade above 25° C and 2 bpm for every mmHg*

above 20 mmHg water vapor pressure. Exercise intensity can be slowed to appropriate safe levels by using target heart rate (unchanged from cool conditions) as a guide.

3. *Use an aquatic environment. Very few aquatic situations impart a heat stress similar to that found in air environments. While body temperature does rise and sweating does occur during aquatic activity, the conductive cooling provided by the water usually limits heat strain. As a rule, the water should feel cool to the touch. Depending on participants and intensity of exercise, 25-29° C (77-84° F) is usually a comfortable range of water temperature when air temperatures are high."*[51]

Dr. Kenney also notes *"the NIOSH guidelines and other proposed standards assume that the participants are free of overt disease which may increase the likelihood of heat illness. Many such conditions exist, including (but not limited to): hypertension (alters control of skin blood flow), diabetes (neuropathies may affect sweating and/or skin blood flow), aging (alters peripheral cardiovascular and sweating responses), various drug regimens (including diuretics, beta-blockers, alpha-agonists, and vasodila-tors), alcohol use (causes vasodilation and enhances dehydra-tion), obesity, and a prior history of heat illness or difficulty acclimating to heat. The exercise professional should be knowl-edgeable about the effects of each of these on temperature regulations."*[52]

Dr. Kenney believes, *"one of the key events in decreasing the risk of exercise program participants developing heat illness is gradual acclimation to exercise in hot environments. Through this process, heart rate and temperature at a given exercise intensity decrease, sweat rate increases, and sweat becomes more dilute. It has been estimated that as much as 25% of the population is heat intolerant in the unacclimated state, and that about 2% remain heat intolerant even after thorough acclimation. The best method of acclimation is to combine aerobic exercise (at intensi-*

ties as low as 30% VO2 max) with heat exposure, beginning with as little as 10-15 minutes and increasing duration gradually. It takes most healthy people 10-14 such exposures to fully acclimate, although illness and alcohol consumption have been shown to slow this process.

[A]cclimation and adequate hydration are the two key events in mitigating the untoward effects of high temperatures. All...programs should have fluids available for participants before, during, and after exercise. The fluid should be cold (45-55°F) and palatable, and with very few exceptions, water is the replacement drink of choice. Participants should be encouraged to drink as much water as is physically comfortable 15-30 minutes prior to exercise, a cupful of water at 15 minute intervals during exercise, and more water than thirst dictates after exercise. This latter point is especially applicable for those participants over the age of 60, since research has shown a decreased thirst sensitivity to body hydration status in this age group. There is little need to replace electrolytes lost during most exercise sessions since these small decrements are typically replenished when the next meal is eaten. For participants on a restricted salt diet, their physician should be consulted with regard to salt balance. Unless the exercise bout lasts in excess of 90 minutes, there is little advantage to supplementing carbohydrates." [53] Inadequate fluid replacement and inappropriate activity in heat and humid conditions may be an area of potential medico-legal concern and should be avoided. [54]

One of the classic examples of heat stroke in a traditional sports medicine related setting is contained in the case of <u>Mogabgab vs. Orleans Parish School Board</u>. [55] In this case a high school football player suffered profound heat stress during practice, which was not timely noted nor appropriately treated by the school's coaches, which in turn lead to the boy's untimely death. The boy's parents subsequently brought suit against the school board, the coaches and administrative personnel contending negligence in that the defendants failed *"to perform their duty of providing all necessary and reasonable safeguards to prevent accidents, injuries and sickness of the football players...and...in failing to provide for prompt treatment when injuries or sickness occur."* [56] The plaintiffs also specifically alleged *"that the defendants did not follow the recommendations of the American Medical Association for the prevention of heat stroke and heat exhaustion during football workouts, which they assert was the cause of...[the decedent's] suffering a heat stroke or that it at least contributed* thereto." [57] It was also further alleged that although the boy's first symptoms appeared at approximately 5:20 pm on the day of the event that he became unconscious by 5:25 pm, *"after which...improper treatment was administered which contributed or caused deterioration...to such an extent that proper medical treatment was of no avail and death occurred."* [58]

The facts of this case were rather dramatic and unfortunate in that no medical personnel were even called until one hour and twenty minutes after the boy became unconscious. Examination and treatment did not commence until almost two hours after the boy became ill. *"[T]he negligence of...[the coaches] actively denied...[the athlete] access to treatment for some two hours after symptoms appeared. When he did see a physician it was too late and he died."* [59] Judgment was thus rendered in favor of the plaintiffs and against the defendant coaches.

While the emergency response practices in this case are unusual and hopefully not indicative of the present day sports medicine standard of care, this case clearly points out what can go wrong. All members of the sports medicine team must be prepared to promptly deal with such incidents.

I.   EMERGENCY RESPONSE PROTOCOLS
AND PROCEDURES

Sports medicine programs absolutely must have well-formulated, adequately written and periodically rehearsed emergency response protocols to be carried out in the event of untoward incident. This is one of those areas of frequent medico-legal concern.[60] Deficiencies in this area often result in claim and suit. The recent suit brought by the estate of Hank Gathers against Loyola Marymount University and several members of its Athletic Department and sports medicine team emphasizes some of the medico-legal concerns in this area[61] as does the foregoing Mogabgab case.[62]

In the Gathers action, specific details of alleged negligence were set forth in a 52 page complaint which among other things contended that the emergency response efforts of the sports medicine team following the collapse of Hank Gathers during an intercollegiate basketball game on national television were inadequate under the circumstances. The complaint in particular alleged that the defendants knew that Hank Gathers prior to the date of his death had a life-threatening cardiac arrythmia, specifically a ventricular tachacardia, which could lead to his death if it went untreated. The complaint further contended that the University in response to this condition, purchased a heart defibrillator for use on the person of Hank Gathers should his heart require defibrillation during a game. Although the complaint alleged that the semi-automatic machine was purchased for Gathers, kept at courtside during games, and that members of the sports medicine team were trained in its use, the complaint also alleged that after Hank Gathers collapsed and went into convulsions and cardiac arrest, nothing was done either by way of CPR or defibrillation to resuscitate Gathers. Specifically, the complaint alleged *"Said individually named defendants intentionally did nothing of a medical nature for Hank Gathers for a period in excess of two minutes and forty-five seconds, which was the entire period of time he laid on the court, although Hank Gathers was in need of immediate medical assistance and was in need of cardiopulmonary resuscitation (CPR) and defibrillation. Said defendants did not apply or touch Hank Gathers' body with the defibrillator during this period of time when he needed it most nor was CPR started or even attempted. Initially, the decedent had a weak and threading pulse and later no pulse. Said defendants abandoned their roles as health care providers and were not acting as physicians within the meaning of [the law]. Said defendants intentionally and outrageously refused to perform their duties so that the 4,500 persons present and those watching on television would not have their sensibilities offended by such acts of resuscitation or electric shock."* In addition to these claims regarding intentional acts, the complaint of the plaintiffs also alleged that the defendants acted negligently and carelessly in not providing appropriate emergency response. While this case was not fully litigated at trial and while the facts were merely alleged rather than proven, the case adequately demonstrates the need to have clear emergency response protocols in place, rehearsed and carried out appropriately in the event of need. Alleged delays in rendering appropriate emergency treatment can lead to a variety of claims like those which arose in this case. Deficiencies in planning for emergency response, even with apparently healthy athletes who have been cleared for participation, are actionable since there is a need to respond to clearly foreseeable events.[63]

To illustrate the need for clear, rehearsed emergency response policies the case of Montgomery vs. City of Detroit[64] should also be considered along with the Mogabgab case.[65] In the Montgomery case, a fourteen year old boy collapsed on a track during participation in his high school physical education class. He was found on the track incoherent, incontinent, breathing hard, sweating profusely and shaking uncontrollably. He was carried to the gym and his mother, the plaintiff, was called for permission to call an EMS unit. This call was placed approximately 15 minutes after the incident itself. An effort was then made by the gym teacher to call an EMS unit but due to some problem with a new phone system the call did not get through. The teacher then called the school office and asked that an EMS unit be contacted. Some 21 minutes after the collapse an EMS unit was contacted but was not dispatched until almost an hour after the incident due to unit unavailability. The student was transported to a hospital about one hour after the collapse but subsequently died of a previously unknown but pre-existing heart condition. His mother later brought suit alleging negligence and gross negligence. She claimed that the delay in transport to a hospital deprived her son of a chance of survival.

Although the court dismissed the case due to state immunity statutes, it is interesting to note that the school, while having a policy to deal with medical emergencies, apparently made no showing of any training or rehearsal to insure that the emergency response plan worked in a timely manner. There may have been no requirement that phone lines be tested or that personnel be trained in their use for such procedures. It seems important that policies for response to medical emergencies be clear and specific and tested to detect if they are workable. Details must not be overlooked or programs may risk serious injury to their participants and later claims and suits. In jurisdictions without immunity laws, claims like this might be substantial indeed as they were in the Mogabgab case.[66]

J. SPORTS MEDICINE RISK MANAGEMENT RECOMMENDATIONS

While the foregoing discussion in this chapter, as well as the topics discussed hereinafter all outline the relevant medico-legal related risks to the sports medicine team, these risks can be minimized in sports medicine settings by the application of appropriate risk management practices. According to Neil J. Dougherty, Ed.D. and Professor of the Department of Recreational Study and Physical Education at Rutgers University, the practice of sports medicine is so broadly defined and diversely applied that no single set of guidelines can effectively prepare the practitioner for every type of risk that might be encountered in each of the many possible delivery situations within the theoretical programming boundaries.

Dr. Dougherty states: *"While the broad spectrum of applications and the diversity of practitioners precludes the development of a single concise listing of the potential risks and recommended management techniques applicable to all sports medicine programs, one need not resort to a multitude of situation-specific guidelines. The general principles of risk management tend to be relatively transferrable and constant across virtually all programs and activities. Therefore, given a clear understanding of such principles, the practitioner should be able to develop specific procedures applicable to his or her particular situation in order to 'manage and minimize risk.'*

Reduced to its simplest terms, risk management is a process of accomplishing two separate but interrelated tasks:

1. *Recognizing the primary risks associated with any given activity and taking all reasonable steps to eliminate or reduce them.*

2. *Recognizing that, despite one's best efforts, not all injuries can be avoided and, therefore, taking appropriate steps to maximize the likelihood of successfully defending whatever lawsuits may arise."*[67]

Dr. Dougherty believes: *"There are three general categories of causal factors which can be found, either singly or in combination, at the root of most preventable injuries. These are: 1) faulty supervision; 2) improper selection and/or conduct of the activity itself; and 3) unsafe environmental conditions. These factors have been found to form the basis for most sport related negligence claims...and, thus, they must be considered in the development of any risk management program for these programs and for sports medicine services."*[68]

FINAL THOUGHT
The broad and diverse nature of expected duties and responsibilities of the sports medicine team, and the variety of statements which could be used as standards on this subject, have far-reaching, medico-legal implication to sports medicine personnel. Practice and game duties and responsibilities are diverse and

include a variety of matters which must take place well before the season commences and long thereafter. Practitioners would be well advised to stay current with the expected standard of care, and those areas of frequent medico-legal concern, along with the implementation of a variety of risk management suggestions to deal with those areas of potential concern on an ongoing and continuous basis.

CHAPTER 4 FOOTNOTES:

1. AAP, SPORTS MEDICINE: HEALTH CARE FOR YOUNG ATHLETES, SECOND EDITION (AAP, Elk Grove, IL 1991) (Reprinted with permission from SPORTS MEDICINE; HEALTH CARE FOR YOUNG ATHLETES, Copyright 1983, American Academy of Pediatrics).

2. AAP, SCHOOL HEALTH, *supra* at 145-146. (Reprinted with permission from SCHOOL HEALTH: A GUIDE FOR HEALTH PROFESSIONALS, Copyright 1987, American Academy of Pediatrics).

3. NCAA, SPORTS MEDICINE HANDBOOK (Fifth Edition) (NCAA, Overland Park, KS 1992).

4. Samples, "The Team Physician: No Official Job Description," *The Physician and Sportsmedicine* 16(1):169-175, 1988; Loeffler, "On Being a Team Physician," *Sports Medicine Digest* 9(2):1-3 (1987); Howell, "Primary Care Sports Medicine: A Part-Timer's Perspective," *The Physician and Sportsmedicine* 16(1):103-114, 1988.

5. Herbert, THE SPORTS MEDICINE STANDARDS BOOK (Professional Reports Corporation, Canton, OH 1992, supplemented 1993).

6. AMA, LEGAL IMPLICATIONS OF PRACTICE PARAMETERS (American Medical Association, Chicago, IL 1990).

7. Abraham, "Specialties race against payers to set standards," *AMA News* 17, January 6, 1989.

8. *See* Mueller & Schindler, ANNUAL SURVEY OF FOOTBALL INJURY RESEARCH 1931-1987 (American Football Coaches Association, et al., 1988) at page 5; *cf., supra,* AAP, SCHOOL HEALTH, at page 147. *See also,* Mueller, et al., "Catastrophic Spine Injuries in Football," *The Physician and Sportsmedicine* 17(10):51-53, October, 1989.

9. *See, supra* footnote 2.

10. *See, supra* footnote 2, at page 146.

11. National Operating Committee on Standards of Athletic Equipment, NOCSAE MANUAL.

12. Hauter vs. Zogalts, 534 P.2d 377 (Cal. 1975); Tirino vs. Kennet Products Co., 341 N.Y.S.2d 61 (Civil Ct. Queens Cty., 1973); Filler vs. Rayex Corp., 435 F.2d 336 (CA 7th Cir. 1970).

13. Herbert, "Equipment Injuries in Fitness Facilities," *The Exercise Standards and Malpractice Reporter* (2):25-27, September, 1988; Herbert, et. al., "A Trial Lawyer's Guide to the Legal Implications of Recreational, Preventive and Rehabilitative Exercise Program Standards of Care," *The American Journal of Trial Advocacy* 11(3):433-452, Spring, 1988.

14. Civil Case CB-81-197255S, Fairfield County, Connecticut 1985.

15. Civil Case No. C339856, Los Angeles, California 1985.

16. Civil Action No. 86 CV 9489, Denver, Colorado 1986.

17. Civil Action No. A85 CV 1249, Arapahoe County, Colorado, 1986.

18. Rabinoff, "An Examination of Four Recent Cases Against Fitness Instructors," *The Exercise Standards and Malpractice Reporter* 2(3):43-47, May, 1988.

19. *Id.*

20. *See* ACSM, STANDARDS & GUIDELINES FOR HEALTH & FITNESS FACILITIES (Human Kinetics, Champaign, IL 1991); Rabinoff & Shaw "The Weight Room - Don't Leave It Alone," *Looking Fit* 88, October, 1987; Herbert, "Avoiding Injuries and Claims," *Fitness Management* 25, October, 1989; Herbert, "Equipment Deficiencies and Improper Instruction," *Fitness Management* 12, January 1989; Herbert, "Legal Aspects of Fitness Management," *Fitness Management* 49, November/December, 1987; Herbert, "Legal Aspects of Fitness Premises Liability," *Fitness Management* 17, September, 1988; Herbert, "Provide Services or Just Facilities? The Legal Concerns Are Different," *Fitness Management* 45, January, 1988; Herbert, "Changing Standard of Care in Club Facilities," *Fitness Management* 36, August, 1989.

21. *See, supra* footnote 13.

22. *See, supra* footnote 20.

23. TRENDS, "Dramatic Increase in Diagnostic Testing for MI Patients Reported," *The Exercise Standards and Malpractice Reporter* 2(2):28, 1988.

24. "Exercise Tests: A Survey of Procedures, Safety and Litigation Experience in Approximately 170,000 Tests," *Journal of The American Medical Association* 217:1061-1066 (1971).

25. Gibbons, L.W., M.D., "Editorial - The Safety of Maximal Exercise Testing," *J. Cardiopulmonary Rehabilitation* 7:277 (1987).

26. TRENDS, "Physician Must be Present For Administration of Graded Exercise Tests," *The Exercise Standards and Malpractice Reporter* 1(5):75, 1987.

27. Figure World vs. Farley, 680 S.W.2d (Tex. App. 3 Dist. 1984), *analyzed in* "Participant Injury Suffered While on Jogging Treadmill can be Facility's Responsibility," *The Exercise Standards and Malpractice Reporter* 1(4):61, 1987. Other cases include: Tart vs. McGahn, 697 F. 2d 75 (2nd Cir. 1982) and Hedgecorth vs. United States, 618 F. Supp. 627 (E.D. Mo. 1985).

28. 697 F.2d 75 (2nd Cir. 1982).

29. 618 F. Supp. 627 (E.D. Mo. 1985).

30. *Cf.*, Deutsch, "The Fast Flooding of Sports Medicine," *Sports, Inc.* 16, March 7, 1988.

31. *See* Herbert, "Is There a Need to Screen Participants Before Recreational Activity?," *The Sports Medicine Standards and Malpractice Reporter* 2(1):11-12, 1990; "Provider's Alleged Advice Allowing Patient to Ski May Result in Liability," *The Sports Medicine Standards and Malpractice Reporter* 2(2):36-37, 1990; "Jogger's Death Deemed Not to Be Physician's Responsibility," *The Exercise Standards and Malpractice Reporter* 2(1):14, 1988; *but see,* Camerena vs. Kaiser Permanente, *analyzed in* "Are GXTs Required For Screening of All Men Over 40?," *The Exercise Standards and Malpractice Reporter* 2(2):30, 1988.

32. "Adolescent Patients Pose Particular Problems: Physical Fitness May Help Prevent Injuries," *JAMA* 259 (23):3380, June 17, 1988.

33. 530 N.Y.S.2d 825 (A.D. 1 Sept. 1988) *reversed* 541 N.E.2d 29 (N.Y. 1989).

34. Herbert, "Coach and Administrator Responsibility for Mismatches and Injuries Due to Fatigue - An Examination of Recent Trends," *The Sports, Parks and Recreation Law Reporter* 2(3):33-38, December 1988.

35. *See, supra* footnote 1.

36. Ball, "Playing by the Rules: Rules and Responsibilities of Sport Care Professionals, Part I," *Sport Care and Fitness* 40-42, March/April, 1989.

37. Lubell, "Potentially Dangerous Exercises: Are They Harmful to All?," *The Physician and Sportsmedicine* 17(1):187-192, 1989; EXERCISE DANGER: 30 EXERCISES TO AVOID PLUS 100 SAFER AND MORE EFFECTIVE ALTERNATIVES (Wellness Australia, 1989 reprint).

38. Herbert, "Medical-Legal Concerns and Risk Management Suggestions for Medical Directors of Exercise Rehabilitation and Maintenance Programs," *The Exercise Standards and Malpractice Reporter* 3(3):44-48, 1989.

39. Herbert, "Liability Associated With Dieting Advice and Publications," *The Exercise Standards and Malpractice Reporter* 4(1):9, 1990.

40. *See, supra* footnote 1 at 33-34 (Use of Tanner Matching Ratings), *see also,* Goldberg "Injury Patterns in Youth Sports," *The Physician and Sportsmedicine* 17(3):175-186, 1989; Roy, et al., "Body Checking in Pee Wee Hockey," *The Physician and Sportsmedicine* 17(3):119-126, 1989.

41. 531 N.Y.S.2d 367 (A.D.2 Dept. 1988).

42. *Id.* at page 368.

43. *Id.*

44. *Id.*

45. Benitez vs. New York Board of Education, 530 N.Y.S. 825 (AD 1 Dept. 1988, *reversed* 541 N.E.2d 29 (New York 1989)), *analyzed in* Chapter 8, *infra.*

46. "Two Corporate Challenge Series Participants Die," *The Exercise Standards and Malpractice Reporter* 2(6):94, 1988.

47. Case No. 86-CV-1368 (U.S. District Court, Eastern District New York, February 8, 1989).

48. 698 F. Supp. 419 (Eastern District of New York 1988).

49. "Why Marathon Runners Collapse - Implications to the Standard of Care," *The Sports, Parks and Recreation Law Reporter* 3(1):19-20, 1989.

50. *See, supra* footnote 1 at pages 142-160. *See also,* "Heat Stress at Police Academy," *The Exercise Standards and Malpractice Reporter* 3(1):8, 1989.

51. Kenney, "Considerations For Preventive and Rehabilitative Exercise Programs During Periods of High Heat and Humidity," *The Exercise Standards and Malpractice Reporter* 3(1):1-7, 1989.

52. *Id.*

53. *Id.*

54. *See, supra* footnotes 47 and 48.

55. 239 So.2d 456 (Ct. of Appeals, LA 1970).

56. *Id.* at page 457.

57. *Id.*

58. *Id.* at page 460.

59. *Id.*

60. Kleinknecht vs. Gettysburg College, 786 F.Supp. 449 (M.D. Pa. 1992) *analyzed in* Lehr, "Medical Emergency Foreseeability a Duty," *The Sports, Parks and Recreation Law Reporter* 7(2):26-28, 1993.

61. Gathers v. Loyola Marymount University, Los Angeles, California, 1990 filing, analyzed in Herbert, "The Death of Hank Gathers: An Evaluation of the Legal Issues," *The Sports Medicine Standards and Malpractice Reporter* 2(3):45-47, 1990.

62. *See, supra* footnote 55.

63. *See, supra* footnote 60.

64. 448 N.W.2d 822 (Mich. App. 1989).

65. *See, supra* footnote 55.

66. *Id.*

67. Dougherty, "Risk Management in Sports Medicine Programs," *The Sports Medicine Standards and Malpractice Reporter* 1(3):47, 50-54, 1989.

68. *Id.*

5 POLICIES, PROCEDURES AND RECORD KEEPING

Given the foregoing definitional references and the general legal background for the sports medicine team, (resulting in at least some question as to who is authorized to deliver certain services), it is clearly advisable for all programs to develop policies and procedures for program activities. Putting aside the legal questions, there are also a number of professional considerations which dictate the need to delineate and specify policies for the delivery of sports medicine services.

THE DEVELOPMENT OF PROGRAM POLICIES AND PROCEDURES

The development of program policies and procedures should provide a blueprint for who does what for whom and under what circumstances within the program setting.[1] Such a manual needs to provide for specific job descriptions for those rendering services developed not only in accordance with service considerations but legal ones as well. Consequently, the development of position descriptions needs to be formulated by reference to state legislation as well as appropriate medical and professional practices. Supervisory responsibility must be focused upon those having authority to provide or control the delivery of care. Such responsibility must generally be derived from the program physician. Delivery mechanisms for service must stem from this provider to others pursuant to law and established standards of care. The program's policies and procedures need to be drafted from this perspective.

Policies and procedures for sports medicine teams must facilitate communication within the group. Such communications must necessarily include both verbal and written modes, all of which must be properly recorded and preserved within program documents. Policies and procedures also need to specify that services will be provided only to those for whom the program is designed. Many times, sports medicine providers will be asked to "look at" employees, parents, relatives or others who are not the intended targets for delineated and defined program services. Inasmuch as program policies and procedures must delineate who is to be served, the exclusion of those outside the contemplated spectrum of service delivery seems only natural and must be specified. Examinations for or service delivery to those outside the defined patient population must be avoided. Even a mere "look at" someone from outside this group can create a physician or provider-patient relationship which can lead to unnecessary and needless claims and suits in the event of some untoward occurrence.

The program manual must provide for and define the essential elements of the program. Once the initial recipient of program services is delineated and job descriptions written, service modalities and procedures must be considered and developed.[2] These include the use of intake forms, including informed consent documents, insurance documents/payment procedure forms, patient reporting documents and other forms related to the duty for follow-up care, preparticipation physicals, re-entry to play decisions, emergency care and procedures, confidentiality and privacy, release of information, as well as other matters.[3]

Program policies and procedures must be developed in accordance with applicable standards of care in the sports medicine setting. There are numerous organizations involved in setting certain standards which may have implication to the practice of sports medicine services.[4]

Standards of practice, guidelines, recommendations, parameters of practice and similar professional statements have been developed by a variety of organizations which have either direct or indirect application to many sports medicine provider activities or programs. These organizations include, but are not limited to, the following diverse groups:

1. Academy For Sports Dentistry;

2. Aerobics and Fitness Association of America;

3. American Academy of Family Physicians;

4. American Academy of Orthopaedic Surgeons;

5. American Academy of Pediatrics;

6. American Academy of Podiatric Sports Medicine;

7. American Academy of Sports Physicians;

8. American Association of Cardiovascular and Pulmonary Rehabilitation;

9. American Athletic Trainers Association and Certification Board, Inc.;

10. American Chiropractic Board of Sports Physicians;

11. American College of Cardiology;

12. American College of Obstetricians and Gynecologists;

13. American College of Sports Medicine;

14. American Council on Exercise;

15. American Heart Association;

16. American Medical Association;

17. American Medical Athletic Association;

18. American Medical Power Lifting Association;

19. American Medical Soccer Association;

20. American Medical Society for Sports Medicine;

21. American Optometric Association, Sports Division Section;

22. American Osteopathic Academy of Sports Medicine;

23. American Osteopathic Society for Sports Medicine;

24. American Physical Therapy Association;

25. Association For Worksite Health Promotion

26. Canadian Academy of Sports Medicine;

27. Canadian Aerobics and Fitness Association;

28. Canadian Podiatric Sports Medicine Academy;

29. IRSA, the Association of Quality Clubs;

30. International Dance Exercise Association Foundation;

31. International Society of Sports Psychology;

32. National Academy of Sports and Vision;

33. National Athletic Trainers Association;

34. National Collegiate Athletic Association;

35. National Strength and Conditioning Association;

36. President's Council On Physical Fitness In Sports;

37. Young Men's Christian Association; as well as many others.

A wide spectrum of professionals are drafters of these standards which might be used in specific sports medicine related claims and suits. Each is drafted to one degree or another by reference to one or more particular professional disciplines. As a consequence, the standards are not uniform nor available for easy implementation to all professionals or programs.[5] Moreover, as a result of the overlapping of many professional disciplines and sports medicine programs, one could readily expect that individuals from one particular licensed or certified profession could set particular standards and later wind up testifying against individuals from a different licensed or certified profession in the event of claim and suit. Under these circumstances, many providers may well have their conduct judged by reference to another profession's standard of care as expressed by expert witnesses from that profession rather than the provider's own profession. While this may be somewhat unique to some, it is not without precedence.

Theoretically, a provider's standard of care is judged by his peers, whose collective opinion would provide the norm of expected professional behavior for use in judging conduct during the course of litigation. However, where a multiplicity of professionals are involved in the rendition of particular services, this is not always possible, practical nor required in a court of law. As a consequence, when examining, for example, provider conduct during a particular preparticipation athletic examination in a given case, that conduct might well be examined in a court of law by a board certified orthopedic surgeon as opposed to a family or general practitioner. In other circumstances, the care rendered by an athletic trainer might well be analyzed by a physical therapist, a physician's assistant or even a physician.

Modern evidentiary rules codified in many jurisdictions would seem to support the admissibility of testimony from a wide variety of individuals in these situations provided they are able to express familiarity as to the appropriate standard of care and are accepted by reason of education, training and experience as "experts". For example, Rule 702 of the Federal Rules of Evidence, which would often be used or cited to decide such questions, provides: *"If scientific, technical, or other specialized knowledge will assist the trier of fact to understand the evidence or to determine a fact in issue, a witness qualified as an expert by knowledge, skill, experience, training or education, may testify thereto in the form of an opinion or otherwise".*

Given the fact that many diverse professionals, licensed and non-licensed, are involved in the provision of sports medicine services, it seems even more logical to presume that testimony from one's "peers" might be broad based indeed! It is clear that professional conduct can be judged from a variety of perspectives and by a number of professionals, utilizing an ever growing body of professional standards.[6]

Aside from the foregoing, it is important to remember that many documents which might be classified in law as "standards" might actually be couched in terms of "recommendations" or even "guidelines" by their drafters. As such, some professionals may arguably view these statements as less than authoritative, certainly not mandatory, nor even indicative of clear professional guidance except in certain areas. Notwithstanding the foregoing, any statement provided by a professional association may have the basic underpinnings to establish a standard of practice, whether or not the statement is referred to as a guideline or recommendation.[7] However, regardless of the label attached to these documents, such statements may well be preferable to the individualized opinions of experts providing testimony in court for a fee. Notwithstanding the foregoing, some groups, including the American Academy of Orthopaedic Surgeons, for example, are still debating whether or not standards should be developed.[8]

National standards of care must be utilized to develop, reference and support a program's policies and procedures manual. In the event of conflict among the published standards, the most defensible and reasonable position should be selected after consultation with program legal counsel and the program's physician.

When examining these standards in the course of developing program policies and procedures it is important for practitioners to know that there are inconsistencies within the standards themselves. Some of the standards impose very broad and yet specific duties upon sports medicine practitioners which need to be addressed within the policies and procedures manual of a particular program.

It is extremely important to remember that once standards of practice are adopted into the policies and procedures manual, these policies must be read, understood and applied by program personnel. Evidence of a failure to follow a specified program policy may be deemed to be negligent by judges or juries engaged in comparing the conduct with self-imposed standards of care.[9] Under these circumstances, expert testimony may not even be required. For example in a recent decision from the state of Arizona,[10] the court held: *"The existence of a hospital protocol is...some evidence of the standard of care...Under the current posture of this case, the trier of fact could conclude that the protocol was a standard of care and that the failure to follow that standard was negligence."*

In essence, this case and others like it, stands for the proposition that a program's own written policies and procedures may be utilized to establish a standard of care. In the eventuality that such a standard is not followed, the facts of the case when compared to the written standard exemplified by the policies and procedures developed by a program, may obviate the need for any expert testimony to prove the standard of care and any breach of that standard. Liability may well follow from such a scenario.

RECORD KEEPING

As stated by Jerald D. Hawkins, one of the members of the Board of Contributing Authors for *The Sports Medicine Standards and Malpractice Reporter, "One of the most important...administrative functions in any sports medicine program is record-keeping. The development and implementation of a comprehensive record-keeping system serves to enhance the effectiveness of organizational communication while, at the same time, helping to minimize the ever-present threat of litigation resulting from the failure to adequately document the nature and extent of care provided to an injured athlete or program participant.*

[T]he first purpose of [any such effort is to establish] a comprehensive record-keeping system to maximize communication within the sports medicine organization so as to provide optimal care to the athlete/patient. Textbooks on organization and administration often classify organizational communications as 'formal communication,' the exchange of important information or ideas which require written documentation, and 'informal communication,' the exchange of less important information which usually takes place verbally, and requires no written documentation. Most of the communication within a sports medicine program is

sufficiently important to be considered to be of the 'formal' type. However, such communication is often treated as 'informal,' resulting in needless, potential claims and litigation. On the other hand, while record-keeping in and of itself cannot shield one from litigation, carefully written documentation of care rendered can be a powerful weapon for refuting claims of negligent behavior. This is assuming, of course, that such documentation reflects a pattern of reasonable and prudent care.

The development and implementation of an effective record-keeping system is a highly personalized process in that the finished product must accurately reflect the specific needs and functions of the organization. Likewise, the number and types of record-keeping forms utilized will vary significantly from one organization to another. Although the specific nature of the record-keeping system will depend upon the needs and functions of the organization, there are a few general suggestions which should be considered when attempting to maximize record-keeping effectiveness.

Every member of the organization should be instructed to document every communication, recommendation, and procedure concerning his/her function as an agent of that organization. Making written documentation a regular part of day-to-day staff duties will go a long way toward establishing record-keeping as an integral and vital part of the injury care process, and will minimize the likelihood that inappropriate or inadequate care will result from poor communication. Furthermore, such practice will maximize the documentation of proper care should documentation be needed to establish the precise nature of care rendered in response to a suit based on a claim of negligent care against the organization and/or employee(s) thereof.

One of the most important concepts in the process is that of maintaining records of important information in more than one location. For example, the basic information concerning an acute sports injury (e.g., name, date, type of injury, immediate care rendered, etc.) should be maintained in several locations such as the athlete's personal medical file, a central file of all injury reports, and a computer data file if the record-keeping system is comput- erized. The purpose of this procedure is twofold. First, practicing cross-file duplication minimizes the danger of losing important data in the event that one of the file sources is misplaced, destroyed, or, in the case of computerized data, erased. Second, maintaining multiple file sources is one way of establishing an image of prudent and conscientious behavior for the organization and its staff.

The use of carbonless, multicopy forms is one effective way of implementing the cross-file plan recommended in the preceding section. When multiple copies of an important form are available, the task of creating multiple file sources is an easy one. Simply file one copy of the form in the athlete's file, another in the central file, and others in other appropriate locations. In this way, information recorded on one form may serve multiple purposes with a minimum of effort. A second important benefit of using multicopy forms is that of improved organizational communication. When multiple copies of a form are available, one or more of these copies may be routed to appropriate members of the organization outside the sports medicine program (e.g., administrators, coaches, etc.), providing them with written information about the injury in question. This eliminates many of the problems inherent with verbal communication.

An interactive form is one which requests and/or requires two- way communication before the form is considered complete and ready for action and/or filing. Interactive forms are especially beneficial for establishing clear communication and precise docu- mentation of information among various members of the sports medicine organization, or between members of the organization and others, such as physicians who may be outside the organiza- tion. When an injured athlete or program participant is referred to a physician for evaluation and treatment, a written reply from the treating physician is always preferable to a verbal reply since the physician's opinion may be the basis for such important decisions as when and if the athlete may return to activity, and how the athlete should be cared for during the important time of recuperation and rehabilitation. Using a form which requires such written interaction enhances both the quantity and quality of communication between the sports medicine organization and the medical community...

[A sample interactive form] designed to maximize communication between the [sports medicine staff] and the physician(s) to which an injured athlete is referred [is hereinafter reproduced]. When an injury occurs, the attending athletic trainer will complete the top portion of the form using information obtained from (1) personal observation and examination; and, (2) the injured athlete. The information recorded on the form is then certified as correct by signatures from both the attending trainer and injured athlete. This feature of the form is intended to minimize the chance that the circumstances surrounding the injury and its immediate care might be described incorrectly. The back copy of the form is held in the training room pending return of the physician's written comments. The remaining three copies of the form are forwarded along with the injured athlete to the treating physician. Upon completion of his/her examination and/or initial treatment, the physician is requested to complete the form, retain the back copy for his/her records, and return the remaining two copies along with the athlete to the training room. Upon receipt of the physician's report, the...staff (1) communicates the physician's findings to the appropriate coach, (2) takes the appropriate injury care actions based on the physician's recommendations, and (3) files one copy of the report in the athlete's file and the other in a central file. If the injured athlete fails to return the complete form to the...staff, he/she is withheld from practice and play until the physician's written report is received. This significantly reduces the possibility of inappropriately returning an injured athlete to activity, and the obvious threat of litigation which such action might precipitate.

(4 PART FORM)

LANDER COLLEGE ATHLETIC INJURY REPORT

REPORT FROM ATHLETIC TRAINER TO PHYSICIAN

Name: _____

Sport: _____

Date of Report: _____ Date of Injury: _____

_____
Person Completing Report   (Athletic Trainer)

_____
(Title)   (Phone)

Body Part Injured: _____

Mechanism of Injury (How? What Happened?):

Physical Findings:

Tentative Evaluation:

Immediate Care:

Comments:

Follow Up: _____ Physician Visit and/or X-rays Recommended
                   on _____
           _____ Physician Visit Not Recommended at This Time

_____   _____
(Athlete's Signature)   (Trainer's Signature)

* LC * LC * LC * LC * LC * LC * LC * LC * LC * LC * LC * LC * LC * LC * LC *

REPORT FROM PHYSICIAN TO ATHLETIC TRAINER

Name   Sport

Diagnosis:

Treatment/Rehabilitation Recommendations:

Copy of Specific Program Attached?   _____   Yes
                                          _____   No

Estimated Time Out of Activity: _____

Follow Up:
___   Must see me/another physician prior to return to practice and/or
       competition.

___   May be checked by athletic trainer in lieu of visit to a physician.

___   May return to practice and/or competition upon successful
       completion of treatment/rehabilitation program above.

___   May return to practice and/or competition immediately with the
       following restrictions: _____

Comments:

_____
(Physician's Signature)   (Date)   (Phone)

Yellow - File Copy * Pink - Physician's Copy * Gold - "In-Process" Copy   9/88

One of the most common problems in every sports injury care program is the lack of specific communication between staff members and coaches regarding the precise type of injury, the injury care recommended, and the playing and/or practice status of the injured athlete. [An] Injury Care Recommendation Form is designed to minimize this problem. This form is a three-copy form which is utilized to provide coaches with written information concerning the injury status of his/her athletes, and to provide...staff members with written documentation of the specific injury care regimen recommended for each athlete. When an athlete experiences an injury which may require a change in his/her activity status, an Injury Care Recommendation Form is completed by the attending athletic trainer. The injury care and modification in activity recommendation may be based upon the recommendation from examining physician(s) and/or the attending athletic trainer [where permitted by law]. Once completed, the back copy of the form is forwarded directly to the appropriate coach, advising him/her of the injury status of the athlete. The second copy of the form is immediately filed in the athlete's medical file. The original copy of the form is posted in the athletic training room so that all staff members may consult it before rendering care to the athlete. Upon completion of the care regimen, the original is filed in a central file. Use of the Injury Care Recommendation Form significantly enhances the communication among...staff, coaches, and athletes."

(3 PART FORM)

INJURY CARE RECOMMENDATION FORM

Name: _____

Sport: _____

Date: _____

Injury: _____

Recommended Care:

_____   May continue regular activity

_____   Should modify activity as follows:_____

_____

_____   No activity, pending re-evaluation on _____

_____   Other: _____

_____
(Trainer's Signature)

Yellow - File Copy * Pink - Coach's Copy

These are but two of the many forms which may be useful in developing and implementing a comprehensive sports medicine record-keeping system. However, they both serve as excellent examples of the types of benefits which may be realized by (1) putting sports medicine communications in writing, (2) cross-filing all records, and (3) utilizing multi-copy and interactive forms whenever possible."[11]

As Dr. Hawkins so aptly points out, the development of adequate record-keeping procedures within a program's policy and procedure manual is of absolute importance. Many times, when untoward incidents occur, which are followed by claim and suit, lawyers representing interested parties will argue that if a matter is "not charted/recorded, it didn't happen." Jurors tend to place much stock in the written word. Disagreements as to whether or not particular matters took place but simply were not recorded will not be effective unless proper records are maintained relating to those activities. It is also important to record not only abnormals but normals as well. When athletes don't listen or follow program recommendations, appropriate notations must be recorded and preserved not only for the benefit of the athlete's care, but for potential use in the event of claim and suit.

FINAL THOUGHT

The development of position descriptions and written program policies and procedures is of absolute importance to any sports medicine program. Such policies and procedures must be developed in accordance with appropriate national standards of practice. Thorough record keeping must be stressed by all personnel. Program policies and procedures must be followed and carried out by all personnel. Detailed records must be maintained from such activities. A failure to do so may result in findings of negligence and substandard care.

CHAPTER 5 FOOTNOTES:

1. Herbert, "Developing Policies and Procedures for Sports Medicine Programs," *The Sports Medicine Standards and Malpractice Reporter* 5(3):43, 1993.

2. Webster, Mason and Keating, GUIDELINES FOR PROFESSIONAL PRACTICE IN ATHLETIC TRAINING (Professional Reports Corporation, Canton, OH 1992).

3. Hawkins, THE PRACTICAL DELIVERY OF SPORTS MEDICINE SERVICES: A CONCEPTUAL APPROACH (PRC Publishing, Inc., Canton, OH 1993).

4. Herbert, THE SPORTS MEDICINE STANDARDS BOOK (Professional Reports Corporation, Canton, OH 1992, Supplement 1993).

5. *Compare,* ACSM, STANDARDS AND GUIDELINES FOR HEALTH/FITNESS FACILITIES (Human Kinetics, Champaign, IL 1992) *with* IRSA, the Association of Quality Clubs, BASELINE MEMBERSHIP ELIGIBILITY STANDARDS FOR IRSA CLUBS (IRSA, Boston, MA 1993). *See* Herbert, "New ACSM Standards for Health Clubs Come Under Attack," *The Sports Medicine Standards and Malpractice Reporter* 4(4):60, 1992; "IRSA Developing New Health Club Standards," *The Sports Medicine Standards and Malpractice Reporter* 4(4):61, 1992.

6. *See, supra* footnote 4.

7. Herbert, "New Standards of Practice and Professional Concerns: Debate Over Provider Standards Is Not New," *The Sports Medicine Standards and Malpractice Reporter* 5(4):49, 52-53, 1993.

8. Abraham, "Specialties race against payers to set standards," *AMA News* 17, January 6, 1989.

9. *See e.g.,* Jarreau vs. Orleans Parish School Board, 600 So.2d 1389 (La. App. 4 Cir. 1992) *analyzed in* "Trainer and Coach Liable for Non-Referral of Student/ Athlete to Physician," *The Exercise Standards and Malpractice Reporter* 7(1):12-13, 1993.

10. Peacock vs. Samaritan Health Service, Case No. 1 CA-CIV 8968, released April 28, 1988.

11. Hawkins, "Sports Medicine Record Keeping: The Key to Effective Communication and Documentation," *The Sports Medicine Standards and Malpractice Reporter 1(2):31-35,* 1989.

6 INFORMED CONSENT, ASSUMPTION OF THE RISK AND PROSPECTIVE RELEASES

INFORMED CONSENT

Informed consent in a medical setting is a process by which patients agree to undergo certain medical examinations, procedures or treatments. It is more than a thing – more than a piece of paper. The process is multi-faceted and is predicated upon the provision of information to the patient, the details and extent of which vary from state to state and are subject to on-going judicial and professional review, followed by a patient decision to undergo or not to undergo the examination, treatment or procedure. In order for an informed consent to be valid, certain requirements must be met.

For a participant to validly consent to a contemplated medical examination, test, treatment or procedure, he/she must:

1. be legally capable of giving consent (*i.e.,* he/she cannot be legally or mentally incapacitated – he/she must be of full age and competent);

2. know and fully understand the relevant and material risks to which he/she is consenting (*i.e.,* he/she must be fully informed as to all material or relevant facts and related dangers so that he/she may make an informed decision as to whether to participate); and,

3. give his/her consent voluntarily and not under any mistake of fact or duress.

The question of whether or not the participant engaged in the proper process is frequently determined subjectively: *i.e.,* did this particular individual rather than an ordinary and reasonable man fully understand and comprehend the facts and the dangers?

In practice, informed consent or a consent to participate should be obtained in written form, and be preceded by a full and adequate disclosure of all relevant and material risks associated with the particular procedure or activity in question. An opportunity for questions by the athlete and answers by the professional must be offered and in fact encouraged. Concurrently with such a procedure, recorded notes should be kept in the patient's chart or file to offer additional evidence if necessary, of consent, and the professional's perception of patient understanding as well as to evidence the question-and-answer period.

In some states, statutory rules have been promulgated and impact this process. For example, in the State of Ohio, statutory procedures for the procurement of a valid informed consent for a medical procedure are contained in Ohio Revised Code §2317.54. This Code section provides as follows: *"Written consent to a surgical or medical procedure or course of procedures shall, to the extent that it fulfills all the requirements in divisions (A), (B) and (C), of this section, be presumed to be valid and effective, in the absence of proof by a preponderance of the evidence that the person who sought such consent was not acting in good faith, or that the execution of the consent was induced by fraudulent misrepresentation of material facts, or that the person executing the consent was not able to communicate effectively in spoken and written English or any other language in which the consent is written. Except as herein provided, no evidence shall be admissible to impeach, modify, or limit the authorization for performance of the procedure or procedures set forth in such written consent.*

(A) The consent sets forth in general terms the nature and purpose of the procedure or procedures, and what the procedures are expected to accomplish, together with the reasonably known risks, and, except in emergency situations, sets forth the names of the physicians who shall perform the intended surgical procedures.

(B) The person making the consent acknowledges that such disclosure of information has been made and that all questions asked about the procedure or procedures have been answered in a satisfactory manner.

(C) The consent is signed by the patient for whom the procedure is to be performed, or, if the patient for any reason including, but not limited to, competence, infancy, or the fact that, at the latest time that the consent is needed, the patient is under the influence of alcohol, hallucinogens, or drugs, lacks legal capacity to consent, by a person who has legal authority to consent on behalf of such patient in such circumstances.

Any use of a consent form that fulfills the requirements stated in divisions (A), (B), and (C) of this section has no effect on the common law rights and liabilities, including the right of a physician to obtain the oral or implied consent of a patient to a medical procedure, that may exist as between physicians and patients on July 28, 1975."

As can be readily determined from a reading of this or any number of other, similar state statutes, the attainment of a proper consent form as specified in the statute, can go a long way toward providing a defensible position for the sports medicine physician or other sports medicine team professional as to claims relating to a lack of informed consent. The consent forms offered at the end of this guide provide examples of forms for current use as do a number of forms contained within publications of the American Heart Association[1] and the American College of Sports Medicine.[2]

Much litigation has arisen over the years as to the disclosure requirements for the informed consent process. Frequently, this litigation has centered upon the question of whether or not sufficient information has been provided to the patient to enable the patient to make an "informed" decision as to the procedure in question.

Several very complex questions sometimes arise relative to disclosure considerations during the informed consent process. Most frequently, with medical or quasi-medical procedures, questions center upon the extent of risk disclosure to the participant. Sometimes the disclosure of all known risks or even all known material risks will so unnerve or adversely affect an anxious participant that additional risks are created as a consequence of the disclosure. This is often very perplexing for many practitioners. In years past, courts would take the position that the degree of disclosure required under these circumstances, rested within the sound medical or professional judgment of the professional making the disclosure. Pursuant to this reasoning, the professional would be held to a standard of care generally exercised by members of his or her profession in similar circumstances.

This requirement is changing. A growing number of state and federal courts are determining these cases from a different perspective, basing disclosure requirements upon the patient's need for information. Unlike the so-called "professional rule" where the physician determines the adequacy of risk disclosure in accordance with his or her professional judgment, the *"patient's need for information doctrine"* requires disclosure based upon the patient's requirements. This later doctrine which has been adopted in nearly half of state jurisdictions to date requires a disclosure of *"all information material to [the patient's] making a truly informed and intelligent decision concerning the proposed medical procedure."[3]*

The risk disclosure requirements associated with the informed consent process are undergoing somewhat distinct change. These changes are reaching and effecting a wide variety of health care providers including those in sports medicine. Consider the 1985 case of Hedgecorth vs. United States.[4] The case, which was tried to the court judge as opposed to a jury, was brought under the Federal Torts Claims Act which allows, under certain circumstances, suits against the federal government and its agencies.

The plaintiff in this case contended that he suffered a stroke or other cardiovascular accident in 1980 while undergoing a physician prescribed and monitored diagnostic graded exercise stress test at a VA hospital in late March of 1980. The plaintiff's relevant medical history included a 1978 and 1979 myocardial infarction, post MI angina pain, a 1970 cardiac catheterization procedure which revealed severely occluded coronary arteries, a 1979 five vessel coronary bypass operation and post surgical PVCs upon exercise, but with no evidence of ischemia. Prior to the stress test in question, the plaintiff, in early March of 1980, in connection with an application for social security disability benefits underwent a graded exercise stress test performed for the Social Security Administration. Later that same month however, the plaintiff returned to the VA hospital for follow-up treatment for his coronary condition and some minimal effort was made by the VA physicians to obtain the results of the earlier Social Security Administration sponsored test. The test results were not obtained as of March 20, 1980, and as a consequence, the VA physicians scheduled the stress test in question to be performed on March 31, 1980. It was during this test that the plaintiff contended that he suffered a stroke or some other cardiovascular event. The court later found that inadequate efforts had been put forth by the VA physicians to secure the stress test results from the March 3, 1980 stress test.

Prior to the administration of the second stress test, a VA physician met with the plaintiff and orally informed him of some of the dangers associated with taking such a test. However, the physician did not inform the patient of the danger of stroke as one of the dangers of taking a stress test.

Once the testing procedure began in the cardiology section of the VA hospital under the supervision of a physician and a technician, the plaintiff complained of a loss of vision in his left eye and chest pain after approximately five and two-tenths minutes into the test. As a consequence, the test was terminated. Suit was later instituted by the patient claiming actual malpractice in the performance of the stress testing procedure.

The court examined all of the evidence including expert testimony evidence offered by the plaintiff which consisted of the testimony of an opthalmologist and an emergency medicine specialist[5] and agreed with the plaintiff in concluding: *"under the facts and circumstances of this case the giving of the stress test was both negligent and the proximate cause of plaintiff's injuries."*[6] The court based its conclusion upon two separate findings. First, as to the giving of a stress test when the results of another recently conducted test were available, the court stated: *"[A] patient should not be given a stress test if there are available adequate results from a prior stress test given less than one month prior to the subsequent test. Because of the dangers associated in giving the stress test, the results from the immediately preceding stress test should be used by the ordinary careful and prudent physician in lieu of retesting the patient."*[7] Second, as to the informed consent process, the court concluded: *"The credible medical evidence presented at trial demonstrates that giving the [VA conducted] stress test to the plaintiff...was a deviation from the appropriate standard of care. The purpose of a stress test is, as the name implies, to place a stress on the heart through physical exercise and thereby derive information concerning the heart's condition. Because of the nature of the test certain dangers accompany its administration. These dangers include the possibility that the patient will suffer a stroke. The patient should be warned that a stroke could result from the administration of the test, and plaintiff Lowell Hedgecorth was not warned of this danger. Thus, plaintiff...did not take the test with informed consent of its dangers."*[8]

The court in assessing the plaintiff's case found: *"As a direct result of the negligent acts and omissions of the defendants, the plaintiff...suffered an infarct in the right occipital lobe of his brain. This stroke directly caused plaintiff...total and permanent disability."*[9] The plaintiff was awarded $750,000 in damages for his injuries and his wife was awarded $75,000 for her loss of consortium, companionship and services.

Although the <u>Hedgecorth</u> decision is not binding precedent outside the Eastern District of Missouri, the court's ruling has some rather broad and far reaching implications. Normally, a physician or other provider is required in the informed consent process to disclose all risks which are material to the procedure about to be performed upon the patient. Materiality is generally equated with probable, anticipated or likely occurrences which might arise. The law does not generally require a disclosure of improbable, remote or unlikely risks or occurrences, which can possibly arise during a procedure.

As a District Court of Appeals in Florida noted in 1984 in the case of <u>Valcin vs. Public Health Trust of Dade County</u>[10]: *"Consent is 'informed' where the person knows the dangers and degrees of danger of a certain procedure to be performed... however, the duty of a medical doctor to inform his patient of the risks of harm reasonably to be expected from a proposed course of treatment does not place upon the physician a duty to elucidate upon all of the possible risks ...[citations omitted]."* [11]

Normally, the informed consent doctrine *"requires a physician to make a reasonable disclosure to his patient of [inter alia]...the more probable consequences and difficulties inherent [in the procedure]...These consequences and difficulties have been termed the 'recognized risks' of the treatment."* [12]

Even though clear statistical evidence of the risk of stroke occurrence during exercise stress testing procedures is not readily apparent, it is very clear that the risk of stroke is very minimal, even unlikely. It is not even listed in the classic risk studies or literature dealing with exercise testing risk.[13] Given this minimal risk of occurrence, the <u>Hedgecorth</u> ruling is extremely troublesome from several perspectives: First, it may now be prudent to disclose the risk of stroke during the informed consent process for such procedures; if so, the question arises as to whether or not the risk of blindness due to stroke should also be disclosed, or the risks of total or partial, temporary or permanent paralysis, or a host of other possible consequences due to stroke? Secondly, is it now also necessary to disclose other remote, possible risks which could occur during such a procedure? If so, which ones? Thirdly, if remote risks must be disclosed, how are the risks which are to be disclosed, differentiated from those risks which will not be disclosed?

The answers to these questions are not susceptible to any quick or ready response. Once an examination of all possible risks is undertaken, it is quite clear that the process of specific risk identification and disclosure could go on ad infinitude inasmuch as anything is possible. Such a scenario provides no answer however to the problems created by the <u>Hedgecorth</u> decision.

As a practical matter, physicians and other providers are faced with the question of what disclosure course is minimally prudent conduct in light of the <u>Hedgecorth</u> opinion? In light of such rulings, sports medicine professionals should review their informed consent process and revise it if necessary and as required by individual state law. For exercise stress testing procedures performed by sports medicine professionals, it may be prudent to include "risk of stroke" and "risk of blindness" due to stroke disclosures in the informed consent risk disclosure section of the informed consent form. However, the inclusion of such remote risks may well call into question, due to omission, the possible lack of disclosure as to any one of a number of other remote risks which in the event of some proximately caused untoward event could lead to a <u>Hedgecorth</u> type suit. Secondly, it may be minimally prudent conduct to review orally with the patient those risks which are associated with a procedure and just simply list in the informed consent form the fact that the risks were disclosed and make an accompanying note in the chart that a discussion as to the risks took place. Then, however in the event of some untoward event and suit, the proof as to whether or not a risk disclosure was made will depend upon what the trier of fact believes after hearing individualized testimony. Thirdly, it may be prudent to include a "catch all" type provision within each informed consent form which provides in general terms that there are other risks of injury and, if appropriate, even death which may occur as a result of certain tests or procedures.

Informed consent questions are a frequent issue in many sports medicine cases.[14] Often such cases deal with the question of whether or not information was withheld from the athlete/patient or whether or not the information was correctly and impartially communicated to the athlete/patient without outside interference.[15] Such cases can be difficult to defend. Deficiencies related to the informed consent process should be avoided by providers.

Informed consent forms utilized by a given facility must be drafted with appropriate medical and legal advice and utilized only after a thorough review of applicable law and professional standards within each jurisdiction. In the long run, adequate statistical studies as to the incidence of untoward events due to risk occurrence, as well as prompt and ongoing professional discussion as to these issues should greatly assist in standards development for risk disclosure. Examples of informed consent forms for these procedures are contained within the Appendix to this work.

Notwithstanding the foregoing discussion, material risks associated with any procedure must be disclosed if there is to be any valid consent to support a defense to battery, negligence/malpractice claims based upon a failure to obtain an informed consent. Traditionally, the courts have ruled that the more remote and unlikely the risk, the less the need for disclosure, especially in the face of a distraught and anxious patient whose condition can sometimes be harmed by a more complete disclosure. Often in these situations, where the professional claims that a more full disclosure would have adversely affected a participant, questions of negligence and intentional tort are considered. In the event that a determination is reached that a fuller disclosure should have been made, negligence as well as battery claims may be available to the injured party as a basis for suit. Resolving this risk/ disclosure problem in a way that is sensitive both to the patient's need for information and his/her ability to adequately comprehend the issues relevant to rendering a consent decision, the professional must apply his best judgment as to whether a further disclosure would threaten the participant's well being or contraindicate the procedure altogether. Such judgments should always be the subject of consultation with family members of the patient and perhaps subject to second opinions. Under no circumstances however may the professional decide to "make the decision" for the non-anxious patient who has an absolute right to such facts.

In cases where consideration is given to partial disclosure of risks because of an anxious patient, program professionals should:

1. disclose all major, known or probable risks associated with undergoing the procedure or not undergoing the procedure where such disclosures will not harm the participant's wellbeing;

2. document a decision not to disclose certain risks of potential or actual adverse harm to the participant;

3. support his non-disclosure reasons by observed and/or supportable facts or documentation, written and noted in the patient's record;

4. corroborate a decision not to disclose with a second professional opinion (perhaps from medical personnel, especially in the event that the professional is not within that group); and,

5. if appropriate, and with the patient's consent, review the risks and reasons for non-disclosure with a member of the family so they may be aware of these modifications and the reasons for individualizing the procedure. A spouse or other family mem-

ber may also need to execute the consent form or a separate consent form which details all of the risks, especially those not disclosed to the participant.

Risk disclosure to a non-anxious patient or apparently healthy exercise or athlete/participant should proceed according to normal disclosure rules and the requirements applicable in the jurisdiction wherein the provider renders service.

Evidentiary proof of informed consent is often essential to the defense of a battery or negligence action. Such a consent should be secured in writing since such a document provides evidence of consent. Proper written documentation of the consent process as well as recorded notes made in the patient's file are especially critical to the professional who may someday have to prove consent to a jury. Adequate documentation simply must be made and maintained for that eventuality. Giving a copy of the consent to the athlete/participant, with individualized notations may also be a desirable means to assure that the participant retains an understanding of the procedures, potential risks/benefits, and agreements. In such an eventuality, however, should any subsequent notations be made upon the program copy, questions may arise as to the changes to such documents. Records like these should never be changed to modify information or to add information which was not originally provided. Claims of fraud or disciplinary actions could well arise in such eventualities.[16] If information must be added, an appropriate and dated and/or timed supplemental notation should be made within the patients' chart or record so no adverse inferences as to that information may be made.

Once a consent is properly obtained, it generally insulates the program and its personnel from successful suit by that participant and usually by his or her estate in the event of death from claims of battery or negligence in obtaining the consent or for negligence due to a failure to obtain an informed consent. However in some states, despite participant consent, the participant's spouse may have an independent but related cause of action against the program, even though the participant's spouse may be precluded from instituting suit directly on these grounds. Even though a spouse cannot generally prevent a procedure to which his/her spouse consents, securing a spousal consent can have practical beneficial results for a program.

In most jurisdictions, a spouse, in the event of injury to that person's wife or husband, has a cause of action stemming from the underlying injury to the wife or husband; this action is generally known as a *loss of consortium* claim. Quite simply this cause of action is designed to compensate for interference with and injury to the marital relationship, including damage to the rights of companionship, conversation, comfort, conjugal relations, and other aspects of life attributable to marriage. In light of potential spousal suit, independent from any participant suit, it may be prudent for programs, after consultation with their legal advisor, to seek and obtain consent from each participant's spouse. In this manner, the program may be able to minimize its own risks in the event of injury or death to the married participant based upon claims of fraud, lack of informed consent, etc. Although in some states, a spouse's cause of action for interference with the marital relationship as a result of injury to the other spouse, may exist as a totally independent cause of action,[17] most states limit recovery to situations where the spouse can recover and not otherwise.[18] That is, if the injured individual cannot recover for his/her injuries, then the spouse similarly cannot recover for interference to the marital relationship. Local counsel must examine each program's state laws to determine the possible applicability of independent spousal suits based upon claims of loss of consortium when founded upon such assertions.

In some states an emerging trend is also developing to allow suits by children for interference with patent/child consortium type rights in the event of a parent's injury. Although such claims are somewhat common in the event of a parent's death under many state wrongful death statutes, such claims for mere injury are somewhat unique. Depending upon the rule of law existing in a given state, it may be wise to provide for this contingency in the participant consent form by making it binding upon others such as heirs, or by providing for indemnification by the patient or his estate in the event of suit by other family members for injuries to the participant. This latter alternative however, must be examined with much care in light of the realities of participant trust in the program and its personnel. Moreover, some states might well declare such prospective indemnification agreements as agreements against public policy or unsupported by adequate consideration and therefore void or voidable by the patient or the family. However, in some circumstances, even in some medical settings such agreements may be lawful,[19] *see* discussion *infra.*

Informed consents should be obtained from each patient (athlete, exerciser, recreational or rehabilitative participant) preferably in writing. If the patient is a minor or otherwise not competent, consent should also be obtained from the patient's parents or legal guardians. The consent should be as clear and distinct as possible and provide for authorization to treat in the absence of the parent/guardian or in the event the patient cannot then and there consent to treatment. The document should provide for the rendition of care by all members of the sports medicine team.

The document should be properly executed, witnessed and signed by the provider making the disclosures and securing the consent. An opportunity for questions and answers should be provided and the patient's chart should be adequately documented with notations as to the process, questions asked and answers provided. Sample informed consent forms are contained in the Appendix to this work, *infra.* However, such forms are protected by copyright and in any case should not be adopted by any program without seeking individualized legal consultation in the jurisdiction where a particular program is located.

A variety of problems sometimes arise in the informed consent process in sports medicine settings. These problems generally center upon the adequacy of risk or treatment disclosure, the withholding of information, conflicts between the team and the athlete which impact the process, and a whole host of similar matters. Most of these concerns arise in the course of preparticipation examinations, return to play evaluations or during physician-patient communications. Due to the importance of these concerns to sports medicine practitioners these matters shall be separately addressed in Chapters 8 and 9, *infra.*

ASSUMPTION OF RISK

Unlike consents which provide *"permission to act in the future...,"*[20] assumptions of the risk are designed to transfer responsibility to the person engaging in a particular activity. Assumptions of the risk will, if effective, act as a judicially approved defense to a personal injury claim, and transfer liability for given conduct from otherwise potentially responsible individuals to those choosing to assume responsibility.[21] These may be "expressed" through the execution of written documents or by specific stated comments or implied in law by reason of particular conduct. For example, express assumption of risk documents are sometimes used in the sports medicine setting for the purposes of allowing individuals to engage in activity despite contrary advice.[22] The actual use of such documents shall be further examined in Chapter 8, *infra.*

Questions related to whether or not a particular individual impliedly assumed certain risks are very often dependent upon particular facts as interpreted by courts examining such issues. In some states, participation in athletic contests will automatically be deemed to be an assumption of risk so as to bar claims related to injuries arising from normal participation.[23] However, in other states this may not be the case. For example, in the case of Kuehner vs. Green[24] the Supreme Court of Florida in analyzing whether or not a participant in a contact sport (karate) assumed the risk of injury, determined that such participants do not auto-matically assume all risks of injury. The court reasoned: *"Express assumption of risk, as it applies in the context of contact sports, rests upon the plaintiff's voluntary consent to take certain chances...This principle may be better expressed in terms of waiver. When a participant volunteers to take certain chances he waives his right to be free from those bodily contacts inherent in the chances taken. Our judicial system must protect those who rely on such a waiver and engage in otherwise prohibited bodily contacts."* [25]

Without question, many sports medicine related programs involve the risk of injury. Some of these risks are obvious and some are not. Studies and statistical evidence have indicated that the kind of injuries and frequency of same can be described and quantified. Given this fact, it is clear that facilities should, when faced with the burdens of proving express assumption of the risk, supply written disclosure of those risks and receive written participant acknowledgment of voluntary and knowing assump-tion of those risks.

While the informed consent process involves a similar disclo-sure requirement which enables facility personnel to engage in a particular process with the participant or to lead or direct a participant in activity, the assumption of risk process when conducted in writing supplies evidence to establish a defense to a possible negligence action. Contrawise, a release or waiver obtained in advance of program participation theoretically pre-cludes successful suit because the participant has prospectively given up or relinquished his right to sue based upon claims of negligence.[26]

Obviously, should there be a failure to include some enumer-ated risk disclosure in the express assumption of risk process, questions of fact for jury determination will certainly arise. After all, in the course of human events, many things are possible even if not probable. Consequently any risk disclosure evidencing an express assumption of the risk must contain a "catch-all" provision providing for the delineation of the possibility of other injuries and where appropriate, even death. In this manner, the specific risk disclosures followed by the "catch-all" should provide as much evidentiary proof as possible.

It may be prudent for programs to develop a three-part risk disclosure process to secure: (1) informed consent; (2) express assumption of the risk; and (3) release. While such forms should only be developed after consultation with legal counsel, they may prove to be invaluable should an injury occur and suit develop. It may be prudent however given the legal underpinnings affecting each process for the forms to be separated upon program documents. Specific drafting requirements for these documents may vary from state to state but language evidencing an express assumption of the risk like that which is offered in the Appendix should serve as a starting point for legal counsel's consideration.

The use of such preprinted forms requiring systematic review, checking, initials and execution, assures consistency of the process. Notes as to questions and answers if any can also be important to the proof of express assumption of risk should such an issue arise after injury. Moreover, the use of similar forms when coupled with informed consents and perhaps even prospective releases, may reduce the likelihood and frequency of claims, suits and adverse findings. Given that result, liability insurance premiums may be stabilized and even reduced by a responsive carrier who actively encourages risk management activities.

The participation forms offered in the Appendix may be subject to criticism by some due to the fact that they include several places for the participant to initial or sign. However, the use of such multiple execution and initialling spaces provides extremely valuable evidence of careful review, thoughtful consideration and acknowledgment of participant understanding as well as agreement. Any inconvenience in obtaining the signatures and initials should be greatly outweighed by the practical benefits associated with the use of such forms. Thought should also be given to the use of audio and video recordation of the process; BUT it should be remembered that what's recorded can be a two edged sword: one for program defense if the process is complete and accurate and one for participant offense if it is not and something later goes wrong. Moreover, if recordation of the process is to be made on either audio or video tapes, additional participation consent for that process must also be obtained. An example of assumption of risk documents are offered in the Appendix to this work.

PROSPECTIVE RELEASES

Aside from issues dealing with assumption of the risk which operate as a defense to claim and suit, the issue of whether or not releases should be used in sports medicine settings is of some import to all providers.

While often the subject of close judicial scrutiny, prospectively executed release documents if properly and lawfully given in accordance with prior judicial requirements, can effectively act as a bar or barrier to lawsuits against those so released. Releases are generally written to provide: *"The participant hereby releases the program from all damages for injury to myself, and I hereby waive for myself, my heirs, administrators, executors, and as-signs, and any and all others, any claims to damages which I may have against the program or its personnel."*

Absent special settings or elective procedures, prospective waivers/releases are almost universally invalid *in medical or medical-related settings* for two basic reasons. First, such waivers may be totally unsupported by consideration (something of value) and as such are not contractually binding upon the participant or other parties claiming by or through him/her. Secondly and most importantly, such waivers are usually construed to be against public policy inasmuch as enforcement of such claims would undermine the provision of competent care and would allow negligent professionals to escape responsibility for their own deficient actions.[27] Despite the probable unenforceability of such documents in most medical settings, there may be circumstances where such forms may be of importance and even enforceable for some sports medicine activities. This may be particularly true for some preventive, recreational or even rehabilitative type activities, or for training, exercise or therapy programs or for the return to play of an athlete who despite medical advice to the contrary, wishes (and may have a right under some federal or state laws) to return to participation.[28] For example In a recently published opinion from Ohio, Yurcich vs. Murray,[29] the Ohio Seventh District Court of Appeals held that: *"[A] release executed by a patient, relieving a physician from liability for negligence is not necessarily a contract against public policy...[Moreover], in a case wherein the circumstances are similar to those at hand, we do not find that such a release in and of itself is shocking."*

In this alleged medical malpractice action, the plaintiff patient prior to undergoing a surgical procedure signed a consent to operation for cosmetic purposes, and an informed consent for the specific surgical procedure, in addition to a release of all claims arising from any act or omission of the defendant, including those due to negligent acts or omissions. Based ostensibly upon the plaintiff's execution of the release, the trial court granted a motion of the defendant doctor for summary judgment, finding that there was no genuine issue of material fact and that the defendant was entitled to judgment as a matter of law due to the plaintiff's execution of the prospective release.

The release used in the Yurcich case simply provided as follows:

> ## RELEASE
>
> I am aware of the risks, hazards and uncertainties connected with this type of surgery.
>
> In consideration of Dr. Richard D. Murray undertaking to perform such surgery upon me, I release Dr. Richard D. Murray, his heirs, executors, administrators, servants and employees from all claims, demands, actions, causes of action, and from all liability for injury, damage or loss of whatsoever kind, nature or description that may arise or be sustained by me while under the care of Dr. Richard D. Murray and this is to include anything which might arise from any act or omission of Dr. Richard D. Murray, including negligent acts or omissions.

Upon review however, the appellate court scrutinized the release and noted: *"It is a fundamental rule in the construction of contracts of indemnity that such a contract shall not be construed to indemnify against the negligence of the...[defendant] unless it is so expressed in clear and unequivocal terms. Upon our purview the contract involved in this cause, clearly and unequivocally, was a release of negligence."*

Notwithstanding this finding, however, the court of appeals reversed the trial court's decision and sent the case back to the trial court because it found: *"There was no evidence properly before the trial court to indicate that...[the defendant doctor], or one of his agents, disclosed to...[the patient] the effect of the execution of the release and there was no evidence that the...[defendant doctor] or any of his agents attempted to ascertain, as fully as possible, that the...[patient] understood the consequences of executing the release in question."*

In examining a physician's duties to the patient when attempting to secure such a release in a medical setting, the court noted that: *"[A] release, executed between a patient and a physician, is not the usual run-of-the-mill contract. The relation of patient and physician is a fiduciary relationship which requires a duty of good faith and fair dealing on the part of the physician, not only as to the professional obligations of the physician but also as to other transactions between the parties...[I]f a physician desires to secure a general release of liability from a patient, because of the fiduciary relationship, he owes a duty to fully disclose to the patient the effect of such release and to ascertain as fully as possible that the patient understands the consequences thereof."*

The Yurcich case is somewhat different than a number of decisions from other jurisdictions which have declared the use of prospective releases in medical settings to be against public policy. These states include California (1963), Georgia (1980), Tennessee (1977), North Carolina (1969) and Kentucky (1969). Although the rationale for these decisions may vary somewhat, most of these courts believe that the provision of medical service is of such import to society that the public interest cannot permit the use of these documents, relieving a provider from liability due to his/her own negligence. As the Tennessee Supreme Court noted in 1977 [30] *"A professional person should not be permitted to hide behind the protective shield of an exculpatory contract and insist that he is not answerable for his own negligence. We do not approve the procurement of a license to commit negligence in professional practice."* [31] Even in the three states where these releases have withstood public policy arguments (Ohio, New York and Washington), the particular fact patterns involved experimental or elective surgical procedures (New York, Ohio), or were such that the patient's refusal to permit a blood transfusion prior to a D & C operation led to the execution of the release in favor of the treating physician (Washington).

A number of sports and sports medicine programs utilize prospective releases even where the services offered and performed are clearly medical in nature.[32] The use of these forms should be undertaken with great care and only after thorough and well reasoned professional advice is first obtained. There appears to be little question that services which are medical in nature, even if carried out under some other label, will be subject to the same rules of law and practice as any other medical service. The use of prospective releases containing exculpatory clauses in medical settings may be lawful however and valid in some states. Prior to adopting any such procedure for the utilization of these documents, the following suggestions should be considered:

SUGGESTIONS FOR THE USE OF PROSPECTIVE RELEASES IN A MEDICAL SETTING

1. Prior to even considering the use of these documents, program administrators, physicians and allied health personnel should determine the professional propriety of using the forms. Moral, ethical and professional concerns should be initially addressed and resolved before proceeding further.

2. Assuming the program's professional staff determines that such forms should be considered, program legal counsel must be consulted to research particular state law to determine the validity of prospective releases in particular sports medicine settings.

3. After legal counsel has determined that such releases are or may be valid, proper contractual forms must be developed to insure that they meet state legal requirements and expressly state that the beneficiary of the document is being released from negligent acts and omissions.

4. Once proper forms are developed, a clear written procedure must be developed by legal counsel, administration and staff which must be regularly followed to insure that adequate disclosure, understanding and form execution by the athlete/participant takes place. An opportunity for questions must be provided to the patient and any such inquiries must be properly addressed. Notations of questions and answers, as well as other statements or indications of patient understanding should be noted by the staff member securing the release. Adequate document comparison, and most importantly, contrast, should be provided if the release is secured along with other documents such as an informed consent. Consideration should be

given to preserving the form execution process on audio or video tape if so determined after consultation with legal counsel and if the patient's additional written consent to same is secured.

5. Records as to the process must be preserved. Dictated and preserved staff remembrances might be of great benefit if later questions or suit should occur.

6. Periodic review, and if necessary, modification, of forms, procedures and record keeping must be consistently completed by staff, administration and legal counsel.

7. Risk management advisors and liability insurers should be consulted as to the development and use of such documents. If the use of the documents can be demonstrated to reduce the frequency of claims or suits, a variety of benefits may be available to the program. These may include continued liability insurance coverage and reduction and/or stabilization of liability insurance premium rates.

8. Consideration should be given to the question as to whether or not it is necessary to secure signatures of the patient's spouse and/or children in addition to the patient himself or herself so as to maximize the effectiveness of any such form and make it as binding as possible upon the broadest group possible.

Notwithstanding the potentially limited availability of prospective releases in some sports medicine settings, the use of prospective release forms has some precedence, and may in fact be beneficial as to other activities or when related to the provision of non-medical or quasi-medical services. For example, with certain dangerous, perhaps ultra-hazardous activities the use of such contracts containing exculpatory provisions have been upheld in some jurisdictions despite public policy arguments. These forms have been allowed for activities such as race car driving,[33] parachute jumping[34] bicycle rental[35] and a whole host of other activities. To be valid in these situations releases must be supported by adequate and valuable consideration (something of value) since they are very strictly construed by the courts.

In the exercise and fitness setting, some courts have allowed the use of release forms.[36] For example in the New York case of <u>Ciofalo vs. Vic Tanney Gyms, Inc.</u>[37] a spa member upon joining a health club executed an assumption of risk agreement within her membership contract which provided that she would *"assume full responsibility for any injuries which might occur to her in or about defendant's premises, including but without limitation, any claims for personal injuries resulting from or arising out of the negligence of the defendant."*[38] The member subsequently fell at the spa pool site and brought suit alleging that the fall was caused by the negligence of the operation due to excessive floor slipperiness and lack of sufficient and competent personnel.

The court in examining her claims, injuries and preceding actions held: *"Defendant, [Vic Tanney], a private corporation, was under no obligation or legal duty to accept plaintiff as a 'member' or patron. Having consented to do so, it had the right to insist upon such terms as it deemed appropriate. Plaintiff on the other hand, was not required to assent to unacceptable terms, or to give up a valuable legal right, as a condition precedent to obtaining employment or being able to make use of the services rendered by a public carrier or utility [organizations required by law to provide services]. She voluntarily applied for membership in a private organization, and agreed to the terms upon which this membership was bestowed. She may not repudiate them now."*[39]

It is important within the context of the court's decision to point out that this involved claims of **passive** spa conduct rather than **active**, **directed** spa activities by spa personnel. Secondly, it is also important to note that no claim was put forth that the club was providing any medical or quasi-medical services of any kind.

In the state of Illinois a similar result as in the Ciofalo case was reached in the case of Owen vs. Vic Tanney Enterprises.[40] In this case the plaintiff, like the injured party in the New York case, fell in an area near the facility's pool and brought suit claiming that the spa was negligent. The plaintiff similarly executed a prospective release form in favor of Vic Tanney Enterprises. The court followed the reasoning of the Ciofalo case and upheld the operations contract form even though it contained exculpatory language.

In another Illinois case, Neuman vs. Gloria Marshall Figure Salon,[41] the court issued its opinion barring the plaintiff's action against the defendant health club. In this case the plaintiff joined the spa in 1982, at which time she signed a contract agreeing to pay a specified sum for a specific number of visits. That membership contract also contained the following language: *"Patron specifically assumes all risks of injury while using any equipment or facilities at the salon and waives any and all claims against Gloria Marshall Management Company and the owners and employees of the salon for any such injury."*

Shortly after joining the facility, the plaintiff allegedly injured her back while using one of the defendant's exercise machines. She contended that one of the defendant's employees, (after her selection of a machine), placed the leg portion of the machine in a downward position before turning it on and leaving the room. When the machine was activated the plaintiff felt sharp, stabbing pains in her back but nevertheless continued with the exercise on the machine. The defendant's employee, she contended, did not determine whether or not she was lying properly on the table prior to leaving the room. After the initial session on the exercise machine, the plaintiff advised the spa employee that she had experienced the excruciating back pain while the machine was operating with the leg portion of the machine in a downward position. The employee advised the plaintiff not to repeat the exercise with the machine in that position. However, the plaintiff completed the program that night, including the use of the same machine with the leg portion in the upward position, even though she continued to experience back pain. Thereafter the plaintiff obtained medical treatment which revealed a ruptured disk. A lumbar laminectomy was required in an effort to treat the plaintiff.

Suit was later filed contending, among other things, that the spa and its employees were negligent. Although the plaintiff attempted to raise several factual issues, the court determined: *"Where an exculpatory clause specifically sets forth in clear language the range of activities to which it applies, the clause is enforceable."*[42] In reviewing the exculpatory clause as contained within its membership application, the court noted: *"The provision explicitly mentions 'injury while using any equipment' and waiving claims against defendant for 'any such injury'."*[43] While finding that the form was sufficient to bar the plaintiff's action, the court held that the use of the word "negligence" was not required. The court concluded *"[I]n this case, plaintiff assumed the risk that due to an employee's negligence and whether or not the employee was an expert, she may be injured by using a machine. As a result, plaintiff could have reasonably altered her conduct, for example, by stopping the exercise immediately after experiencing the excruciating pain or by consulting an employee of the defendant immediately regarding the possibility of improper usage."*[44] Inasmuch as the court found that the exculpatory clause in this case was not against public policy or otherwise invalid, the plaintiff's cause of action was dismissed.

Even though a great many of the release cases involving exercise facilities have resulted in findings upholding such documents, other cases have not been so favorable to some defendants. In the case of <u>Brown vs. Racquetball Centers, Inc.</u>,[45] the plaintiff fitness club member was required to sign a two-page document upon his admission to the center which included a release provision. The release provided as follows:

"I, Leroy F. Brown, voluntarily enter the Westend Racquet Club...to participate in the athletic, physical and social activities therein. I have inspected the premises and know of the risks and dangers involved in such activities as are conducted therein and that unanticipated and unexpected dangers may arise during such activities. I hereby and do assume all risks of injury to my person and property that may be sustained in connection with the stated and associated activities in and about those premises.

In consideration of the permission granted to me to enter the premises and participate in the stated activities, I hereby, for myself, my heirs, administrators and assigns, release, remise and discharge the owners, operators and sponsors and the premises and its activities and equipment and their respective servants, agents, officers, and all other participants in those activities of and from all claims, demands, actions, and causes of action of any sort, for injury sustained to my person and/or property during my presence on the premises and my participation in those activities due to negligence or any other fault."

After joining, the plaintiff slipped and fell on a wet tile floor in the club shower area and was injured. The plaintiff instituted suit and contended that the club had negligently maintained the shower room floor which proximately resulted in his injuries. In analyzing the facts and the release the court however stated that the release did not specifically *"spell out the intention of the parties with the necessary particularity. The language does not set forth in an unambiguous manner that the releaser, in signing the agreement intends to absolve the lessee of liability for the lessee's own negligence. Instead, the language can more clearly be interpreted to relieve the club of liability as a result of injuries sustained by a member while participating in certain activities of the club."*[46] Based upon the foregoing, the court determined that the release did not satisfy the requirements of Pennsylvania law and therefore ordered that the case proceed to trial.

In another similar decision,[47] the plaintiff filed a negligence action against the defendants for injuries she sustained while utilizing a free-fall simulator. Prior to her use of the simulator however, the plaintiff signed a liability release form, purportedly releasing the defendants of any liability due to their negligence that might occur while the plaintiff was using the simulator. At the trial court, the defendants filed a motion for summary judgment and urged the trial court to determine their liability by reference to the signed release. The district court upon the basis of the motion granted the summary judgment in favor of the defendants. The plaintiff appealed.

The appellate court in addressing the issues involved in the case determined that in order for the defendants to be relieved from liability based upon the plaintiff's assumption of risk, two requirements must have been met: *"First, there must have been voluntary exposure to the danger. Second, there must have been actual knowledge of the risk assumed... 'A risk can be said to have been voluntarily assumed by a person only if it was known to him and he fully appreciated the danger'."*[48] In applying the facts as determined by the trial court, the appellate court found that the plaintiff denied appreciation of the risks associated with the free-fall simulator. The appellate court also acknowledged that there was some dispute as to whether or not the plaintiff knowingly and voluntarily assumed the risks not associated with the simulator. Based upon these factual disputes, the appellate court returned the case to the trial court with the notation: *"It is necessary for the fact finder to hear testimony and assess credibility."*[49]

Each case must be determined upon the basis of its own merits and the law of the particular jurisdiction involved. Care must be taken to review the law in each jurisdiction and to develop proper waiver forms in accordance with that jurisdiction's law.[50]

Even though releases in some sports medicine settings may not be void as against public policy, deficiencies in the execution process itself may result in a nullification of the document. For example, in the case of <u>Stalnaker vs. McDermott Corporation</u>,[51] the plaintiff, a seaman, filed suit pursuant to federal law in the state of Louisiana for injuries which he suffered while serving as a seaman. The defendant employer contended that the plaintiff had executed a release and settled his claim for injuries prior to filing suit. As a consequence, it offered the release into evidence and moved for the entry of summary judgment in its favor.

The plaintiff responded to this motion and alleged that genuine issues of material fact were presented for jury determination which precluded the entry of judgment in favor of the defendant. The plaintiff contended that the release was invalid for several reasons:

1. He was under the influence of prescriptive drugs at the time the release was executed;

2. He was not represented by counsel when he executed the document;

3. He signed the release only as to specific injuries but not for all injuries; and,

4. He executed the release under duress.

The trial court granted the summary judgment motion and the plaintiff appealed.

Although the appeals court noted that peculiarities of federal maritime jurisprudence placed a "heavy burden" on the ship owner to establish that a seaman's release was valid, the court based upon a transcript of the seaman's testimony held: *"After review of the evidence, we are of the opinion that a material issue of fact does exist with respect to the possibility of plaintiff being under the influence of medication when executing the release."*[52]

The plaintiff's testimony with reference to the release execution process was as follows:

"Q. Are you on any medications?

A. Yes.

Q. What medications are you taking?

A. I don't know the name of them.

Q. O.K. What is it for?

A. But it's for esophagitis.

Q. O.K.

A. It's nothing that would hamper my thinking in any way whatsoever.'

...

Q. Okay. What medication were you under for pain?

A. I believe he had given me muscle relaxers. I don't know the name of the muscle relaxers. And also, I believe Percodan.

...

Q. Okay. Now, what effect did that [which] you were taking have on you during the Receipt and Release [process] that you feel makes the Receipt and Release invalid at this time?

A. I didn't fully understand totally all of the ramifications of this."[53]

Given this testimony, the Louisiana Appellate Court concluded that the trial court could not decide that the release was valid due to the fact that genuine factual questions existed as to the release execution process. The case was therefore remanded to the trial court level for evidentiary hearing.

Even the most complete and properly worded releases may be declared invalid in a particular case due to some flaw or deficiency in the execution process. The party executing such documents must have some understanding and comprehension of the legal effect of the release. If such a person's mental faculties are impaired due to drugs, medication, age, physical or mental infirmities or other valid reason, the release execution process may be suspect. At the very least jury questions will be raised which must depend upon factual determinations at time of trial rather than through less costly and less time consuming summary proceedings.

When release documents are used, an affirmative statement should be included for the participant to acknowledge through signature or initialing that the signer is not impaired, is not taking any drugs or medication and understands the effect of the release. In this manner claims like the one at issue in the Stalnaker case might be precluded. Examples of clauses which could be used to refute claims as to the execution process could include the following suggestions:

➤ I AM NOT TAKING ANY DRUGS OR MEDICATIONS, ALCOHOL OR OTHER SUBSTANCE, NOR AM I IMPAIRED IN ANY WAY. x_____

➤ I HAVE READ AND UNDERSTOOD THIS RELEASE DOCUMENT BEFORE SIGNING IT. x_____

➤ WARNING! READ THIS RELEASE DOCUMENT BEFORE SIGNING IT! x_____

➤ WITH THE INTENT TO GIVE FULL LEGAL EFFECT TO THIS RELEASE DOCUMENT I SIGN IT THIS ____ DAY OF _____, 19____. x_____

Although the exact language to be used in this document will depend upon the nature of the activity for which the release is sought, the circumstances at hand, and the jurisdiction within which the matter is to be determined, (which must be drafted by local legal counsel in accordance with particular state law), these examples should be of some assistance.

In other situations, it is important for sports medicine providers to realize who can lawfully execute a release document, under what circumstances and for whom. For example, in a case from Washington,[54] certain school districts had required students and their parents to execute a standardized preparticipation release form, relieving the school district from liability arising from any ordinary negligence that might arise in connection with the student's participation in the district's interscholastic and scholastic activity programs. Such forms were required by the defendant school districts prior to allowing students to participate in any athletic program.

The parents in these consolidated cases sought to have the releases declared invalid as being against public policy. The court, in examining the releases, and considering various public policy considerations, determined that even though students had no fundamental right to participate in interscholastic activities, such activities were a matter of great public importance in the state of Washington. The court also determined that the law of Washington required school districts to employ ordinary care and to anticipate reasonably foreseeable dangers, so as to take precautions to protect children under its jurisdiction from injury or harm. Based upon all of the foregoing, therefore, the court held *"To the extent that the release portions of these forms represent a consent to relieve the school districts of their duty of care, they are invalid, whether they are termed releases or express assumptions of risk."*[55] The court also determined that while the state legislature might consider the adoption of such release forms, they could not, absent express legislative authorization, uphold the use of such forms.

If a program serves minor patients, releases cannot be effectively obtained from such persons due to the fact that they are not of "legal" age to sign contractual documents. Even a child's parents may not be able to effectively and lawfully execute releases on behalf of their children in some instances.[56] In this case, a child gymnast had been injured on uneven bars at a

Pennsylvania gymnastic facility. Prior to her participation, the child and her parents executed a release purportedly barring suit in the event of the child's injury. In examining the situation, the court held: *"The parents did not possess the authority to release the claims or potential claims of a minor child merely because of the parental relationship."*[57]

In another case,[58] the plaintiff's parents sought to facilitate their son's admission to the Valley Forge Military Academy by executing an agreement releasing the Academy *"from all claims and damages arising from or related to or in any way connected to their son Jerry's hemophilic condition"*. The court refused to uphold the Release because under Pennsylvania law, the parents did not possess the authority to release the claims or potential claims of a minor child merely because of the parental relationship.

In some circumstances however, parents may be in a position and have the legal authority to execute such documents to bind their children to certain agreements.[59]

Some contend that these decisions, prohibiting parents from lawfully executing releases on behalf of their children, could be devastating to program offerings and their continuing viability. Until now, some gymnastic centers, high schools, little leagues, etc., have required potential participants to execute a release or consent prior to participation, in order to limit the organization's exposure to liability claims (*see* examples in the Appendix). Now, however, many of these efforts may be unenforceable. Schools, youth leagues and perhaps some sports medicine programs will be faced with a decision about how to otherwise insulate themselves from suit or, at least, how to limit their exposure to suit.

One somewhat untested alternative might be to have participants execute some form of an acknowledgment of injury and have parents execute an indemnification agreement to become effective in the event the minor disaffirms the release and brings suit. While still not an enforceable contract as to the minor, it may provide a defensible position at the time of any trial based upon assumption of the risk. An example of such a form is included in the Appendix to this work.

The use of prospective releases containing exculpatory clauses in some program activities has some authority in some states. Other states have taken the position that such documents are against public policy and unenforceable. Even where enforceable, defects in the execution process can render such documents invalid. Local program counsel will simply have to review his/her state's statutes and case precedents to determine the enforceability of the clauses for his/her program. However, some general rules would appear to be readily apparent:

1. Prospective releases in the medical or quasi-medical setting will not in all probability be upheld by the courts who will probably view such clauses as being contrary to public policy, except in rare instances (elective procedures) and even then, only in a few states;

2. Exculpatory clause contracts when used for certain adjunct services – exercise, preventive or rehabilitative activity, recreation, etc., may be valid if supported by adequate consideration and fully and properly prepared and executed;

3. Prospective waivers/releases of liability may be sufficient to protect sports programs and perhaps even sports medicine providers in attempting to insulate themselves from suit where an adult athlete wishes to participate but his or her medical condition is questionable or where the athlete asserts that his/her rights are being violated by excluding him or her from play.[60]

4. Such contracts will probably be upheld as to the more dangerous participant activities where the participant knows and appreciates the related risks and dangers.

Based upon the rule in some states it would appear that some programs could reduce their own risks by the use of such forms especially as to participants who are not receiving purely or solely medical or medical support services from the program. These might include test subjects seeking measurement of their functional capacity for work or sport, as opposed to those seeking or needing evaluation of disease or injury. Moreover, those healthy or apparently healthy individuals participating in exercise or training programs for non-therapeutic reasons may also validly execute such contracts in some states. Lastly, the use of such forms for athletes seeking the right to participate in sports programs may also be of some value to the program and perhaps members of the sports medicine team where the athletes have a questionable or debatable condition, such as to make them disabled or handicapped under federal or state laws and they are otherwise qualified or able to participate (*see* Chapter 8, *infra*). If such clauses are to be used, they must be supported by adequate consideration; consequently the program should obtain them at the inception of the participant's entry and acceptance into the program or at other critical times such as when an athlete is returned to participation.

FINAL THOUGHT

The concept of informed consent in any medical or quasi-medical procedure is inviolate in this country. Every patient has the right to be informed of the examination, treatment or procedure recommended and of the risks associated therewith as well as expected benefits to be derived therefrom and the available alternatives. Upon the basis of this information patients can then make "informed" choices – informed decisions as to whether or not to undergo the recommended process. Conflicts within the sports medicine setting which might tend to interfere with this process must be minimized if not excluded entirely so as to allow the athlete complete freedom of choice and information. The use of assumption of risk documents or releases in the sports medicine setting must be carefully considered by program personnel and their legal counsel and used, if at all, only in appropriate and lawful settings and for appropriate and lawful purposes.

CHAPTER 6 FOOTNOTES:

1. AHA, "Exercise Standards – A Statement For Health Professionals," *Circulation* 82(6):2286-2322, 1990.

2. ACSM, GUIDELINES FOR EXERCISE TESTING AND PRESCRIPTION, Fourth Edition (Lea & Febiger, Philadelphia, PA 1990).

3. Paucher vs. Iowa Methodist Medical Center, No. 86-364 (Super. Court, Iowa, June 17, 1987. *See* Herbert, "Risk Disclosure in The Informed Consent Process: Judging the Adequacy of Disclosure in Light of the Patient's Need for Information, An Emerging Trend," *The Exercise Standards and Malpractice Reporter* 2(4):56-57, 1988.

4. 618 F. Supp. 627 (Dist. Ct., E.D. Mo.).

5. Herbert, "Who Will Judge Your Professional Conduct in Court?," *The Exercise Standards and Malpractice Reporter* 1(1):14-16, 1987.

6. *See, supra* footnote 4 at page 631.

7. *See, supra* footnote 4 at page 632.

8. *Id.* at page 631-632.

9. *Id.* at page 632.

10. 473 So.2d 1297.

11. *Id.* at page 1302.

12. McNiece, "Legal Aspects of Exercise Testing," *New York State Journal of Medicine,* July 15, 1972, 1822-1824, at page 1823.

13. *See e.g.,* Rochmis and Blackburn, "Exercise Tests: A Survey or Procedures, Safety and Litigation Experience in Approximately 170,000 Tests," *JAMA* 217(8):1061-1066, 1971.

14. *See e.g.,* Krueger vs. San Francisco Forty Niners, 234 Cal. Rptr. 579 (Cal. App. 1 1987) *analyzed in* Leslie, "War and Peace With Hippocrates – A Modern Dilemma Facing Sports Medicine," *The Sports Medicine Standards and Malpractice Reporter* 2(2):21, 24-28, 1990; Martin vs. Casagrande, 559 N.Y.S.2d 68 (AD Dept. 1990) *analyzed in* Herbert, "Conspiring to Withhold Information Against Professional Hockey Team and Physician Dismissed," *The Sports Medicine Standards and Malpractice Reporter* 3(1):8-9, 1991.

15. *See e.g.,* Gathers vs. Loyola Marymount University, Los Angeles, California 1990 filing, *analyzed in* Herbert, "The Death of Hank Gathers: An Examination of the Legal Issues," *The Sports Medicine Standards and Malpractice Reporter* 2(3):45-47, 1990; Sherwin vs. Indianapolis Colts, Inc., 752 F. Supp. 1172 (N.D.N.Y. 1990) *analyzed in* "Another Suit Based Upon Information Withholding Allegations," *The Sports Medicine Standards and Malpractice Reporter* 3(3):55-

56, 1991; Hendy vs. Losee, 274 Cal. Rptr. 31 (Cal. App. 4 Dist. 1990) *analyzed in* "Professional Football Player's Malpractice Action Against Team Physician to Proceed," *The Sports Medicine Standards and Malpractice Reporter* 3(2):26-28, 1991.

16. *See e.g.,* Jimenez vs. Dept. of Pro Regulation, 556 So.2d 1219 (1990) *analyzed in* "Physician Disciplined For False Entries Regarding Fitness Testing," *The Exercise Standards and Malpractice Reporter* 5(3):47, 1991.

17. *Cf., e.g.,* Arnold vs. Shawano Cty. Agr. Soc., No. 81-1039, Wisc. Sup. Ct. March 1, 1983.

18. *See e.g.,* Byrd vs. Matthews, 571 So.2d 258 (Mass. 1991) *analyzed in* "Husband's Execution of Release Bars Wife's Claim," *The Exercise Standards and Malpractice Reporter* 5(5):78, 1991. *But see,* Brown vs. Kil-Kare, Inc., 63 Ohio St.2d 84 (1992) *analyzed in* "Husband's Release Does Not Bar Wife's Lawsuit," *The Exercise Standards and Malpractice Reporter* 6(3):42, 1992.

19. *Cf.* Comodeca, "Acknowledgment of Risk Forms: The Best Defense for Sports Medicine Practitioners," *The Sports Medicine Standards and Malpractice Reporter* 4(4):49, 51-54, 1992; "The Use of Releases to Clear Athletes for Participation," *The Sports Medicine Standards and Malpractice Reporter* 4(3):45, 1992.

20. THE PRACTICAL LAWYER 32(6):58, 1986.

21. *See, supra* footnote 14.

22. *Id.*

23. *See e.g.,* Hendy vs. U.S. Fidelity & Guaranty Insurance Company, 594 So.2d 584 (La. App. 5 Cir. 1992) *analyzed in* "Raquetball Player Not Liable For Opponent's Injuries," *The Sports, Parks and Recreation Law Reporter* 7(4):57, 1993; *but see,* Clark vs. Weigand, 617 N.E.2d 916 (Ind. 1993) *analyzed in* "Will More Sports Related Injuries Become Questions For Jury Determination?," *The Sports, Parks and Recreation Law Reporter* 7(4):54-55, 1994.

24. 436 So.2d 78 (1983).

25. *Id.* at page 80.

26. *See, supra* footnote 19.

27. *See e.g.,* Tunkl vs. Regents of U. of Calif., 60 Cal.2d 92 (1963).

28. *See, supra* footnote 19.

29. Case No. 85 CA 28 (Court of Appeals, Seventh District, Mahoning County, December 27, 1985) (relying on two earlier pronouncements: Magull vs. Murray, Case No. 80 CA 126 (Court of Appeals, Seventh District, Mahoning County, August 14, 1981 and Guido vs. Murray, Case No. 84 CA 109 (Court of Appeals, Seventh District, Mahoning County, February 20, 1985).

30. Olsen vs. Molzen, 558 S.W.2d 429.

31. *See, supra* footnote 27 at page 432.

32. "The Use of Releases to Clear Athletes for Participation," *The Sports Medicine Standards and Malpractice Reporter* 4(3):45, 1992.

33. Seymour vs. New Breman Speedway, Inc. 31 Ohio App.2d 141 (Auglaize Cty. 1971); Hine vs. Dayton Speedway Corp., 20 Ohio App. 2d 185 (Montgomery Cty. 1969).

34. Cain vs. Cleveland Parachute Training Center, 9 Ohio App.3d 27 (Geauga Cty. 1983); *but see* Renand vs. 200 Convention Center, Ltd., 728 P.2d 445 (Nov. 1986) *analyzed in* "Releases Are Not Always Valid," *The Exercise Standards and Malpractice Reporter* 1(2):34, April, 1987, Jones vs. Dressell, 582 P.2d 1057 (Colo. Appeals 1978).

35. Gimpel vs. Host Enterprises, Inc., 640 F. Supp. 972 (E.D. Pa. 1986).

36. *See* Herbert, "The Use of Prospective Releases Containing Exculpatory Language in Exercise and Fitness Programs," *The Exercise Standards and Malpractice Reporter* 1(6):89-90, October, 1987.

37. 177 N.E.2d 925 (Ct. Appeals 1961).

38. *Id.* at page 926.

39. *Id.* at page 927.

40. 199 N.E.2d 280 (Appeals Ct. 1964).

41. 500 N.E.2d 1011 (Second District, November 13, 1986).

42. *Id.* at page 1013.

43. *Id.* at page 1014.

44. *Id.* at page 1014

45. 534 A.2d 842 (Pa. Super. 1987).

46. *Id.* at page 843.

47. Renaud vs. 200 Convention Center, Ltd., 728 P.2d 445 (Nev. 1986).

48. *Id.* at page 446.

49. *Id.*

50. *See* Herbert "The Use of Prospective Releases Containing Exculpatory Language in Exercise and Fitness Programs," *The Exercise Standards and Malpractice Reporter* 1(6): 89-90, 1987; "The Use of Prospective Releases in Exercise Facilities: An Update," *The Exercise Standards and Malpractice Reporter* 3(2):32-35, 1989.

51. 505 So.2d 139 (La App. 4th Cir. 1987).

52. *Id.* at page 140.

53. *Id.*

54. Wagenblast vs. Odessa School No. 105-157-166, 758 P.2d 968 (Washington 1988).

55. *Id.* at page 974.

56. Simmons vs. Parkette National Gymnastic Training Center, et al., 670 F. Supp. 140 (Pa. Dist. Ct. 1987). *See also,* Ehrlich, "Release Signed By Minor Gymnast Deemed to be Unenforceable," *The Sports, Parks and Recreational Law Reporter* 2(2):30-31, 1988. *See also,* Herbert, "Protection From Claims in Fitness Activities for Kids," *Fitness Management* 5(3):15-16 (March, 1989).

57. *Id.*

58. Apicella vs. Valley Forge Military Academy, 630 F.Supp. 20 (E.D. Pa. 1985),

59. Bukler vs. French Woods Festival of Performing Arts, Inc., 546 N.Y.S.2d 591 (A.D. 1 Dept. 1989).

60. *See,* "The Americans With Disabilities Act: Its Effect on Sport, Sports Medicine and Activity Programs," *The Sports Medicine Standards and Malpractice Reporter* 3(4):66-68, 1991; Herbert, THE AMERICANS WITH DISABILITIES ACT: A GUIDE FOR HEALTH CLUBS AND EXERCISE FACILITIES (Professional Reports Corporation, Canton, OH 1991).

7   PREPARTICIPATION EXAMINATIONS

Sports medicine practitioners have traditionally and histori-cally been called upon for the purposes of conducting physical examinations of athletes and other individuals seeking medical clearance prior to engaging in sport or similar exertional activities. The purpose of the sports or clearance examination has been to *"determine whether the...athlete is prepared to engage in a particular sport."*[1] According to several written pronouncements as to the standard of care owed during such examinations, it seems that a review of an individual's health history, a physical examination, tests as appropriate and evaluation are necessary components of an appropriate examination.[2] While each of these statements are couched in terms of recommendations rather than mandates, it appears that these basic examination elements would be judged in a court of law to be minimal portions of the standard of care owed to the examinee during a preparticipation examination rather than optimal recommendations as to same.

FORMS OF EXAMINATION

There are several different forms of examination available for sports teams seeking preparticipation medical clearance. These are:

1. personal physician conducted examinations;

2. station examinations conducted by several physicians of entire teams or groups of athletes during each of which the examining physician concentrates upon a particular area of the body or some system therein contained; and

3. locker room type examinations during which a team of physicians examines participants en masse.

These forms of examination were the subject of a 1987 study by DuRant, et. al.[3] The study examined these three methods of preparticipation physical examinations to determine whether or not one was more effective than another in detecting potential problems of those undergoing examination. The results of this study indicate that the station, multi-physician examination method probably is more thorough, and may result in greater detection of potential muscular/skeletal and orthopedic problems and limitations, than either of the other methods. This study also reported that the station examination method resulted in more recommendations for further evaluation and referral.

While this study does not follow up on the post-examination injuries of the athletes tested by one of the aforementioned methods to detect if the examination practices helped screen out potential problems or conditions, this study may well be cited as authority for a standard of care for advocation of multi-station, multi-physician, preparticipation examinations, especially where a post-examination injury is due to a failure to detect a muscular-skeletal or orthopedic problem or limitation during another kind of preparticipation examination, or where further referral and evaluation should have occurred as to the subsequently injured athlete.

It may well be as to those facilities or physicians engaging in personal physician or locker room type examinations, that particular emphasis should be placed on muscular-skeletal and other orthopedic problems or limitations, and even more careful screening of those prospective athletes who may require further specialized evaluation or care. Anything less in the face of studies like the foregoing may result in a failure to adhere to the proper standard of care.

In another recently published article in *The Physician and Sportsmedicine,*[4] certain survey results for preparticipation physical examinations were reported. Based upon the survey results, the authors concluded that there was a need for appropriate guidelines and recommendations for preparticipation physical examinations. In the article, the authors developed a rather strong case for more uniform national guidelines as to the preparticipation physical examination process. In the absence of such recommended guidelines, the preparticipation physical examination process may be subject to attack on a variety of bases and may be subject to individualized expert opinions provided in a court of law in the event of claim or suit even though some standards exist. The development of nearly universal and uniform national standards of practice for preparticipation examinations has now occurred[5] which may preclude more individualized opinions as to what is necessary or required for preparticipation physical examinations.

HISTORICAL REVIEW OF STANDARDS FOR PREPARTICIPATION EXAMINATIONS

A number of standards related to preparticipation examinations have been developed over the years. In 1976, the American Medical Association last revised a list of disqualifying conditions to be used by those conducting these examinations.[6] A more recent, comprehensive and updated list of recommendations for participation in competitive sports was also prepared by the American Academy of Pediatrics through its Council on Child and Adolescent Health, Committee on Sports Medicine. This publication entitled RECOMMENDATIONS FOR PARTICIPATION IN COMPETITIVE SPORTS was published in 1988 by the AAP.

The recommendations as developed by the American Academy of Pediatrics Committee on Sports Medicine began with a classification of various sport activities into subsets of:

CONTACT/COLLISION SPORTS
LIMITED CONTACT/IMPACT SPORTS
STRENUOUS/NON-CONTACT SPORTS
MODERATELY STRENUOUS/NON-CONTACT SPORTS
NON-STRENUOUS/NON-CONTACT SPORTS

Thereafter, these groupings were utilized for the purposes of assessment of certain common medical and surgical conditions to determine whether or not participants would be exposed to a substantial risk of injury in the event of participation. The listing and grouping of medical and surgical conditions was such that the recommendations were easy to use in conjunction with preparticipation medical examinations for those desiring to participate in various athletic-type activities.

Aside from the foregoing, a new effort was undertaken in 1992 to develop comprehensive standards for preparticipation physical examinations which was then being compiled by five nationally prominent sports medicine organizations. These associations include the American Osteopathic Academy of Sports Medicine (AOASM), the American Medical Society for Sports Medicine (AMSSM), the American Academy of Family Physicians (AAFP), the American Academy of Pediatricians (AAP) and the American Orthopedic Society for Sports Medicine (AOSSM). The effort was aimed at the development of universal preparticipation examination guidelines for use nationally to bring together a uniform statement on the subject.[7] The publication recommends an entry level complete evaluation followed by annual re-evaluations and assessments of athletes. In this regard it is similar to an NCAA publication in part devoted to the same subject.[8] The latest association publication follows a sport clearance classification system like that originally developed by the AAP and includes concussion guidelines developed by the Colorado Sports Medicine Committee.[9] Given the stature of these organizations, these standards are sure to have a dramatic impact upon the practice of sports medicine clearance of athletes for participation and even for re-entry to play decisions.

PRE-ACTIVITY CLEARANCE EXAMINATIONS

The need for preparticipation clearance is not and should not be limited to competitive athletes. Sports medicine practitioners will in some situations be called upon in ever-increasing numbers to clear individuals for participation in a variety of activities including: youth camp attendance,[10] admission to health clubs or other similar facilities,[11] or for the clearance of adults or children prior to their beginning a program of planned activity, exercise, recreation or sport.[12] As a result of one 1988 California malpractice arbitration award in the matter of <u>Camerena vs. Kaiser Permanente</u>, some are claiming that graded exercise stress testing is a necessary prerequisite to clearing *all* asymptomatic men, forty years of age and older for silent ischemia prior to a physician's authorization of a plan of physical activity.[13] In this particular case, the decedent had requested a physical examination for clearance prior to beginning an activity program. He completed a health questionnaire, had his blood analyzed, was given a resting ECG and subsequently a physical examination. While he was put on a low cholesterol diet and told to report back in three months, no restriction on activity was apparently placed upon him. He died suddenly while jogging shortly after the physical. A subsequently filed suit resulted in an arbitration award for his family of $500,000.00. The plaintiffs contended that since the physician did not test for silent ischemia (which in all probability would have demonstrated multiple coronary artery disease since the decedent had occlusion of some coronary arteries and complete occlusion of the right coronary artery) the physician was negligent and thus responsible for the activity related death which the patient was not apparently warned to avoid.[14]

Awards or verdicts in cases like this one may well impose greater and greater obligations upon physicians and other health care providers who are asked to screen many individuals for a wide variety of activities.[15] For example, in the case of <u>Contino vs. Lucille Roberts Health Spa</u>,[16] a chiropractor allegedly advised the plaintiff to take an aerobics class to improve a back condition. During activity the plaintiff-patient fell, further injured her back and brought suit against the facility alleging negligence. The facility instituted a third-party action against the chiropractor seeking indemnification in response to the plaintiff's suit. The club facility claimed that the chiropractor's advice to the plaintiff was negligent and directly contributed to the injury. While the chiropractor sought to be dismissed from the case as a matter of law, the court held that *"the pleadings set forth an ample basis for holding that it is*

*possible that the negligence of both the [spa]...and the [chiroprac-
tor]... contributed to and was responsible for the...injury to the
plaintiff."* [17] In other situations, physicians can also be held liable
for clearing individuals for inappropriate activity given known
physical conditions or limitations. [18]

Current and on-going developments in the promulgation of
standards related to the screening of individuals for participation
in exercise, recreation and sport is sure to impact this crucial
sports medicine practice area. The American College of Sports
Medicine has now finalized standards and guidelines for health
and fitness facilities. These standards, published in 1992, include
statements regarding the need for screening and physician
evaluation of individuals seeking clearance for participation in
activity. [19] Due to the stature and expertise of this association,
these standards and guidelines are sure to rather dramatically
impact this crucial area of concern in addition to the preparticipation physical examination standards recently developed by the
AAFP, AAP, AMSSM, AOSSM and AOASM.

LEGAL CONTROVERSIES AND CASES

Legal controversies have arisen over the preparticipation
examination of athletes and others seeking to be medically
cleared for participation in sport or activity. While we shall examine
a number of cases dealing with return to play issues in Chapter 8,
it is important to note that there has been a "preponderance of
litigation" related to evaluations of athletes for admission to
various programs. [20] While much of the litigation in this area has
centered upon professional or high profile athletes, there has
been a noted absence of lawsuits against sports medicine providers at the amateur level, [21] except for recent litigation involving the
estates of college basketball stars Hank Gathers [22] and Ernest
Killum. [23] Aside from these cases, the sparsity of litigation may be
due to a variety of reasons including the fact that some states
provide immunity to volunteer health care providers who render
health care services to athletic teams. [24]

Litigation related to preparticipation physicals, particularly in those instances where physicians are retained by a club, facility, team, school system, university or other similar entity, may also be limited for other reasons. This is due to the fact that in some jurisdictions, under some circumstances, these physicians may owe only a limited duty to the patient – that is the duty to conduct an examination in a reasonable manner.[25] In some instances this is referred to as a "limited physician-patient relationship" because the physician is not retained to treat and take care of patients, but merely to examine team members and report examination findings to a third party.

For example, consider a recent ruling from the New York Supreme Court, Appellate Division, in an action against a physician who was charged with the responsibility of conducting referee physicals for the National Basketball Association (NBA). In this case, Murphy vs. Blum,[26] the plaintiff, who was employed as a referee for the NBA, was required to undergo (and pass) a yearly physical *"to ensure that he would be able to withstand the rigors of his job."*[27] In 1987, the plaintiff was put through an exercise stress test as part of his examination which was analyzed by the defendant physician. The physician concluded that the test was "abnormal" and so advised the NBA and the plaintiff's personal physician. The following season, the plaintiff suffered a cardiac arrest and *"could no longer maintain his position as an NBA referee."*[28] He then brought suit against the examining physician sounding in medical malpractice which also resulted in a third party action against the NBA.

In response to the lawsuit, the trial court dismissed the action due to a failure to state a cause of action against the physician. The referee appealed. On appeal, the appellate court examined the relevant issues and stated: *"A doctor engaged only for the purposes of examining a person for workers compensation or similar purposes is under a common law duty to use reasonable care and his best judgment when conducting the examination...*

Such a doctor, however, only assumes the duties associated with the functions undertaken ...no duty exists concerning treatment or the giving of expert opinions if the doctor was retained solely to examine the plaintiff..."[29]

The court concluded that since the defendant doctor *"was retained by the NBA solely for the purpose of advising it whether [the plaintiff] would be physically capable of performing his duties as a referee, and not to treat or advise the plaintiff, no physician-patient relationship existed in this case...therefore, the [trial] court correctly dismissed the plaintiff's action for failure to state a cause of action."*[30]

As in all negligence cases, including malpractice claims, the plaintiff must prove four basic requirements:

1. Duty;
2. Breach of Duty;
3. Proximate Cause;
4. Injury to the Plaintiff.

Absent any one of these elements, no cause of action may be successfully maintained. If no physician-patient relationship exists, then no duty (at least in the normal sense of the physician-patient relationship) exists. Since no duty exists, there can be no breach of duty, even if the other elements of actionable negligence are present. Therefore, no successful suit upon such a basis may be maintained where no duty exists.

Given this circumstance, sports medicine physicians who are retained for the purposes of conducting "clearance" type physical examinations, may wish to have their duties and responsibilities contractually stated with the retaining entity. If such statements are obtained which delineate that the physician is retained by a non-patient for the purposes of assessing another's status and condition, then it may be possible to avoid malpractice claims related to alleged breaches of the physician-patient relationship, which never really existed, at least in a traditional sense.

In other situations where professional athletes are concerned and the sports medicine examiners are employed by the club along with the athletes, worker's compensation rules may bar suits against such physicians who would be co-employees of the athletes: *"[T]he exclusive remedy provision [of worker's compensation laws] bars an employee from bringing a common law negligence [or malpractice] action against a co-employee,"* <u>Bryant vs. Fox</u>.[31] In this particular case, two professional football players brought a medical malpractice action against their team and an orthopedic surgeon retained to treat the members of the team. The team and the physician moved to dismiss the complaint against them on the basis that the plaintiff's exclusive remedy was through worker's compensation and that they could not therefore proceed in a negligence action against them.

While the trial court agreed with the defendants and dismissed the case, the appellate court on appeal reversed the trial court and sent the case back to the lower court for a determination as to whether or not the Bears were covered by worker's compensation as of the date of the plaintiffs' injuries. Despite the foregoing however, they found that the physician in this case was not an employee of the team [and therefore not a co-employee] but rather an independent contractor whose function as a team physician was not subject to team control, which the court deemed to be determinative of this case. Consequently, the worker's compensation laws did not bar the common law action against the physician in this case even though upon proper facts, such a result would likely occur.

In still other situations, the terms of player-management agreements may preclude the judicial determination of these and similar issues and make such matters the subject of contractual arbitration.[32] However, such contractual arbitration claims may not apply to team employed physicians so as to preclude judicial as opposed to arbitration determinations of such issues.[33]

One of the areas which has brought the court system to bear upon the conduct of preparticipation examinations relates to situations of sudden death in athletes. While such events are fortunately infrequent,[34] such occurrences particularly of late, capture strong media and public attention (including the very recent and tragic death of NBA star Reggie Lewis.)[35] While some contend that a properly obtained history and adequate cardiovascular screening can "pinpoint" and thus identify athletes at risk for cardiovascular complications which require further evaluation and testing, sudden death on the court or the field can lead to very complex litigation over a variety of equally complex medical issues.[36]

While an extremely important and legally significant statement was developed in 1984 related to the screening of athletes for cardiovascular abnormalities, only partial answers can be supplied for very "complex questions" regarding cardiovascular abnormalities as to an athlete's eligibility for competition.[37] The 1990 death of Loyola Marymount basketball player Hank Gathers and the subsequent filing of a multi-million dollar lawsuit dealing with his clearance for participation or return to play has fueled this debate.[38] It is sure to be some time before this particular debate is resolved, particularly due to the fact that the Gathers case was resolved without trial in 1992.[39] In the meantime, however, questions naturally arise as to what testing is necessary to clear athletes or others in the sports medicine examination process at least for cardiovascular abnormalities. *"These [questions] include...[an assessment of] the adequacy of medical screening techniques and technology applied to assess...risks for cardiovascular sudden death...."[40]*

Sudden death related to screening for cardiovascular abnormalities during the preparticipation or re-entry to play process is not the only cause of sudden death of athletes which has led to sports medicine related litigation. For example, in the case of Sorey vs. Kellet,[41] a black football player at the University of Southern Mississippi became ill during practice and collapsed. He was apparently taken to the USM on-campus clinic but was later transferred to a local hospital where he died. Although the circumstances of the practice and the facts of the incident itself are not entirely clear, the player's mother filed suit against USM, its board of trustees and the head coach, trainer and physician alleging that the physician and athletic trainer were unable *"to recognize, diagnose or treat a case of sickle-cell crisis...common among black athletes."*[42] She also contended in her original and amended complaint that the trainer and coach were negligent in treating her son after he collapsed at practice and that the coach *"failed to perform a non-delegable duty of responsibility for the custody and care of football players [including her son]."*[43]

The trial court dismissed all claims against the institution and the board of trustees upon the defendant's motion. The United States District Court of Appeals (849 F.2d 960, 5th Cir. 1988), also later dismissed the wrongful death, negligence and breach of contract claims against the physician, coach and trainer upon state sovereign immunity grounds. Consequently the actual merit of the plaintiff's claims were not determined.

The Sorey case however, raised several significant medico-legal questions which sports medicine practitioners may wish to consider especially in light of the research findings to date. These concerns, some of which may have implications to the preparticipation assessment process, include the following:

1. What is a head coach's responsibility for the provision or supervision of competent and adequate medical care for team participants or to otherwise care for team players?;

2. What steps should be undertaken to screen players for the sickle-cell trait and by whom?;

3. What steps should be undertaken and by whom to test, screen, recognize, diagnose and treat a case of sickle-cell crisis?;

4. What steps should be undertaken to alter practice schedules, times, techniques, or methods to protect those at practice suffering from the sickle-cell trait?;

5. What independent responsibilities of care does an athletic trainer have to team players, separate and apart from those owed by the team physician?;

6. Can team trainers be jointly and severally liable along with team physicians for alleged negligent acts or omissions in the overall management of player health care as well as for alleged failures in player health screening, testing and preparticipation assessment duties?;

7. What are team physician responsibilities for screening for the presence of the sickle-cell trait in players, or for that matter any other similar conditions?; and,

8. What is the responsibility of team physicians/trainers in rendering advice to team coaches as to the scheduling of practice times, methods and workout intensities, giving due deference to known and changing environmental factors of temperature, humidity and other conditions, which when taken together with conditions such as the sickle cell trait, may adversely affect those who are participating, especially when such conditions are not generally known.

More litigation related to such occurrences may be likely. In 1970, the *New England Journal of Medicine*[44] reported that the sickle-cell trait was a possible cause of death of four black army recruits who died suddenly during basic training. In 1987 in that same publication in another article,[45] the authors reported that individuals with the sickle-cell trait *"have a substantially increased, age-dependent risk of exercise-related sudden death unexplained by any known pre-existing cause."*

Many providers including those in sports medicine have been troubled in *"advising athletic associations, the military services or persons with...[the] trait."*[46] Despite the concern, some knowledgeable authorities believe that the case reports of sudden death and the case findings should not be subject to *"over interpretation"* and that the *"findings do not provide a reason for taking otherwise healthy blacks and screening them for sickle-cell trait before they undertake normal daily activities, or for using sickle-cell trait as a reason for denying certain types of employment or insurance."*[47] Others have also contended: *"Black athletes need not be alarmed by this new report. Athletes with [the] sickle-cell trait need take only the same common sense precautions as any other athlete – no more, no less ... [T]he sickle-cell trait is no barrier to outstanding athletic performance."*[48]

Despite the lack of clear opinion, the United States military has taken certain measures to perhaps prevent sudden death in such instances. These measures include:[49]

1. monitoring of heat stress through the use of wet bulb thermometer readings as often as every hour or half hour;

2. stricter rules regarding activity in hot, humid climates;

3. utilization of lighter weight fabric drill clothing; and,

4. improved training for drill instructors.

Even though these conclusions and the research findings to date are somewhat unclear, the legal implications associated with death or injury due to an alleged failure to diagnose and deal with such a condition have already, as we have seen, been raised in litigation and will likely be raised again in the near future. Questions related to preparticipation screening for the trait in an athletic preparticipation examination setting have not as yet been fully addressed. However the NCAA has undertaken an effort to develop policies related to such conditions which should be considered by sports medicine practitioners.[50] Preparticipation examinations which result in medical determinations, excluding individuals from play or participation are a very frequent source of litigation. Due to the frequency of claims related thereto as well as the legal reasoning associated therewith, these claims shall be examined separately in Chapter 8.

FINAL THOUGHT

Appropriately performed preparticipation examinations are part of the standard of care owed by members of the sports medicine team to their patients. Existing standards or guidelines related to these examinations are continuing to undergo evolution and have recently been rather comprehensively updated. The screening or medical clearance of a wide variety of patients desiring to participate in sport, exercise or recreation is undoubtedly increasing. While litigation outside of the professional or highly visible collegiate athletic arenas related to preparticipation physicals has been infrequent, this may not continue to be the case. The medico-legal issues related to these examinations are complex and the stakes can be very high. Knowledge of the latest and most appropriate standards of care and performance in accordance therewith would seem to be absolutely necessary.

CHAPTER 7 FOOTNOTES:

1. NCAA, SPORTS MEDICINE HANDBOOK, Fifth Edition (Overland Park, KS 1992).

2. American Academy of Family Physicians (AAFP), American Academy of Pediatrics (AAP), American Medical Society for Sports Medicine (AMSSM), American Orthopedic Society for Sports Medicine (AOSSM) and the American Osteopathic Academy of Sports Medicine (AOASM), PREPARTICIPATION PHYSICAL EVALUATION (Middleton, WI 1992).

3. "The Preparticipation Examination of Athletes," A.G.D.C. 657-661, 1987.

4. Ronald A. Feinstein, M.D., et al., "The National Survey of Preparticipation Physical Examination Requirements," *The Physician and Sportsmedicine* 16:51-59 (1988).

5. *See, supra* footnote 2.

6. *See,* American Medical Association, MEDICAL EVALUATION OF THE ATHLETE: A GUIDE (revised edition, Chicago, IL 1976).

7.   "New Preparticipation Physician Evaluation Monograph Now Available," *The Sports Medicine Standards and Malpractice Reporter* 5(2):22-23, 1993.

8.   *See, supra* footnote 1.

9.   Colorado Medical Society, REPORT OF THE SPORTS MEDICINE COMMITTEE, GUIDELINES FOR THE MANAGEMENT OF CONCUSSION IN SPORTS (Revised); *see,* "Commentary on the New Concussion Evaluation Guidelines," *The Sports Medicine Standards and Malpractice Reporter* 4(2):26, 1992.

10. Benda, "Pre-Camp Physical Examinations: Their Value May be Greater Than You Think," *The Physician and Sportsmedicine* 17(5):167-169, 1989.

11. Herbert, "Is There a Legally Mandated Duty to Screen Exercise Participants Prior to Exercise?," *The Exercise Standards and Malpractice Reporter* 1(1):10-12, 1987.

12. Litigation and Court Rulings, "Are GXTs Required for Screening of All Men Over Forty?," *The Exercise Standards and Malpractice Reporter* 2(2):30, 1988.

13. "Lawsuit Could Mandate Screening," *Medical World News* 19, March 28, 1988.

14. *But see,* Gonzales vs. Roth, Case No. 90CV1570 (District Court, City and County of Denver, Colorado 1991 defense verdict) *analyzed in* Herbert, "New Litigation: Exercise Without GXT Results in Defense Verdict," *The Exercise Standards and Malpractice Reporter* 5(6):90-92, 1991.

15. "Prescription of Activity: What Are the Legal Risks?," *The Sports Medicine Standards and Malpractice Reporter* 2(3):54-55, 1990.

16. 509 N.Y.S.2d 369 (A.D.2 Dept. 1986).

17. *Id.* at page 370.

18. Mikkelsen vs. Haslam, 764 P.2d 1384 (1988) *analyzed in* Litigation and Court Rulings: "Provider's Alleged Advice, Allowing Patient to Ski May Result in Liability," *The Sports Medicine Standards and Malpractice Reporter* 2(2):36-37, 1990. *But see,* "Exercise Testing Results in Two Rulings for the Plaintiff – One for the Defense," *The Exercise Standards and Malpractice Reporter* 7(5):73-74, 1993.

19. ACSM, HEALTH/FITNESS FACILITY STANDARDS AND GUIDELINES (Human Kinetics, Champaign, IL 1992).

20. Kaiser, LIABILITY IN LAW AND RECREATION, PARKS AND SPORTS, at 174 (Prentice-Hall, Englewood Cliffs, NJ 1976).

21. Appenzeller, SPORTS IN THE COURTS at 238 (The Miche Company, Charlottesville, VA 1980).

22. Herbert, "The Death of Hank Gathers: An Evaluation of The Legal Issues," *The Sports Medicine Standards and Malpractice Reporter* 2(3):45-47, 1990.

23. Herbert, "Another Basketball Star Dies," *The Sports Medicine Standards and Malpractice Reporter* 5(2):17, 19-20, 1993.

24. *See e.g.,* Ohio Revised Code §2305.23.1 which provides as follows: *"...No medical practitioner who volunteers his services as a team physician or team podiatrist to a school's athletics program, and no registered nurse who volunteers his services as a team nurse to a school's athletic program, is liable in damages in a civil action for administering emergency medical care, other emergency professional care, or first aid treatment to a participant in an athletic event involving the school, at the scene of the event or while the participant is being transported to a hospital, physician's office, or other medical facility, or for acts performed in administering the care or treatment, unless the acts of the medical practitioner or registered nurse constitute willful or wanton misconduct..."*

25. Sitomer vs. Half Hollow Hills Central School District, 520 N.Y.S.2d 37 (A.D. 2 Dept. 1987) (*analyzed in* Chapter 8 *infra*).

26. 554 N.Y.S.2d 640 (AD 2 Dept. 1990).

27. *Id.* at page 641.

28. *Id.*

29. *Id.*

30. *Id.*

31. 515 N.E.2d 775 (Ill. App. 1 Dist. 1987).

32. *Cf.* Sherwin vs. Indianapolis Colts, Inc., 752 F. Supp. 1172 (NDNY 1990) *analyzed in* "Another Suit Based Upon Defendant Withholding Allegations," *The Sports Medicine Standards and Malpractice Reporter* 3(3):55-56, 1991.

33. *See,* Hendy vs. Losse, 274 Cal. Rptr. 31 (Cal App. 4th District 1990) *analyzed in* "Professional Football Player's Malpractice Action Against Team Physician to Proceed," *The Sports Medicine Standards and Malpractice Reporter* 3(2):26-28, 1991.

34. Braden & Strong "Preparticipation Screening for Cardiac Death in High School and College Athletes," *The Physician and Sportsmedicine* 16(10):128-141 (1988).

35. Gallup, "Death on The Court: A Look at the Tragic Death of NBA Star Reggie Lewis," *The Sports Medicine Standards and Malpractice Reporter* 6(1):12, 1994.

36. Herbert, "The Death of Hank Gathers: Implications to the Standards of Care for Preparticipation Screening?," *The Sports Medicine Standards and Malpractice Reporter* 2(3):41-45, 1990; Herbert, "The Death of Hank Gathers: An Examination of the Legal Issues," *The Sports Medicine Standards and Malpractice Reporter* 2(3):45-47, 1990. *See also*, Robertson, "Hank Gathers Case Challenges the Role of Team Physicians," *Medical Malpractice Law And Strategy* 3, May, 1990.

37. 16th Bethesda Conference, CARDIOVASCULAR ABNORMALITIES IN THE ATHLETE: RECOMMENDATIONS REGARDING INELIGIBILITY FOR COMPETITION, October 3-5, 1984.

38. Munnings, "The Death of Hank Gathers: A Legacy of Confusion," *The Physician and Sportsmedicine 18(5):97-102* (1990); Straus, "Editor's Notes: Learning About Risks the Hard Way," *The Physician and Sportsmedicine* 18(5):3, 1990; Straus, "Sports Physicians: Caught Between Health and the Pursuit of Happiness," *The Physician and Sportsmedicine* 18(5):26, 1990; Thomas & Cantwell "Case Reports - Sudden Death During Basketball Games," *The Physician and Sportsmedicine* 18(5) 75-78, 1990.

39. "Gathers Case Resolved," *The Sports Medicine Standards and Malpractice Reporter* 4(2):27, 1992.

40. *See, supra* footnote 36.

41. 673 F.Supp. 817 (U.S. District Court, Southern District of Mississippi, 1987).

42. *Id.* at page 824.

43. *Id.* at page 821.

44. Jones, et al., "Sudden Death In Sickle-Cell Trait," 282:323-5.

45. Kark, et al., "Sickle-Cell Trait As A Risk Factor For Sudden Death In Physical Training," *New England Journal of Medicine* 317 (13):781-7, 1987.

46. Eichner "Sickle-Cell Trait And Risk Of Exercise-Induced Death," *The Physician and Sportsmedicine* 15(12):41-43, December 1987.

47. Monahan, "Sickle-Cell Trait: A Risk For Sudden Death During Physical Activity?," *The Physician and Sportsmedicine* 15(12):143-145, December, 1987, at page 144.

48. *See, supra* footnote 46 at page 43.

49. *See, supra* footnote 47 at page 145.

50. NCAA, *supra* footnote 1 at Guideline 3C, "The Student-Athlete With Sickle Cell Trait," pp. 37-38.

8 EXCLUSIONS FROM PLAY/RE-ENTRY TO PLAY DECISIONS

EXCLUSION FROM PLAY DECISIONS

While exclusion from play and re-entry to play decisions may be inextricably connected with preparticipation examinations as well as practice and game duties and responsibilities, it has been the subject of enough medico-legal controversy as to require its separate examination, discussion and analysis. Two basic and distinct medico-legal problems are presented when dealing with these two separate but related issues. Troublesome questions[1] and litigation[2] can arise from a sports medicine determination to exclude individuals from play under circumstances where the individuals, despite advice to the contrary, wish to commence or continue with activity. Cases can also arise in situations where individuals are cleared to enter or recommence play who are subsequently injured and later contend that they should not have been allowed to re-enter play and therefore that the clearing physician is responsible for their injuries.[3]

As to those instances where litigation commences based upon exclusion from play decisions, an examination of the basic suit contentions would seem to be in order. For example, in a case arising from the state of New York,[4] the defendant school officials refused a junior high school student the opportunity to try-out for the high school tennis team because they determined that the student was not physiologically mature enough to participate, *see* Chapter 7, *supra*. Their determination was based upon the results of a screening test designed by the State Education Department which was administered by the school physician. As a result of their refusal to allow the student to try-out, the student, by his father, commenced the action against the school district and the school physician (sounding in medical malpractice) contending that the district's actions were arbitrary, capricious, unlawful, and deprived the plaintiff of an opportunity to develop as a tennis player. The suit further contended that the school physician negligently failed to exercise reasonable medical judgment, and failed to follow proper medical practice in evaluating the infant/plaintiff's level of physiological maturity.

In analyzing the plaintiff's contentions, the court determined that public policy concerns dictated that courts not second guess the *"professional judgments of public school educators and administrators in selecting programs for particular students."*[5] The court determined that the complaints of the plaintiff really sounded in educational malpractice which was not cognizable in the courts of New York.

As to the claims against the school physician, who was an employee of the school district, the court determined that he *"owed the infant/plaintiff no duty other than to administer the screening test in a proper manner"* (relying upon two prior New York cases) *see* Chapter 7, *supra.* The court reasoned that since there was no allegation that the examination was improperly conducted, the physician could not have breached any duty owing to the plaintiff, and consequently, the court of appeals upheld the trial court's determination to dismiss the plaintiff's complaint.

It is interesting to note that the request of the junior high student was to participate at a higher level of competition. He was still allowed to participate at the junior high level, but, based upon the recommended screening procedures, the court followed the physician's determination that the student had not reached a physiological maturity *"sufficient to allow him to try out for the high school tennis team."*[6]

This case is similar to another New York case decided in 1976.[7] In this particular action, the plaintiff, a 15 year old student under the jurisdiction of the defendant high school, and his parents, brought action against the school district after they conducted, at the plaintiff's request, a physical examination of the student to determine whether or not he should be permitted to participate in contact sports at the high school level. The examination was conducted pursuant to certain regulations of the state of New York, which provided that it was the duty of, among others, the Board of Education *"to provide adequate health examinations before participation in strenuous activity and periodically through the season as necessary, and to permit no pupil to participate in such activity without the approval of the school medical officer."*[8]

During the physical examination the school medical officer noted that the plaintiff student was totally deaf in his right ear, and that he had a 50% loss of hearing in his left ear, which problem had existed since birth. The medical examiner also noted that the student was wearing a hearing aid in his left ear, and, based upon his examination and findings the medical officer concluded *"there is a marked impairment of the hearing when [he] clicked his fingers on the right or left side of [the student's]...head,"* and that even with loud finger clicking there was *"an impairment in determining the directional course of the sound."*[9] Based upon these findings, the medical officer determined that the student should not be permitted to play football, lacrosse or soccer because he believed that the deafness had left the student with a permanent *"auditory blind side and a diminished sound perception on his other side, and as such was unable to directionalize the source of sounds, leaving him at increased risks of bodily harm as compared with students with full sensory perception."*[10]

In arriving at these conclusions, the medical examiner took into consideration the American Medical Association's 1972 revised edition of a work entitled: A GUIDE FOR MEDICAL EVALUATION OF CANDIDATES FOR SCHOOL SPORTS, which had previously been approved by the State Education Department. The guide (as well as its updated counterpart which was reviewed in Chapter 7, *supra*) provided disqualifying conditions for participation in certain contact sports, due to impairment under certain circumstances.

The plaintiff student and his parents contended that the guidelines did not take into consideration other relevant factors such as the student's ability to participate in sports, the student's unusual and extraordinary talents, the student's and the parents' absolute and unqualified consent to participation, the fact that the student had never sustained any injury in any contact sport theretofore, that the student had played football previously in organized, non-school groups, and that a prohibition against participation would psychologically damage the plaintiff.

The court analyzed all of these contentions and the evidence presented at time of hearing, and concluded that *"it is thus abundantly clear that there are at least conflicting views with respect to whether [the student's] participation in contact sports represents a danger to his physical well being, or the safety of other students with whom he might participate in such games."*[11] Based upon the conflict in the testimony, the court determined that the decisions of the educational institution should not be set aside by courts attempting to construe administrative decisions. The court found, citing from a prior case: *"In cases where a diversity of medical opinions exist, it is well settled that a school district may rely upon the opinion of its own physician."*[12] The court also quoted from a prior New York decision, which determined that a Board of Education, on the advice of its physician, had a duty to act in the best interests of the pupil, even if the pupil and the pupil's parents may be willing to undertake a particular risk.

In conclusion, the court noted that *"it is sound judgment for the school district to follow the advice of its own medical director and the A.M.A. Guide, and prohibit the student...[from participating in contact sports]."*[13] Based upon the foregoing, the case was dismissed and the student was excluded from participation. It is interesting to note that even though the student and his parents were willing to assume the risks of injury and to even indemnify the school board against any damages arising from untoward events, the court determined that the school board's decision, absent clear evidence of capricious and arbitrary conduct, would be upheld by the courts. The court placed particular emphasis on the AMA GUIDELINES and clearly used this publication as an authoritative standard in determining the relevant issues in the case.

In some circumstances unlike the foregoing cases, other courts may be willing to mandate participation over team physician objections if the athlete and/or his/her parents want the right to participation **and** the athlete is otherwise qualified to participate, despite the infirmity. Such cases turn on the operation of the Rehabilitation Act of 1973, 29 USC §794, *"which prohibits discrimination against an 'otherwise qualified handicapped individual in federally funded programs solely by reason of his handicap'".*[14] The provisions of this Act could apply to any program receiving federal financial assistance which could undoubtedly include most high school and collegiate programs. Section 504 of the Rehabilitation Act states: *"No otherwise qualified handicapped individual...as defined in Section 701(7) of this title, shall, solely by reason of his handicap, be excluded from participation in, be denied benefits of, or be subject to discrimination under any program or activity receiving federal financial assistance."* An examination of the issues involved in alleged violations of this Act would seem to be in order.

In <u>Poole vs. South Plainfield Board of Education</u>,[15] the defendant school board refused to allow the plaintiff student the right to participate in varsity wrestling his junior and senior years. The plaintiff *"was a vigorous, athletically inclined high school student in good health. His only physical problem was the absence of one kidney from birth. His single kidney was, however, a healthy one...the Medical Director of the...[defendant] advised the Board that it should not allow...[the plaintiff] to participate in its wrestling program because of his physical condition. Both...[the plaintiff] and his parents wanted...[him] to participate in the high school wrestling program, even after they were made aware of the school system's concern over possible injury to his kidney. Despite protests and an offer to sign a waiver...the Board decided to heed...[the Medical Director's] advice...[and therefore] denied [the plaintiff the right of] participation..."*[16]

The plaintiff's family physician and another medical expert both felt that the student could participate. Although the defendant school board knew of these opinions, as well as the student's and parents' wishes, it imposed *"its own rationale decision over the rationale decision of the...[parents]."* In examining this decision under the Act, the court concluded that the defendant board *"had neither the duty nor the right...to do so,"[17]* due to the fact that the purpose of the Act *"is to permit handicapped individuals to live life as fully as they are able, without paternalistic authorities determining that certain activities are too risky for them."[18]* In essence the court concluded that the plaintiff was otherwise qualified to participate in athletics except for his handicap (only one kidney) since he met all the requirements for participation and had two knowledgeable and experienced physicians medically clearing his participation. Under these circumstances, the court concluded, an athlete may not be discriminated against by a denial of participation.

In another similar case,[19] the plaintiff was sighted since infancy in only one eye. He desired to participate in the defendant's intercollegiate football program and was, he contended, "otherwise qualified" to participate and was willing, along with his parents, to release the defendant from any liability which might arise by reason of his participation in the football program. Despite his desire, and assessment to which the team's coaches agreed, which was buttressed by *"proof through a highly qualified opthalmologist, that no substantial risk of serious eye injury related to football exists,"[20]* the plaintiff was denied the right to participate. He brought suit alleging a violation of the Rehabilitation Act and sought injunctive relief so that he could gain entry onto the team for participation.

In granting his request the Court *"enjoined [the defendant] from denying [the] plaintiff the opportunity of participating in the intercollegiate football program because of his visual handicap."[21]*

It is important to note that both of these decisions were predicated upon the fact that the athlete had authoritative medical opinions clearing the athlete for participation. Once these opinions were presented and deemed credible, the athletes were thus deemed "otherwise qualified" under the Act for participation. Absent such opinions, an athlete would not be otherwise qualified and discriminatory exclusion from participation would not be at issue.[22]

Given the relationship brought about by reason of this federal enactment (or another similar federal enactment, the Americans With Disabilities Act, or analogous state laws) there may arise circumstances where athletes may inherently have to be allowed the right to participate despite contrary sports medicine team advice. However, the sports medicine team must continue to weight their decisions upon the basis of rational and authoritative medical judgment and then determine if qualified contrary opinions are presented so as to render the athlete "otherwise qualified." At such junctures appropriate professional advice should be obtained.

The foregoing cases reflect, if you will, the other side of the coin from the typical lawsuit brought once an athlete is injured based upon what he or she contends was an inadequate preparticipation physical examination. Decisions to exclude prospective participants from play can be met with extreme emotion, claims and even suits as the foregoing cases readily demonstrate. Some practitioners may feel in light of these occurrences that their actions will be questioned and challenged no matter what they do. In many instances in fact, the athlete or the athlete's relatives will seek out additional opinions so that re-entry to play or participation may be granted.[24] Often times this involves inherent conflicts between the sports medicine team and outside practitioners. An absolute policy must be developed for all sports medicine programs, providing that the sports medicine team's decision will be final under all circumstances, at least insofar as possible. This will avoid the inherent conflicts involved in physician shopping for the purposes of getting second and/or third opinions allowing participation. However, in those instances where policy is lacking or policy allows for outside evaluations or where the Rehabilitation Act, the Americans With Disabilities Act or similar state enactments come into play, the question arises as to what should be done with the athlete. In these circumstances, coaches and sports medicine team personnel are faced with a clear dilemma. This dilemma involves a number of ethical, medical and legal questions:

- Should outside advice be allowed to control over contrary in-house opinion?

- Should such advice prevail only when accompanied by concurrent athlete/parent requests to allow participation?

- Should participation be allowed without a contemporaneous and favorable medical opinion when the athlete and his parents are willing to assume all risks of harm or injury from re-entry to play or participation?

- Can parents and/or athletes lawfully execute express assumption of risk forms or even waivers or releases so as to allow participation without risk of claim and lawsuit in the event of further injury or aggravation of same?

- Should they be allowed to do so in any case?

All of these concerns involve different and complex moral, ethical, professional, familial and legal issues. Frequently, such concerns can be compounded by a variety of other potential problems. If athletes are not allowed to participate despite a willingness to assume all risks can their potential college or professional careers be precluded or adversely affected and if so, can decisions to exclude from play result in successful litigation against a program? If athletes are allowed to play in spite of contrary team medical opinions, can such decisions lead to litigation in the event of subsequent and relevant injury or disability? If either decision can result in litigation, which decision for legal or other reasons should be made, and why?

As a starting point, it is perhaps important to review some basic underlying legal concepts. Schools, programs, administrators, coaches and sports medicine personnel owe a duty to provide reasonable and proper care to those in their charge in full accordance with the applicable standard of care. While this basic concept can differ from state to state, deviations from the appropriate standard of care can be actionable.

Particular professionals on the coaching and sports medicine team have the principal duty to protect their athletes. These individuals are **primarily** charged with that responsibility by virtue of their relationship with the program, the team and the players. Outside professionals may also have certain duties once they assume a physician/patient relationship with an athlete. However, the **last** and **final** authority on the issue of who will or will not participate subject only to the applicable legal constraints previously discussed herein, is with the program's personnel and **not** with outside consultants or practitioners. While such practitioners may be **concurrently** liable along with program personnel for erroneous and negligent decisions to allow re-entry to play in the event of athlete injury or death, program professionals may be deemed to be guilty of **superseding** or **peremptory** negligence for allowing participation after outside medical clearance, followed by injury, aggravation of injury or death. Such professionals may not be able to escape liability by pointing to others and saying that the negligence is chargeable to those others when the program professionals had the final say-so and either knew or should have known, through the exercise of appropriate judgment, that some other course of conduct was required.

When faced with what program professionals believe is an erroneous, outside clearance to participate or to re-enter play, program personnel must adhere to the appropriate standard of care or face the potential consequences from a contrary course of action. In the face of significant potential harm arising from a re-entry to play, the decision to ignore outside advice will be easy, even in the face of athlete/parent willingness to assume all risks of harm or even prospectively release the program from claim or suit except where the protections of the Rehabilitation Act, the Americans With Disabilities Act or analogous state laws come into play. Where the decision is less clear however, a decision to exclude from play may be more difficult in the face of well-reasoned outside opinions which support participation, especially when a specialist may be involved in rendering that opinion as to an injury which is within his or her realm or specialty. In the face of such an opinion, a re-examination of the patient or the patient's condition or the progress of rehabilitation of the injury may be in order. Whether or not the program decision needs or justifies change depends upon the exercise of independent professional judgment in the application of the appropriate standard of care which is owed to the athlete patient and an application of relevant principles of federal and state laws.

If an athlete presents an outside medical opinion purporting to release the athlete to play or to re-enter play which is well reasoned and supported but which is contrary to the program's initial decision, **and** the outside opinion is accompanied by an athlete's and/or parents' willingness to execute an express assumption of risk or prospective waiver/release form what should the program and it's personnel do (especially if the Rehabilitation Act, the Americans With Disabilities Act or similar state statutes are applicable to the program)? In this regard it is important to remember that express assumption of risk forms or waiver/releases are contractual documents in nature. Only competent adults may contract or waive their rights – and even then, only in certain court approved areas. The use of releases in the medical setting has been generally disfavored and is often deemed to be contrary to public policy.[25] However, such documents have been used in the sports medicine setting and may serve to protect programs who allow participation in spite of contrary medical advice.[26]

Most high school athletes will not be deemed, by reason of their minority, to be legally capable of executing any such documents. Parents[27] and even spouses[28] in some states moreover, do not have the ability to lawfully release or contract away their children's or their spouse's rights. In these states, parent or spouse executed documents may be of little or no value in protecting a program which decides to allow participation in what may later be deemed to be a questionable situation from suit by a minor or the spouse of the athlete who will often have an independent right to sue for injury to the spousal relationship. For these reasons, parents/spouses may be completely unable to execute effective express assumption of risk contracts or releases for their children. Moreover, a husband or wife executed release may not bind the non-executing spouse from suing independently of the husband or wife. It may be possible however in other circumstances where not against public policy, to have parents and athletes execute prospective releases or waivers either independently of or in conjunction with express assumption of risk documents which require the parents or one spouse to hold the program harmless if the contract should ever be deemed to be unlawful or unenforceable as to the minor child or if the minor child or spouse should ever attempt to bring suit against the program or any of its personnel despite the existence of the document. An example of one such form appears in the Appendix to this work. No such form however should ever be adopted or used without review and modification by local program legal counsel in accordance with local jurisdictional rules and requirements. Even where the use of such forms may be justified in some circumstances, legal rulings in particular states may preclude their use.

For example, in the case of, <u>Wagenblast vs. Odessa School District</u>,[29] certain school districts had required students and their parents to execute a standardized preparticipation release form, relieving the school district from liability arising from any ordinary negligence that might arise in connection with the student's participation in the district's interscholastic and scholastic activity programs. Such forms were required by the defendant school districts prior to allowing a student to participate in any athletic program.

The parents in these consolidated cases sought to have the releases declared invalid as being against public policy. The court, as we previously noted, considered various public policy reasons and determined that the use of such releases was invalid.

Many athletic programs, including those at the youth, high school and college levels, have considered the use of such releases to limit a program's liability in the event of injury and claim.[30] Under certain circumstances the use of such releases may be found to be valid and not against public policy. Even in some medical settings, the use of releases can be valid, and will be upheld in certain instances.

The law on the topic of releases varies from state to state, and programs should not be reluctant after consultation with program counsel to consider the use of such forms to reduce their own liability risks where appropriate. Despite the decision in the <u>Wagenblast</u> case, *supra,* sports medicine practitioners should also consider the use of such releases, especially where they may be acting upon a compensation rather than a volunteer basis when making re-entry to play decisions and especially where the provisions of the Rehabilitation Act or the Americans With Disabilities Act or similar state laws may come into play.

Decisions to allow an athlete to re-enter or commence play with an injury or other adverse condition, in light of mixed professional opinions between "inside" and "outside" personnel should be treated most carefully. All of the foregoing factors must be considered and evaluated prior to making any decision – and then only after consultation with knowledgeable legal and medical counsel. The recent and unfortunate death of NBA Celtics star Reggie Lewis points up the various medical and ethical concerns which can arise in this area.[31]

RE-ENTRY TO PLAY DECISIONS

Aside from issues dealing with decisions to exclude athletes from participation and litigation related thereto, the more common medico-legal concern in this area centers upon decisions allowing re-entry to play. While we have heretofore reviewed the facts of the Hank Gathers litigation against Loyola Marymount University, it is important to remember that this litigation involved a variety of allegations including those dealing with alleged negligent determinations made by sports medicine personnel to allow Gathers to participate, despite his having gone through several pre-date of death untoward events and despite several tests indicating certain cardiac abnormalities. The complaint in fact alleged that the defendants negligently allowed Gathers to return to full participation and in addition that they fraudulently misrepresented to the decedent that he could return to play.

The complaint in this case quoted a release letter allegedly provided by one of the defendant physicians to the University which stated: *"This letter should serve as the release for Mr. Eric Hank Gathers to return to full participation with the Loyola Marymount basketball team. It is the request that both myself and [another defendant physician]...the cardiologist who assisted in Mr. Gathers' care, that Hank's full return to participation is a gradual one. We would also like to monitor his initial session with a Holter monitor to ensure that he is in normal cardiac rhythm during these early practice runs. Both...[the cardiologist] and myself will be available to assist in Hank's return to full participation. It is our impression that this should occur over an interval of seven to ten days. This interval of course will depend upon Hank's abilities and physical endurance. Please feel free to contact me should you have any questions."* After this release letter was written, the physicians according to the complaint, did indeed monitor Gathers' heart during practice and allegedly followed up with a written report indicating that the ventricular arrythmias including long runs of non-sustained ventricular tachacardia as well as erratic and at times quite elevated blood pressure needed treatment through a beta blocker even though it had a potential detrimental side effect to athletic performance. Although a beta blocker was originally supplied to Gathers at a therapeutic level, the complaint alleged that through interference by members of the athletic staff, the beta blocker was eventually reduced to a non-therapeutic level which in turn allegedly led to Gathers' death. Although this particular aspect of the case will be discussed in Chapter 9 dealing with communications by members of the sports medicine team with athletes, it is important to note that all of these allegations were cited by the plaintiffs in this case as a basis for their claims of negligence and fraud in returning Gathers to play when they contended he should not have been permitted to return to play. The complaint in fact specifically cited the findings and recommendations of the Sixteenth Bethesda Conference on Cardiovascular Abnormalities and the Athlete and contends that these standards were violated in returning this particular athlete to participation. In light of the subsequent settlement of this case, these issues will probably not receive full attention and will not be judicially determined. Another similar case however was recently filed by the estate of Oregon State University basketball star Earnest Killum which may address some of these concerns.[32]

A recently issued jury verdict and appellate court opinion from the state of New York[33] may well indicate what may become an alarming trend to many involved or active in providing sports medicine services to various athletic programs. The decision follows a rather substantial jury damage award in an area which has traditionally been thought to be beyond judicial resolution. The decision directly focused upon sports medicine responsibility for athletes who are injured in the course of play. The decision has indirect application to sports medicine practitioners in light of some association statements as to sports medicine responsibilities toward athlete patients. The decision may also have a variety of chilling effects to the whole sports staff (including those who are involved in indirect roles), even though the original jury verdict was later overturned, An examination of this case may provide insight into these concerns since it deals with continuation to play, (some would say, "re-entry to play") decisions, (although not those of a traditional nature).

The case involved injuries to a 19 year old high school player who broke his neck during participation in a league game in 1983. His school's team had been "promoted" to "A Division" play prior to the 1982 season. However, certain school authorities had requested a transfer back to the less competitive "B Division" citing the poor performance of the team in 1982 and raising concerns that continuation of the team in "A Division" would be unsafe. The school's request was apparently denied.

Prior to the 1983 game during which the plaintiff was injured, the player's coach had expressed a view that the game should not be played and that there was "a very high risk of injury."[33] The game, however, proceeded and the plaintiff was injured approximately one minute before the close of the first half. He had been on the field for virtually the entire game up to the point of his injury and had played on the defensive, offensive and special teams. The evidence disclosed that he was fatigued at the time of the injury which occurred as he was trying to block an opposing lineman. Although there was some contention as to whether or not he was properly blocking, the plaintiff's expert indicated that *"a mismatch or playing while tired increases the risk of injury."*[34] The plaintiff's coach also testified that *"it was unsafe for plaintiff to be out there playing as he was playing [both ways] – full time."*[35] Even the defendant's expert contended that *"[T]iredness... would affect the coordination level of a player."*[36]

Based upon the foregoing evidence, the jury awarded the plaintiff over $1.2 million but the verdict was reduced to $875,000 due to the plaintiff's comparative negligence. Upon appeal, over the vigorous dissent of Presiding Justice Murphy, the Court of Appeals affirmed the verdict believing that a finding of liability would *"not open the flood gates"* of liability by similar cases nor *"lead inevitably to the total collapse...of any scholastic sports program[s]."* [37]

In analyzing the facts of the case however, the court concluded *"the evidence here indicates that defendants unreasonably enhanced or increased the risk of the player being injured by playing him in a game between mismatched teams and by playing him for virtually the entire game, while he was tired, because there was no adequate substitute for him."* [38] In rejecting defense arguments that the plaintiff assumed the risks of his own injuries, or that he was liable for his own injuries because he did not complain of being tired or ask to be removed from the game, the court stated, *"while plaintiff was a voluntary participant in the game [and] never...complained of being tired, the law does recognize, especially in student-teacher relationships, that a degree of indirect compulsion exists...The rationale is that the student is understandably reluctant to refuse to participate for fear of the negative impact that such refusal might have on his or her grade or standing. Such reasoning applies here."* [39] In conclusion the court held that *"defendants were negligent in permitting plaintiff to play in a game in which his team was greatly outmatched and circumstances in which the likelihood of his being injured was really enhanced."* [40]

Considering the sports medicine practitioner's role in this process, [especially in light of some association standards including those previously identified in this work (*see* Chapter 7)] many practitioners will have to modify and perhaps expand their present practices.

As previously indicated, this decision and jury verdict was later reversed by New York's highest court.[41] In examining the lower court's ruling, the New York high court: *"A board of education, its subordinate employees and interscholastic athletic organizations must exercise only reasonable care to protect student athletes in sports competition from injuries arising out of unassumed, concealed or unreasonably increased risks."*[42]

In applying this standard to the facts of this case this opinion indicated: *"Players who voluntarily join an extracurricular interscholastic sport assume the risks to which their roles expose them but not risks which are 'unreasonably increased or concealed'..."*[43]

This court further noted: *"Fatigue, and unfortunately, injury are inherent to team competitive sports, especially football. Benitez was...an excellent athlete, properly equipped and well trained. He was playing voluntarily in the same manner as he had for the previous year and one-half against Division A competition and had not requested rest or complained. Within the breadth and scope of his consent and participation, plaintiff put himself at risk in the circumstances of this case for the injuries he ultimately suffered. On his own proof, he has failed to meet the burden of showing some negligent act or inaction referenced to the applicable duty owed to him by these defendants."*[44]

In essence, the court based its decision upon the assumption of risk defense and concluded: *"The injury in this case, in sum, was a luckless accident arising from the vigorous voluntary participation in competitive interscholastic athletics."*[45]

Although the court's decision was based upon assumption of risk grounds, the court did not specifically discuss the mismatch allegations raised in the original Benitez trial except within the context of the overall concept of assumption of the risk. Perhaps further commentary must await the final outcome of another New York case dealing with this same concept which we discussed previously herein.[46]

While normal re-entry to play decisions may be made over sufficient time to allow a team physician to reflect upon his or her decision, those re-entry to play decisions which must be made in light of the Benitez type allegations must be made on the spot. A physician or other sports medicine practitioner may have to make determinations as to whether or not the fatigue or other condition of the player is such as to require that a player be removed from the contest in order to avoid injury to the participant. Records of player participation should be maintained along with playing time, notes as to observations during the contest, etc. to avoid situations like the Benitez case.

It may seem in light of decisions like this one that the sports medicine practitioner's role is constantly changing and in fact expanding. New re-entry to play or continuation to play decisions which may be required as a result of this case, or other similar ones, may become very serious to practitioners in the years ahead.

FINAL THOUGHT

Medico-legal issues regarding exclusions from play and those dealing with re-entry to play decisions which are later claimed to be negligently formulated, provide a variety of complex issues for sports medicine practitioners. Litigation in this area is sure to continue inasmuch as a number of competing interests are all at stake. Practitioners must first and foremost develop a clear policy regarding exclusion from play. The sports medicine team must have the final say as to what is to occur in this regard, except in those instances where other requirements must be met due to various medico-legal considerations related to such enactments as the Rehabilitation Act and the Americans With Disabilities Act as well as similar state laws. Re-entry to play decisions must be based upon clear standards and carried out in accordance therewith. New developments in this area must be tracked by the sports medicine team and practices adapted as necessary and appropriate in light of these developments.

CHAPTER 8 FOOTNOTES:

1. *See, e.g.,* Blackstone, "Should an Athlete be allowed to risk his life to play?," *The Dallas Morning News,* Thursday, November 15, 1990, p. 28; A.P., "Testing wasn't through: Lewis wanted his heart monitored before deciding on return to pro basketball," *The Beacon Journal,* Friday, July 30, 1993, p. B3; DiGiovanna, "Looking for a way to play: Haggins, Arizona State differ on heart defect," *Los Angeles Times,* Monday, November 15, 1993, p. C-1.

2. *See e.g.,* Larkin vs. Archdiocese of Cincinnati, Civil Case No. C-1-90-619, United States District Court, Southern District of Ohio, Western Division, 1990.

3. *See e.g.,* Gathers vs. Loyola Marymount University, Los Angeles, California 1990 filing, *analyzed in* Herbert, "The Death of Hank Gathers: An Evaluation of the Legal Issues," *The Sports Medicine Standards and Malpractice Reporter* 2(3):45-47, 1990.

4. Sitomer vs. Half Hollow Hills Central School District, 520 N.Y.S.2d 37 (A.D.2 Dept. 1987).

5. *Id.* footnote 3, at page 38.

6. *Id.*

7. Colombo vs. Sewanhaka Central High School District No. 2, 383 N.Y.S.2d 518 (Supreme Court Special Term Nassau County 1976).

8. *Id.* at page 519, citing 8 N.Y.C.R.R. §135.4(C)(7)(I)(H).

9. *Id.* at page 519.

10. *Id.* at page 519.

11. *Id.* at page 521.

12. *Citing* The Matter of Herrington, Decision of Commissioner of Education, No. 9058, August 4, 1975.

13. *See, supra* footnote 7 at page 522.

14. Southeastern Community College vs. Davis, 442 U.S. 397 (1979).

15. 490 F. Supp. 948 (U.S. Dist. Ct., B.N.J. 1980).

16. *Id.* at page 951-952.

17. *Id.* at page 954.

18. *Id.* at page 953-954.

19. Wright vs. Columbia University, 520 F. Supp. 789 (1981).

20. *Id.* at page 793.

21. *Id.* at page 795.

22. *See* footnote 2 (Partial Transcript of Proceedings before Weber, District Judge).

23. *See also,* The Americans With Disabilities Act (ADA) Public Law 101-336[S.993], July 26, 1990, codified in 42 U.S.C. §12101-12213 (1991) *analyzed in* Herbert, THE AMERICANS WITH DISABILITIES ACT: A GUIDE FOR HEALTH CLUBS

AND EXERCISE FACILITIES (Professional Reports Corporation, Canton, OH 1992).

24. Emery, "Doctor Shopping Can Be Deadly: Celtic Lewis Got the Diagnosis He Wanted," *The Independent* (from *The Providence Journal*) Thursday, July 29, 1993 at page B-4.

25. *See* Herbert, "The Use of Prospective Releases Containing Exculpatory Language in a Medical Setting," *The Exercise Standards and Malpractice Reporter* 1(5):75-78, 1987. *See also* Chapter 5.

26. Comodeca, "Acknowledgment of Risk Forms: The Best Defense for Sports Medicine Practitioners," *The Sports Medicine Standards and Malpractice Reporter* 4(4):49, 51-54, 1992.

27. *See,* "Release Executed by Minors and/or Their Parents May be Unenforceable," *The Exercise Standards and Malpractice Reporter* 3(2):32-35, 1989.

28. *See,* "Husband's Release Does Not Bar Wife's Lawsuit – Implication for Sports Medicine," *The Sports Medicine Standards and Malpractice Reporter* 4(3):41-42, 1992.

29. 758 P.2d 968 (Washington, 1988).

30. *See* footnote 24, at pages 52-53.

31. VanCamp, "What Can We Learn From Reggie Lewis' Death," *The Physician and Sportsmedicine* 21(10):73, 1993.

32. Herbert, "Another Basketball Star Dies," *The Sports Medicine Standards and Malpractice Reporter* 5(2):17, 19-20, 1993.

33. Benitez vs. New York City Board of Education, 530 N.Y.S.2d 825 (A.D. 1 Dept. 1988) *reversed in* 541 N.E.2d 29 (NY 1989).

34. *Id.*

35. *Id.* at page 826.

36. *Id.* at page 826.

37. *Id.* at page 827.

38. *Id.* at page 827.

39. *Id.* at page 827.

40. *Id.* at page 828.

41. Benitez vs. New York City Board of Education, 541 N.E.2d 29 (N.Y. 1989).

42. *Id.* at page 30.

43. *Id.* at page 33.

44. *Id.* at page 34

45. *Id.*

46. Tepper vs. City of New Rochelle School District, 531 N.Y.S.2d 367 (A.D. 2 Dept. 1988).

9   COMMUNICATIONS WITH ATHLETES

Although the informed consent process was separately discussed in Chapter 6, litigation surrounding sports medicine communications with athletes (or the lack thereof) has been of
significant frequency and intensity as to require its separate
consideration. While an examination of this issue necessarily
deals in part with provider duties to disclose relevant information
to athlete-patients, it also deals with broader concepts – conflict
of interest, administrator, coach, parent, player or fan interference
with or adverse impact upon the duty to communicate,[1] negligent
non-disclosure of information, intentional non-disclosure of information and even fraudulent misrepresentation of information. All
of these issues have been and continue to be the subject of some
concern to sports medicine providers while also being the subject
of well known and on-going claims and suit. An examination of
these issues separate and apart from the discussion of informed
consent contained in Chapter 6 should be of benefit to all sports
medicine practitioners.

CONFLICTS IN COMMUNICATIONS

Sports medicine service providers have a duty to provide
clear, accurate and complete information to their athlete-patients
as to the athlete's condition, any need for examination, treatment
or rehabilitation, plus the benefit of the provider's advice and
counsel as to such matters. Sometimes outside pressures are
brought to bear on this duty which can create potential conflicts of
interest for the physician.[2] These conflicts may in turn lead to
breaches in care and interference with the communicative process with athletes. When such interference causes the patient
harm, claim and suit can result.

INTERFERENCE WITH INFORMED CONSENT

The classic sports medicine case illustrative of this potential
conflict is <u>Krueger vs. San Francisco Forty Niners</u>.[3] While this
case was not the first to deal with these issues,[4] it was one of the

first to be fully litigated. In this case, which at trial resulted in a defense verdict, the plaintiff-appellant (Charles Krueger) began playing professional football with the San Francisco 49ers in 1958. He played as a defensive lineman until retiring in 1973. While playing however, he suffered innumerable injuries, particularly, a series of injuries to his left knee which were the focus of the lawsuit. The injuries consisted of a 1955 pre-professional football torn meniscus, a 1963 ruptured medial collateral ligament, surgically "repaired," followed by rehabilitative therapy and four years of knee brace support during play, and a 1963 operative note finding that the anterior cruciate ligament *"appeared to be absent from the left knee."* In the absence of this ligament, the tibia was subject to shifting forward on the femur. The plaintiff-appellant testified at time of trial that he was not told of this ligament's absence.

The plaintiff-appellant apparently received treatment from 1964 to 1978 for the injuries to the left knee consisting of aspirations of bloody fluid by means of a syringe and contemporaneous injection of novocaine and cortisone, a steroid compound (the plaintiff-appellant testified that he received approximately 50 such treatments during the year 1964 and an average of 14 to 20 per year from 1964 to 1973, while the physician testified that his records indicated only seven such treatments); and a 1971 operation to remove "loose bodies" in the left knee resulting from chronic chondromalacia patella (a thinning and loss of cartilage on the under surface of the kneecap, a condition the court concluded was fully consistent with known adverse reaction to prolonged steroid use).

At issue on trial was the disclosure (or lack thereof) of medical information to the plaintiff-appellant by the team physicians. The plaintiff-appellant testified that he was never told that he lacked the anterior cruciate ligament, noted in the operative report of 1963; that he was never told of the dangers associated with steroid injections during the period 1964 to 1973; and, that he was never told that the 1971 operation to remove so-called "loose bodies" from his left knee was a condition fully consistent with known adverse reactions to "prolonged steroid use."

The plaintiff-appellant also testified that in a game in 1970 he suffered a hit to his left knee and felt "a piece of knee" break off. He further testified that he was given a codeine substance and told to return to the game. Although he could feel a "considerable piece of substance" dislodged on the outside of his left knee joint, he played the remaining five games of the season. He further testified that no one ever advised him of the risks of permanent injury which he faced by continuing to play without treatment.

The plaintiff-appellant retired in 1974 and in 1978 for the first time, he contended, was shown his x-rays of the left knee and told that he suffered chronic and permanent disability in the knee. A subsequent operation was performed by another team physician which did nothing to alleviate the discomfort and pain and in fact after the operation, the plaintiff-appellant developed calcification in the knee.

The appellate court found that the plaintiff-appellant *"suffers from traumatic arthritis and a crippling degenerative process in the left knee. He cannot stand up for prolonged periods, and cannot run. He is also unable to walk on stairs without severe pain. His condition is degenerative and irreversible."*[5]

At trial the lower court concluded that the plaintiff-appellant failed to prove all of the elements of fraudulent concealment. Most significantly the trial court concluded that the plaintiff-appellant would have continued playing football even if he had been advised of the complete nature and extent of his injuries, thus negating proximate cause between the alleged breach of duty and the injuries and disabilities.

In evaluating the evidence in light of the plaintiff-appellant's claimed fraudulent concealment, the appellate court concluded that the elements of the action were: a misrepresentation or suppression of a material fact; knowledge of any falsity; intent to induce reliance; actual and justifiable reliance and resultant damages. In evaluating the facts against the elements of the action and Sections 1709 and 1710 of the California Civil Code which provided as follows in §1709: *"[O]ne who willfully deceives another with intent to induce him to alter his position to his injury or risk, is liable for any damage which he thereby suffers,"* and §1710(3): *"[T]he suppression of a fact by one who is bound to disclose it or who gives information of other facts which are likely to mislead for want of communication of that fact..."*. The court concluded that the relationship of physician and patient was fiduciary and created a duty to disclose.

The appellate court also concluded: *"The evidence offered by the [defendants]...never directly contradicted appellant's testimony...the requisite disclosure was never made."* [6]

The court further concluded: *"In our opinion, the duty of full disclosure within the context of a doctor-patient relationship defines a test for concealment or suppression of facts under...[California law §1710(3)]. The failure to make such disclosure constitutes not only negligence, but where the required intent is shown – fraud or concealment as well. A physician cannot avoid responsibility for failure to make full disclosure by simply claiming that information was not withheld."* [7]

Although the court indicated that the physicians neither minimized nor concealed the plaintiff-appellant's medical condition for the purposes of prolonging his career, and that the physicians were never advised by the team to suppress information regarding the plaintiff-appellant's knee, the court held: *"[I]n its desire to keep appellant on the playing field, respondent consciously failed to make full, meaningful disclosure to him respecting the magnitude of the risks he took in continuing to play a violent contact sport with a profoundly damaged left knee. The uncontradicted record shows that the [plaintiff-appellant]...was in acute pain from 1963 on, that he was regularly anesthetized between and during games, and endured repeated, questionable steroid treatments administered by the team physician... respondent's claim of no concealment cannot be substituted for the professional warnings to which [plaintiff-appellant]...was at this point so clearly entitled. And it is in this palpable failure to disclose, viewed in the light of the 49ers compelling obvious interest in prolonging appellant's career, that we find the intent requisite for a finding of fraudulent concealment." [8]*

In evaluating the players own responsibility for seeking knowledge of his injury, the court noted that players like the plaintiff-appellant are entitled *"to rely upon [team] physicians for medical treatment and advice without consulting outside sources or undertaking independent investigation."[9]* After this appellate ruling, the Krueger case was ultimately tried, resulting in a verdict in excess of two million dollars,[10] although the case was reportedly settled for a sum in excess of one million dollars (but presumably less than the jury's verdict).[11]

In another more recent case, Martin vs. Casagrande,[12] alleging facts remarkably similar to those litigated in Krueger, a New York Court of Appeals upheld a trial court's decision granting summary judgment in favor of all defendants upon claims related to an alleged withholding of medical information from an athlete. In this action, *"Richard Martin, a former professional hockey player with the Buffalo Sabres, brought an action against Sabres, Sabres General Manager Scotty Bowman and team doctor Peter Casagrande for damages resulting from a knee injury he sustained on November 9, 1980, in a collision with an opposing goaltender during a home game. Martin was immediately examined by Dr. Casagrande, the Sabres team physician and an orthopedic specialist for over 30 years. He found no evidence of swelling or fracture and made a preliminary diagnosis of a sprained knee due to hypertension.*

Martin missed 20 consecutive games and returned to the ice on December 28, 1980, approximately seven weeks after the injury. Dr. Casagrande performed arthroscopic surgery on January 2, 1981. No ligament or meniscal damage was discovered during the surgery. Martin played in eight games between January 7-21, 1981. After January 21, 1981, Martin never played professional hockey again for the Buffalo Sabres.

On February 3, 1981, Dr. Jackson, a Canadian surgeon whom Martin contacted for a second opinion at the suggestion of Bowman and Dr. Casagrande, performed arthroscopic surgery and discovered two tears of the lateral meniscus, fractured cartilage and other debris not previously discovered or diagnosed. Dr. Jackson predicted that Martin could resume play in four to five weeks. Martin began skating again on February 18th, but the Sabres did not play him and traded him to the Los Angeles Kings on March 10, 1981. Martin played sparingly and retired the following season.

Martin commenced two separate actions, later consolidated. These actions charge the various defendants with failing to discover the ligament and meniscal damage later found by Dr. Jackson. In a fourth cause of action Martin alleges that Dr. Casagrande intentionally concealed the risks and true condition of his right knee; in a fifth cause of action Martin alleges that all defendants intentionally conspired to play him despite knowing that he was physically unable to play."[13]

Based upon these allegations the team and its general manager were granted summary judgment on the grounds that the plaintiffs' prior determination as to the injury by a state Workers' Compensation Board and his acceptance of benefits therefrom was his exclusive remedy and thus barred his action. As to the action against the team physician, the trial court also granted a summary judgment in his favor finding no evidence of fraud or concealment.

As to this later claim, the Appellate District Court noted: *"Martin's claims of intentional concealment and fraud against Dr.*

Casagrande lacks merit. Dr. Casagrande did not order or even suggest that Martin return to the ice in late December, 1980. Rather he left that decision to Martin. Martin was an all star and key player for the Sabres. It is highly unlikely that defendants would do anything to injure him intentionally or to diminish his trade value, which proved to be substantial as evidenced by the Kings deal. Moreover, Martin himself acknowledged in deposition testimony that he knew he risked permanent damage to his right knee if he played on December 28, 1980, and that defendants did not specifically order him to play against his wishes. Thus, on his record, there is no evidence that defendants intended to harm Martin...Moreover, once the court granted summary judgment to the Sabres and Bowman, it was appropriate for Dr. Casagrande to move for similar relief. If the Sabres and Bowman did not commit an intentional tort against Martin then neither did Dr. Casagrande, since he could not conspire with himself to deceive Martin. The fact that Dr. Casagrande earlier moved unsuccessfully for sum-mary judgment [based upon the worker's compensation co-employee rule], did not preclude him from moving again solely on the basis of the success of the Sabres and Bowman in their motions based on similar facts,"[14]

The appeals court distinguished the case from the Krueger decision on both legal and factual grounds. Legally it noted that the Krueger case did not deal with any consideration of workers' compensation issues and therefore was not controlling. It also noted:

"Moreover, Krueger is distinguishable on the facts. There, although x-rays had been taken and fully depicted the extent of the football player's degenerative condition, defendants never in-formed him of this result. Here, the initial x-rays and arthrograms did not indicate the meniscal and ligament damage to Martin's right knee that was later discovered by Dr. Jackson."[15]

While there still may have been a cause of action against the team physician sounding in medical malpractice as the court indicated in its decision, the plaintiff's claims of conspiracy and intentional tort were dismissed. The medical malpractice claim against the team physician proceeded to trial in late 1993 and resulted in a jury verdict in favor of Mr. Martin for some $2.5 million dollars.[16]

In yet another case related to alleged team physician withholding of information from a professional athlete, a United States District Court in New York has ruled that such disputes are subject to mandatory grievance and arbitration provisions of the players collective bargaining agreement.[17]

In this case, somewhat like the case of Hendy vs. Losse,[18] Timothy F. Sherwin, a former professional football player brought suit against his former team, the Indianapolis Colts, and the team physicians. He alleged that while he was under contract with the Defendant Colts, he suffered an injury for which the team and its team physicians *"failed to provide adequate medical care, and that the defendants intentionally withheld information regarding the true nature of his injury."*[19] Specifically, the plaintiff player alleged *"breach of contract, negligence, medical malpractice, fraud, negligent misrepresentation, and negligent and intentional infliction of emotional distress."*[20]

In response to these claims, the team moved to dismiss the case claiming that the controversy arose out of the player's agreement between the players and management and as a consequence had to be arbitrated. The individual defendant team physicians moved for dismissal due to a lack of personal jurisdiction over them.

In response to these claims, as in the Hendy case, *supra,* the court determined that the actions were not cognizable in court, but were instead subject to arbitration pursuant to the terms of the collective bargaining agreement. The court ruled that the causes of action against the team exclusive of the breach of contract claim might be condensed to the following:

"1. That the Colts, 'by and through its team physicians, trainers, agents, servants and/or employees has knowingly committed a fraud upon the Plaintiff...by intentionally and willfully with-holding the true nature and extent of his injuries from him, and by misrepresenting to the Plaintiff...that he was in satisfactory condition to continue to play.' Complaint, ¶50

2. That the Colts were 'under a duty to provide its players, including the Plaintiff herein, with appropriate and necessary care, attention and treatment if injured,' and that the Colts negligently failed to provide such care and treatment and negligently failed to disclose to the plaintiff his true medical condition. Complaint ¶55-59

3. Negligent infliction of emotional distress. Complaint, ¶103-04.

4. Intentional infliction of emotional distress. Complaint, ¶108-10."

The claims against the individual team physicians were determined not to be cognizable in the state of New York. These defendants were licensed to practice medicine in Indiana as opposed to New York. The doctors' only contact with New York was the physicians' annual trips to Buffalo when the Colts played the Bills. In analyzing these issues the court held:

"Plaintiff's causes of action must be directly and proximately related to the business transacted in New York in order to provide a basis for section 302(a)(1) jurisdiction. Conversely, a cause of action which bears only a remote and indirect relationship to the New York transaction will not support jurisdiction... Plaintiff's claims are not remotely related to the doctors' activities in New York.

Although it is unnecessary to decide this point since plaintiff's claims do not bear a relationship to the doctors' activities in New York, it could also be argued that the doctors did not transact business or supply services in Buffalo. As previously stated, the doctors have no contact with New Yorkers while in Buffalo, other than with Buffalo Bills' medical staff to coordinate their services. Their purpose for being in New York is not to solicit or transact business, but to provide services to members of the Colts, which have already been contracted for in Indiana."

As a result of all of the foregoing, the claims against the team and the physicians were dismissed. Depending upon the outcome of ongoing applicable arbitration proceedings or suit filed against the individual physicians in a court which has jurisdiction over them, the merits of these claims will have to wait further determination.

MINIMIZING CONFLICTS AND INTERFERENCE

Based upon the findings in the <u>Krueger</u> decision several points deserve to be made:

1. Specific policies and procedures should be adopted at the team level acknowledging provider independence from team management in the course of their rendition of professional care toward athlete patients;

2. Team/participants/provider conflicts over the health status of an athlete must be avoided. All decisions regarding the athlete's condition must be based upon what is best for the athlete regardless of the employment of the health care provider by the team or organization;

3. If appropriate medical judgment requires that a participant be denied the right to participate or re-enter play, the participant must not, it would seem, be allowed to play despite his or her insistence as to same.[21]

4. Accurate and complete records regarding the provision of information, discussions with athlete players and the like must be accurately recorded and maintained by the team provider.

In light of the principles litigated in the <u>Krueger</u> and related cases, several matters also deserve discussion and evaluation:

1. What is the duty of team physician/trainer/administrative team personnel (and the team itself as the employing entity) to provide accurate and complete medical/health information to a player as to his own medical condition or state of well being?; and, what is the scope of that duty?

2. Is there a conflict between the physician/trainer's duty to the team which employs him and the player who relies upon his professional services and advice; and, if there is such a conflict, how can it be resolved?; and,

3. What policies, procedures, guidelines and forms should be considered to fulfill physician/trainer duties toward players while at the same time minimizing the risks of claims like that occurring in fraudulent or intentional concealment of medical information cases?

Although the law varies from state to state, physicians and other providers of health care and related services (which would seem to include most athletic trainers and some other team employees or agents when construed rather broadly), are under a duty to render their services competently and in accordance with applicable standards of care. In the course of provision of service to fulfill that duty, providers, traditionally physicians, are almost always charged with the duty to provide complete information to their patients as to the patient's condition, the provider's examination or diagnostic findings and the recommended or preferred treatment and prognosis. Exceptions to this rule sometimes arise with a patient who is under age or under some other mental or physical disability which would grossly impair that person's powers of understanding, where the patient is comatose or unconscious, or where the communication of information would, based upon a reasonable medical certainty (as might later have to be supported by expert review), harm the patient or worsen his condition. Even in these situations however, communication with close family members or natural/legal guardians is necessary so that provider obligations can be fulfilled.

Communication of information has always been part of the so-called "informed consent" process, during which generally, patients have a right to full and complete information as to their medical condition. When deciding to undergo medical treatment or other procedure, individuals are entitled to be informed of their condition, the procedure they are asked to undergo, the material risks associated with that procedure, the available alternatives and an explanation of the benefits to be expected.

In light of this trend, team health-care providers should insure that their discussions with players are accurate, complete and meaningful. Information as to a player's condition, the ramifications associated with his/her continued play and the treatment alternatives must all be discussed with the patient. Providers may not have a right to rely upon the patient's failure to ask "the right questions." As the Krueger Appellate Court noted, *"A physician cannot avoid responsibility for failure to make full disclosure by simply claiming that information was not withheld."*[22]

Certainly all diagnostic test results, findings, and conclusions as well as the potential ramifications of those results should be reviewed with the patient athlete. When possible, anatomical models, x-rays, positive print films or other tangible, physical evidence of a procedure should be utilized to heighten and improve the communicative process regarding the athlete's injuries and the proposed treatment or consequences of continued play. Documentation of this procedure is a must. A failure to comply and document such matters might well result in a Krueger type finding in the right case.

While it may be true that team physicians may have a greater fiduciary duty than other members of the sports medicine team towards their athlete patients, the same principles would seem equally applicable to athletic trainers and other administrative team personnel who have knowledge of information regarding the athletes within their programs. Under those circumstances it would seem that these latter persons also have an inherent duty to see to it that information is appropriately communicated to athlete patients.

It seems clear that team/participant conflicts can develop over the health status of athletes. The physician/trainer can often be caught in the middle of such conflicts. Provider decisions which vary from what is deemed to be in the best interest of the athlete will probably be condemned. While many teams may say that athletes want to play and often will play in and through "pain and injury,"[23] absent specific evidence of full and complete disclosure of all risks associated with continued play after an injury and an informed decision to continue, such findings may be deemed to be "mere conjecture,"[24] and may even be equated with fraudulent or negligent nondisclosure. Such scenarios, moreover, may result in findings against providers for full or partial damage awards even where athletes knowingly wish to continue to play despite a medical opinion to the contrary.[25]

Physicians and other providers (even though often in the employ of a team) must exercise independent professional judgment. While to be sure, non-physicians will usually not be held to the same standard of care as physicians, such providers would seem to have similar disclosure/communication duties to the athlete.

In light of all of the foregoing, specific policy guidelines and procedures should be adopted at the team level acknowledging provider independence from team management in professional duties toward the athlete/patient. The well being of the player should be stressed within these guidelines. Policy statements should also acknowledge the inherent risks of player participation, especially with contact sports. The policies and guidelines should be developed to encourage and promote prompt and complete player disclosure of injury, pain or problem. Likewise that policy should provide complete, open and deliberate discussion of all such injuries and stress athlete well being.

Such policies need not be cumbersome or lengthy. A simple policy like the following may suffice to affirmatively provide guidance for all providers, coaches, administrators, fans and most importantly patient-athletes:[26]

1. The (name of sports medicine program) (hereinafter Program) is charged with the responsibility of examining athletes to determine if they are physically able to participate in competitive sport activities – either initially, before participation begins, or after some illness or injury which required their temporary removal from participation.

2. In the course of conducting such examinations and in making medically related decisions and recommendations, applicable professional standards of practice will be followed to assist in making these determinations.

3. The Program and its personnel will always place the interests and well being of athletes ahead of any other concerns including those which would be medically unsound or contraindicated, as well as those from any outside source, including parents, coaches, booster clubs, fans or others which would be contrary to appropriate medical advice.

4. The Program will communicate with athletes as to their respective conditions, diagnoses, treatment options and alternatives, procedures including testing, surgery or rehabilitation and will hold all medical communications with athletes and all medical information about athletes as confidential and privileged information. Medical information

will not be communicated or released to any other party whatsoever unless athletes have formally authorized the release of such information and then only if athletes (and their parents, if a particular athlete is a minor) have signed a written authorization allowing the release of such information to third parties, or when the program may be required to release information as a matter of legal requirement.

5. In the event that a determination is made with which athletes as patients do not agree, athletes are advised to seek other medical opinions. However, the Program and its personnel will provide their own recommendations based upon the exercise of independent medical judgment, taking into account any other professionally derived recommendation or opinion – but always putting the well being of athletes first, with all other considerations being of a secondary nature.

Records evidencing such policies must be developed and systematically utilized and preserved. In the event of an incident or lawsuit, such records will assist in determining the truth of allegations made or positions asserted. Any failure to follow such policies however, can provide ready proof of negligence or breach of duty.

According to Clark J. Leslie, Esq. of San Mateo, California, the lawyer who represented Charlie Krueger in the previously described case, there is a tremendous amount of pressure that accompanies the appointment of a physician as a "team doctor." Regardless of the pressure however, Mr. Leslie believes *"Whether management or the player are making...demands... [on] the physician, the duty of the doctor is clear, precise and express: the best interest of the patient is the sole criterion upon which advice, care and treatment should be based. However, the present system actively undermines this sacred trust to such an extent that even otherwise highly ethical and well respected physicians may succumb to the unrelenting pressures and conflicts unavoidably inherent under the present system of sports medicine."*[27]

Mr. Leslie believes that the inherent conflict between team, coach, player and team physician can be resolved by the adoption of *"an independent medical staff which would virtually eliminate any spectre of conflict, lack of informed consent or other improper medical ethic...Teams would continue to retain a medical staff for simple injuries and post-injury monitoring and rehabilitation but any injury which required any form of hospitalization or otherwise met agreed upon injury criteria would immediately be referred to the independent clinic.*

The rule for treatment would be very simple: the independent physician would have the absolute final say on what treatment should be issued and when the player could return to play. Second opinions could be obtained from a different physician at another independent clinic or from the player's personal, non-team affiliated doctor.

By not having to answer to the coach, owner, fans or even the player's protestations, the patient-athlete would be afforded a much greater opportunity to obtain an objective opinion of his condition while significantly increasing the probability of his receiving truly independent treatment.

The cost, while initially and admittedly expensive, may actually reduce medical expenses in the long-term by reducing the number of serious and catastrophic (or career ending) injuries that seem to inevitably follow from a player released too early to return to the playing field. The exposure to liability will also experience a concomitant decrease.

Informed consent is the patient's greatest weapon in obtaining an accurate and meaningful appraisal of the nature and extent of an athlete's injury. The abolition of the inherent conflict of interest which exists in every professional sport between the player, physician and management must be addressed immediately. [I]ndependent clinics would vastly reduce this needless evil from the sports scene." [28]

The allegations made in the Krueger case were not unique nor were they completely original. Another suit had been brought in 1976 by former Chicago Bears linebacker Dick Butkus along the same lines and another suit was filed in 1989 by former Seattle Sea Hawks football player Kenneth Easley, wherein he contended that his team physician and trainers did not inform him of the adverse effects of large doses of Ibuprofen, which he contended were given to him and damaged his kidneys. [29] Even more recently, as has been mentioned earlier herein, the estate of former college basketball star Hank Gathers filed suit alleging many of these same claims against, among others, his university, Loyola Marymount University and its athletic director, basketball coach, athletic trainer and various physicians. Among other allegations, the 52 page complaint filed in this case alleged fraudulent concealment of information, which was tantamount to claims related to interference with the informed consent process. While the case was settled prior to trial, it had broad and far reaching consequences to the informed consent process in the sports medicine setting. [30] Another similar case involving another college basketball player, Earnest Killum, is now pending in the state of California. [31] This case, which also makes allegations of interference with appropriate medical treatment and the provision of appropriate communication, has sent another "shock waive" through the sports medicine provider community. [32]

Despite all of the pressures which can be brought to bear upon the provider and the athlete in the physician-patient relationship, the bottom line is that clearance decisions related to participation or return to play are and must always be medically oriented and based upon the application of the appropriate standard of medical care. A deviation from this perspective will invariably lead to a "clouding" of the real issues, as all of the various competing interests and potentially adverse consequences of different medical decisions appear on the horizon.

Once such interests come to bear upon medical decisions related to the clearance of athletes for participation, the duty to athlete-patients may be compromised and thus adversely affected. If the clearance which is made is unduly affected by coaching or administrative personnel and injury results therefrom substantial claims and litigation can be put forth.[33]

In the case of Gathers vs. Loyola Marymount University, et. al., the plaintiffs made very serious and specific allegations regarding coach interference with medical care and medical decisions by the decedent's treating physicians. In one of the allegations of the complaint, which included a letter from one of Gathers physicians to another physician, the letter reportedly stated:

"Hank and I met last week to discuss whether or not he was satisfied with his level of performance, vis-a-viz, changes in medications. He indicated to me at that time that he felt his performance was fine, and that there were no depressing effects of the medication at the dose he was taking. Later on over the weekend, I got a call from his coach, indicating that his [Hank's] athletic performance was still substantially sub-par, and that he felt strongly that the medication should be changed. I met with Hank again today, and had another discussion with him. I explored the options of changing to another beta blocker (such as Tenormin) vs. changing to Verapamil. I did emphasize, however, again, that the efficacy of Verapamil could not be predicted, and that in any case, a change-over to that agent would require at least 4 to 5 days with the possibility of missing a game during the adjustment period. Hank felt that decreasing Inderal from 40 t.i.d., to 40 b.i.d. would be his preference; I therefore decreased his dosage to that level and plan on repeating a Holter examination in 48 hours..."

The complaint further alleged that two days prior to Gathers' death the basketball coach called one of the treating physicians *"and stated that decedent was not performing well and again argued that the medication be decreased. In response to the pressure…[the complaint alleges][the physician] instructed decedent to decrease the dosage of…[medication] to a non-therapeutic level."*

Based upon these and other allegations the complaint charged the defendant basketball coach *"with the knowledge and agreement of the [defendant athletic director and university] contacted and induced…[the defendant physician] on more than one occasion to reduce and/or change the heart medication …[which had been] prescribed for decedent Hank Gathers for non-medical reasons, specifically to increase the basketball playing ability of Hank Gathers, without regard to the physical detriment to decedent, and with a conscious disregard for his life and safety."* The complaint further alleged *"[The defendant treating physician]…agreed to reduce and/or change decedent's medications on several occasions, based solely on the inquires of said defendant…[coach]."* The complaint also alleged a conspiracy between the coach, the athletic director and the physicians to institute a scheme and plan to deprive Gathers of information as to his true condition essentially to induce him to return to playing basketball when he should not have done so.

While these allegations were never established in court through trial inasmuch as the case was subsequently settled, and while similar allegations in the other cases previously mentioned are either pending or were resolved without full litigation, cases similar to this one have resulted in successful legal outcomes for the athlete.[34]

In order to avoid these claims as previously indicated herein, administrators and coaches should develop clear and explicit policies and procedures for application by members of the sports medicine staff. The policies should provide that the athletes health is **always** of paramount importance and that the medical staff will **always** have the final say as to the clearance to participate or return to play. Moreover, procedure must always be followed in accordance with these policies. Oral or written commentaries (which are previously authorized by the athlete)[35] between administration/coaching staff and providers should **always** be documented with notations that the administrative staff members are relying upon the medical personnel to make medical decisions without interference or pressure and that the main concern is for the athlete's health and safety.

By establishing and following such a scenario, claims relating to administration/coach interference with medical decisions may be minimized.[36] A failure to do so may well open up a "Pandora's Box" which should best be kept closed.

FINAL THOUGHT

Sports medicine providers must guard the physician-patient relationship most closely — perhaps more so than any other practitioner. The competitive interests which may be brought to bear upon the relationship can potentially create conflicts, interfere with communications with the athlete and lead to claims for the negligent and even fraudulent misrepresentation of an athlete's injuries and condition. Suits against practitioners, administration and coaches can be brought to bear alleging many other claims, including conspiracy, the unlawful practice of medicine and interference with appropriate medical practice. The athlete's condition and treatment must always be of paramount concern to providers who must put aside any competing interests and provide proper and appropriate information during communications with athletes.

CHAPTER 9 FOOTNOTES:

1. *See* Herbert, "Coach/Administrator Interference With Medical Care For Athletes," *The Sports Medicine Standards and Malpractice Reporter* 3(1):1, 3-5, 1991.

2. "Legal and Ethical Conflicts Arising From The Team Physician's Dual Obligation to The Athlete and Management," *JOSM* 15-26, December 1987, reprinted therein with permission from *Seton Hall Legislative Journal* 10:299-325, 1987.

3. 234 Cal. Rptr. 579 (Cal. App. 1 Dist, 1987). *See also,* <u>Martin vs. Casagrande</u>, 559 N.Y.S.2d 68 (AD 4 Dept. 1990), *analyzed in* Herbert, "Conspiracy to Withhold Information Case Against Professional Hockey Team and Physician Dismissed," *The Sports Medicine Standards and Malpractice Reporter* 3(1):8-9, 1991; A negligence based malpractice award against the team physician was rendered in late 1993, *analyzed in* "Sabre's Injured Knee Earns $2.5 Million Dollars," *National Law Journal,* February 7, 1994, p. 10.

4. *See e.g.,* <u>Butkus vs. Chicago Bears</u>, *reported in New York Times,* September 14, 1976, at p. 50.

5. *See, supra* footnote 3 at page 582.

6. *Id.* at page 583.

7. *Id.* at page 584.

8. *Id.* at page 585.

9. *Id.*

10. *See,* Leslie, "War and Peace With Hippocrates – A Modern Dilemma Facing Sports Medicine," *The Sports Medicine Standards and Malpractice Reporter* 2(2):21-28, 1990.

11. *See,* Update on Litigation, "<u>Krueger</u> Settlement Announced," *The Sports, Parks and Recreation Law Reporter* 2(3):44, December, 1988.

12. 559 N.Y.S.2d 68 (AD 4 Dept. 1990).

13. *Id.* at page 69.

14. *Id.* at page 70.

15. *Id.* at page 71.

16. *See, supra* footnote 3.

17. <u>Sherwin vs. Indianapolis Colts, Inc.</u>, 752 F. Supp. 1172 (NDNY 1990) *analyzed in* "Another Suit Based Upon Information Withholding Allegations," *The Sports Medicine Standards and Malpractice Reporter* 3(3):55-56, 1991.

18. 274 Cal. Rptr. 31 (Cal. App. 4th Dist., 1990), reviewed in "Professional Football Player's Malpractice Action Against Team Physician To Proceed," *The Sports Medicine Standards and Malpractice Reporter* 3(2):26-28, 1991.

19. *See, supra* footnote 17 at page 1173.

20. *Id.*

21. *But see,* Federal Rehabilitation Act and the Americans With Disabilities Act provisions and discussion, *supra* Chapter 8.

22. *See, supra* footnote 3 at page 583.

23. "Playing in Pain: Player and Sports Medicine Responsibilities," *The Sports Medicine Standards and Malpractice Reporter* 6(2):27, 1994.

24. *See* Herbert, "Coach/Administrator Interference With Medical Care For Athletes," *The Sports Medicine Standards and Malpractice Reporter* 3(1):1, 3-5, 1991.

25. Mitten, "Team Physicians and Competitive Athletes: Allocating Legal Responsibility for Athletic Injuries," *The University of Pittsburgh Law Review* 55(1):129, 161-168, 1993.

26. Reprinted from Herbert, "Developing Policies and Procedures for Sports Medicine Programs," *The Sports Medicine Standards and Malpractice Reporter* 5(3):43, 1993.

27. Leslie, "War and Peace With Hippocrates – A Modern Dilemma Facing Sports Medicine," *The Sports Medicine Standards and Malpractice Reporter* 2(2):21, 24-28, 1990.

28. *Id.* at page 27-28.

29. *See,* "Negligent/Fraudulent Concealment of Medical Information Claim Surfaces Again," *The Sports Medicine Standards and Malpractice Reporter* 1(3):63-64, 1989.

30. *See,* discussion of case in Chapter 7.

31. *See* Herbert, "Another Basketball Star Dies," *The Sports Medicine Standards and Malpractice Reporter* 5(2):17, 19-20, 1993.

32. *Id.*

33. *See, supra* footnote 3.

34. *See, supra* footnote 3.

35. "A Primer for Sports Medicine Risk Management Practices – Preserving The Confidentiality of Records," *The Sports Medicine Standards and Malpractice Reporter* 5(2):20, 1993.

36. *See, supra* footnote 24.

10 DISPENSING PRESCRIPTION MEDICATIONS TO ATHLETES

Many respected association statements recommend that physicians be present for all athletic contests, as we have previously stated, *see* Chapter 7. Unfortunately, the financial limitations of many programs and/or the practical realities of having such professionals attend all such events, may prevent these recommendations from actually being carried out on a day-to-day basis. Many significant medico-legal implications can potentially arise from a failure to implement and follow such recommendations – especially if they are ultimately judged to be part of or tantamount to the standard of care owed to athletes and athletic programs. Even when physicians do attend all athletic contests and practice sessions, situations often arise where such practitioners must use adjunct personnel for the provision of some services. Moreover, in those situations where physicians are not actually present but are "available," *i.e.,* by telephone contact, certain needed services must be provided to athletes by others or not provided at all.

THE USE OF STANDING ORDERS

In response to certain simple realities, given the obvious need to provide appropriate responses when faced with a need for care, physicians have long delegated the actual provision of some care via standing orders or specific protocols. While variously defined, standing orders are simply orders which have been predetermined by a physician but carried out under certain circumstances by other qualified health care providers. A number of legal concerns however can arise with the use of standing orders. Frequently, the question can become whether or not the order is "legally sanctioned" – that is – is the order properly delegable to the actual provider.[1] The question becomes even more significant when the person carrying out the order is a non-nurse or even a non-licensed provider.

In a majority of programs, athletic trainers rather than nurses will be the one member of the sports medicine team most frequently available during many athletic contests and practice sessions. Given this reality, when coupled with the need or desire to act under certain circumstances, the question related to the delegation of care delivery frequently centers upon the permissibility of care delegation for athletes by the physician to the actual provider – most frequently a non-licensed trainer.

While the practice of athletic training is not regulated by state law in about half of the states,[2] athletic trainers have worked closely with team physicians in the care of athletes for many years. Despite this close relationship, the delegation of care is often determined by reference to state law: *"[M]any states have chosen to exclude athletic trainers from the list of health-care professionals whose duties are specifically regulated by state law. In many cases, this places the athletic trainer, even one who possesses extensive advanced professional education and national certification, in a very precarious position. To provide even the most basic of sports medicine care for an athlete in a state where such care is specifically limited by law to physicians, nurses and physical therapists is to perform outside the apparent authority (and perhaps in violation of many medical/allied health statutes) of the law."[3]*

When an inappropriate or legally impermissible delegation of authority is attempted by a physician to another, the provider as well as the physician may face a number of legal consequences – including the possibility of criminal sanctions. This may be particularly true in the prescription and dispensing of medication to athletes.[4]

Such a delegation of service delivery, involving the dispensing of prescription medications made national headlines in 1989 as a trainer, physician and pharmacist were charged with a variety of criminal offenses related to the prescription and provision of medications for students, some of whom were athletes at Kent State University.[5] The university trainer and pharmacist were subsequently acquitted at trial and the charges against the physician were dismissed.

In these cases, the charges centered upon the alleged pre-scription of medications by the physician and the claimed provi-sion of those medications to student athletes when physicians were not available, through telephone authorization given by the physician to the trainer. As a result of this claimed scenario, the trainer was charged with practicing medicine without a license and the physician was faced with charges related to the writing of false prescriptions. The pharmacist, in a somewhat unrelated case was charged with filling a prescription for a student which had not been written by a physician [a prescription was written by a physician's assistant pursuant to a physician issued oral protocol].

Despite the favorable outcomes for all providers in these cases, the charges which were filed bring into rather sharp focus the potential problems facing the sports medicine team dealing with the day-to-day realities of treating injured athletes. The question of who can do what as a member of the sports medicine team is complex and multi-faceted.

The various state statutory definitions put forth for the practice of medicine and certain allied health professions are of particular import to sports medicine practitioners facing concerns in this area: *"While not universally defined, the practice of medicine is generally regarded as the diagnosis of an individual's symptoms to determine with what disease or illness he is afflicted, and then to determine upon the basis of that diagnosis, what remedy or treatment should be given or prescribed to treat that disease and/ or relieve the symptoms."*[6] The actual practice of medicine is governed by particular state statutory enactments and may be very broadly defined as we discussed in Chapter 3 herein.

In the Kent State University provider cases, the Ohio statutes were utilized to determine the authority of the providers. Ohio Revised Code §4731.41 prohibited the practice of medicine without the proper certification (licensure). Ohio Revised Code §4731.34 defined the practice of medicine as: *"A person shall be regarded as practicing medicine...who examines or diagnoses for compensation of any kind, or prescribes, advises, recommends, administers, or dispenses for compensation of any kind, direct or indirect, a drug or medicine, appliance, mold or cast, application, operation, or treatment, of whatever nature, for the cure or relief of a wound, fracture or bodily injury, infirmity, or disease...".*

As can be readily determined from a review of this statute, the enactment is very broadly written and all encompassing. Since such statutes are often determined to be enacted for the public good they are subject to broad judicial interpretation.

Despite such medical practice acts, other statutes typically define and regulate other licensed providers such as physician assistants, nurses, and therapists. Often these enactments provide that these professionals must work under the supervision of or pursuant to the direction of a physician in certain defined and limited areas. At least one court has determined that such professionals *"although obviously skilled and well trained...[are] not in the same category as a physician who is required to exercise his independent judgment on matters which may mean the difference between life and death."*[7]

Despite such statutes and the interpreting case law arising therefrom, standing orders are typically used to allow the **rendition** of treatment or the provision of service under certain circumstances by non-physician providers. The lawfulness of such practices has been confirmed at least in the state of Ohio, through an Ohio Attorney General's Opinion,[8] and has been recognized as a means *"to foster proper medical care and reduce costs."*[9] When a non-physician provider such as a nurse *"treats a symptom* *pursuant to a standing order…[such a provider] is not diagnosing or prescribing. Rather, in such a situation…[the provider] although exercising judgment, is simply applying a treatment or giving a medication pursuant to an order of a physician. It is the doctor who is practicing medicine and not the…[provider]."* [10]

Although nurses are typically empowered by state enabling statutes to administer injections and oral medications to patients pursuant to physician orders, the reasoning from the foregoing Ohio Attorney General's Opinion and the Ohio Supreme Court case previously cited may well assist others on the sports medicine team who need legal authority to provide such services pursuant to physician standing orders even when they are not licensed by state health-care provider acts. Perhaps the acquittal of the KSU trainer can also be cited as further authority for the proposition – although such reliance would seem to be tenuous at best – given the number of factors which may have led to the acquittal.

Given this legislative and judicial background and the realities of certain sports medicine practices, the dispensing of any medications by non-physician members of a sports medicine team should be preceded by:

1. a thorough legal evaluation of state statutory enactments defining the authority of various members of the sports medicine group;

2. a legal review of judicial precedent analyzing state provider practice acts under specific circumstances; and

3. a legal analysis of federal enactments which impact the prescription and dispensing of medication by various members of the sports medicine team.

Once these basics are analyzed and completed by the group's legal counsel (assuming of course, that there are no direct prohibitions against same) specific **written** standing orders may be developed by the physician to be utilized and carried out when the physician is not present, when the need arises and then only by properly trained and authorized personnel pursuant to the requirements of relevant state and federal law. Perhaps additional consideration should be given to the utilization of the telephone system for the actual authorization to proceed in the absence of a physician pursuant to a written standing order, where legally authorized by state/federal law. The ability of non-licensed trainers to actually dispense prescriptive medication to athletes even upon the direction of a physician may be tenuous at best. In those states where trainers are licensed but not authorized to dispense medication, the authority may even be more suspect. Federal constraints may further complicate the situation.

The question remains however, as to whether or not any other non-physician member of the health care provider team, may under any circumstance, prescribe, provide or dispense medications to patients, including athletes. Typically, pharmacists have been granted statutory authority to dispense various medications to patients but only upon the instructions and prescription of a licensed physician. In addition, nurses and other members of the health care provider team have typically provided care, including the administration of medications to patients under a physician's care upon a physician's orders. These orders typically take the form of direct communication from the physician while the physician is present, or through the previously described standing order process. The use of standing orders to provide care delivery has been approved by those courts examining same.[11]

Given this background, the pivotal question centers upon whether or not non-licensed or even licensed trainers may lawfully provide pharmaceuticals to athletes, pursuant to physician issued standing orders? In light of the legal analysis issued to date, coupled with the practical ramifications associated with this issue, the answer to say the least, is complex and subject to ongoing debate and diverse opinion. In some states it may well be sufficient to say that any member of the sports medicine team acting under the standing or express order of a physician may dispense medications to athletes, assuming the direct provider is qualified to do so and is acting within the scope of the physician's authorization and within the confines of state and federal law. In other states, depending upon the interpretation associated with the scope and breadth of allied health care provider statutes, it may well be that only those allied health care providers who are expressly authorized to do so by law may dispense or provide medications to their athlete patients.

STATUTORY AUTHORIZATION TO PROVIDE MEDICATIONS

In some states, there may also be additional legislative authorization for the provision of some prescription medications by non-licensed members of the sports medicine team to the athletes in their charge. For example, in Ohio there exists a generalized statute allowing local, preparatory boards of education to adopt a policy for the administration of prescribed drugs to students through a school employee with appropriate training, except as otherwise prohibited by federal law.[12]

Statutes like these may well provide some authorization for the dispensing of all but federally controlled substances to student athletes by non-licensed members of the sports medicine team. However, given the lack of a specific legislative response to this issue, there appears to be a dire need to address the problem by legislative enactment. Until then, sports medicine practitioners may well find themselves in a legal quandary without clear solution. While athletic body actions may assist in developing policy,[13] the final solution may require more authoritative action.

FINAL THOUGHT

The dispensing of medications to athletes by non-physician members of the sports medicine team is fraught with legal pitfalls.

Commentary and discussion is desperately needed to address this ongoing problem. Standing orders or procedural protocols may well fill the void of clear legal authorization until specific legislative attention is directed at this area.

CHAPTER 10 FOOTNOTES:

1. *See,* SCHOOL HEALTH *supra,* at page 175.

2. *See* Herbert, "Should Athletic Trainers Be Held To The Standard Of Care Of Physicians," *The Sports, Parks and Recreation Law Reporter* 1(4):56-58, 1988.

3. Hawkins, "The Legal Status of Athletic Trainers," *The Sports, Parks and Recreation Law Reporter* 2(1):6-9 1988.

4. *See* Bradley, "Legal Aspects of Drug Distribution in Athletic Training Rooms," *The Sports Medicine Standards and Malpractice Reporter* 5(1):6-9, 1993; Herbert, "NCAA Drug Distribution Study for University Athletic Programs," *The Sports Medicine Standards and Malpractice Reporter* 5(1):5-6, 1993.

5. *See* NEWS AND REPORTS, "Whose Responsibility Is It To Dispense Prescription Medication To College Athletes," *The Sports Medicine Standards and Malpractice Reporter* 1(3):62, (1989).

6. Herbert and Herbert, LEGAL ASPECTS OF PREVENTATIVE AND REHABILITATIVE EXERCISE PROGRAMS, Third Edition (PRC Publishing, Inc., Canton, OH 1993) at page 113.

7. Richardson vs. Doe, 176 Ohio St. 370 (1964).

8. *See e.g.,* 1980 Ohio Attorney General Opinions 023,

9. *Id.*

10. *Id.*

11. *See e.g.,* Sermchief vs. Gonzales, 660 S.W.2d 683 (Mo. 1983), *analyzed in* Brent, "Risk Management in Home Health Care: Focus on Patient Care Liability," *Loyola University Law Journal* 20:775-795, 1989.

12. *See e.g.,* Ohio Revised Code §3313.713.

13. *See,* "NCAA hopes to set up drug-dispensing plan," *The Beacon Journal* p. B-1, Wednesday June 21, 1989.

11 DRUG TESTING, COUNSELING, CONFIDENTIALITY AND INFECTIOUS DISEASE CONTROL

DRUG TESTING

Drug testing appears to be becoming more deeply entrenched in the athletic area than ever before. Recent Olympic, NFL and NCAA actions, as well as those of a more local nature, have all moved toward more frequent and demanding drug testing policies and procedures for athletes. Team physicians and other sports medicine personnel are sometimes asked to participate in these efforts. While most consider these efforts to be necessary and beneficial to virtually everyone, a number of sports medicine related issues are necessarily raised as a result of such proposals.

It seems relatively certain that sports medicine personnel should be a part of the planning team for the development of any drug testing policy. Such individuals clearly have the insight and expertise necessary to develop overall goals, objectives, policies and procedures, and otherwise provide a unique professional perspective to the planning phase of any such effort. Moreover, such practitioners can provide invaluable insight into the various professional and ethical concerns which accompany these programs.

Sports medicine professionals are also "naturals" for at least two aspects of most programs – education and counseling. Few other professionals will be in the position to provide relevant and necessary information to those athletes in search of information – answers and solutions to the myriad of problems associated with substance use and abuse. The confidential nature of the traditional relationship between the physician and the athlete-patient lends great credence to the participation of the physician in such roles. However, the mere existence of such factors also ameliorates against the physician's role in the mechanical as well as the "search" or "selection" aspects of the testing procedures.

Given the confidential nature of the relationship between sports medicine physicians and athlete-patients, these physicians should not be involved in the selection of athletes for testing, in actually testing those athletes nor in communicating medical information or testing results to third parties unless they are specifically authorized to do so by the athlete or are required to do so by law. The basic nature of the physician-patient relationship really precludes and contraindicates any more physician involvement. The athlete-patient is simply no less the patient just because he or she is an athlete. Treating physicians should remember the basic tenants of that relationship and act accordingly.

If physician involvement in such programs is necessary beyond education and counseling, outside physician involvement clearly seems appropriate. To do otherwise, may well involve the sports medicine physician in a variety of ethical and legal dilemmas for which there is no easy solution.

There are a variety of legal and ethical issues involved in drug testing practices. A number of physician groups for example have condemned the use of such mechanisms for adolescents based upon a variety of factors.[1] Others have contended however that the use of drug testing is absolutely necessary for the purposes of countering the massive drug abuse problem among a wide variety of groups including those in the athletic arena.[2]

The sports medicine professional's role in these programs should be limited and separated from the search, selection or sanction aspects of such activities. Appropriate steps should be taken to distance the sports medicine team from such activities.

COUNSELING AND CONFIDENTIALITY
While a sports medicine physician's role in some aspects of drug testing may be inappropriate given the nature of the relationship of a physician to his/her patients who would be the subject of

such testing, the physician is of course naturally situated at all times to provide counseling, education and recommendations to the athletes. This should include information not only about street drugs but the use of such substances as steroids. Recommendations against such use should be provided and under no circumstances should any member of a sports medicine team turn his or her back upon an athlete who is using steroids or engage in the provision of same.[3]

Direct liability may attach to any member of the sports medicine team who engages in the provision of steroids for athlete use even as to third parties who may be injured by the athlete's actions. For example, in a rather dramatic ruling, an Indiana Court of Appeals held in 1990 that a steroid prescribing physician may be liable to third parties who are injured by the using patient who becomes aggressive due to the medications so provided or prescribed.[4] The facts of this interesting case would indicate that the physician defendant, who also held a Ph.D. in pharmacology, began treating one Michael Neal in November of 1977. Mr. Neal suffered from chronic anxiety and depression and was treated by the defendant doctor with various psychotropic drugs. Aside from these prescriptions, the physician also *"regularly prescribed anabolic steroids for Neal and frequently allowed Neal to take dosages greatly in excess of the manufacturer's recommended dosage. Neal took the steroids to gain weight and enhance his performance in the police olympics. [The defendant], Dr. Webb, prescribed the steroids to give Neal a 'running start' for the police olympics. Additionally, Neal received numerous testosterone injections from Dr. Webb."[5]*

The patient Neal became a deputy sheriff during his period of treatment by Dr. Webb, and held that position until he was disabled in early 1985. He had a large private weapons collection and began to threaten his wife with a gun. He also told her that he would kill her if she told anyone of his violent behavior, although he beat her at regular intervals during this period. Eventually, the patient's wife went to the home of the plaintiffs, Madeline and Thomas Jarvis to report the violent behavior and to seek help. Madeline was her sister and her husband, Thomas, was an Indiana State Police Detective.

As a result of this meeting, others, including the defendant doctor, became aware of the patient's violent behavior and attempted to intercede. However, the patient became irritated and shot the plaintiff's husband, and another police officer in addition to killing a nurse during this same period. Jarvis and his wife subsequently brought suit against the patient's physician alleging negligence. Specifically the plaintiff asserted that *"Dr. Webb negligently over-medicated Neal with anabolic steroids and testosterone to the point that Neal became a toxic psychotic resulting in Neal's attack on [the plaintiff]...a foreseeable victim."* [6] The defendant doctor contended that even if he was negligent he owed no duty toward the plaintiff, a third party, resulting from his treatment of Neal.

As in all negligence actions, the question of whether or not actionable negligence was present so as to permit a lawsuit to be maintained was dependent upon proof of duty and breach of duty proximately causing injury. The question of duty is always a matter for judicial determination as a question of law. In this case, both the trial court and the appellate court held that the physician owed a duty to the plaintiff who the latter court determined was a "foreseeable" victim under Indiana law. In arriving at this conclusion, the court cited previous case law holding physicians liable when over-medicated or epileptic patients cause automobile accidents, or other injuries to third parties, deemed to be due to negligent physician acts or omissions. [7] In applying this reasoning to the issue of whether or not Neal's conduct was foreseeable, the court concluded that the plaintiff *"by virtue of coming into contact with Neal was a foreseeable victim of Neal's uncontrolled behavior."* [8]

Citing from a prior Indiana case,[9] the court determined *"fore-seeability does not mean that the precise sequence of events or exact consequences which were encountered should have been anticipated. Rather the question is whether [the] defendant should have foreseen in the abstract, in a general way, the injurious consequences of its act."*[10] The court in the instant case noted that if the plaintiff *"proves Neal was a toxic psychotic and that the psychosis was the result of Dr. Webb's negligent over-medication, then liability might follow."*[11] Based upon all of the foregoing, the case was remanded to the lower court for trial. A subsequent appeal to the Supreme Court of Indiana reversed the appellate court ruling and found that the physician was not liable to an "unknown" third party.[12]

The <u>Webb</u> court's ruling was based upon legal principles developed in a number of cases, including those relied upon by the appellate court. For example, in cases where physicians negligently certify that an epileptic driver's condition is under effective medical control as required by state law, they may face liability if the physician's actions fall below the standard of reasonable medical care.[13] Similar holdings have also been reached in a number of other cases.[14]

While the appellate court ruling in the Webb case was reversed on appeal to the Indiana Supreme Court, sports medicine provider's potential liability to identifiable or known third parties who may be harmed by the patient under the physician's care can create a number of concerns for such providers.[15] Sports medicine providers should stay informed as to developments in this area.

CONFIDENTIALITY

All information obtained from athletes in the course of rendering services except as otherwise appropriately authorized by the athlete or his or her parents if the athlete is a minor, must be held in the strictest confidence by the sports medicine staff.[16] Quite simply, the physician-patient relationship gives rise to a privilege between the physician and patient as well as a protected confidentiality in information arising out of that relationship. The trust arising therefrom must not be breached by those providing service to the athlete. Appropriate procedures must be integrated into the program to ensure that all patient records and information are maintained in this manner and are not inappropriately released.

Under certain circumstances, physicians may have a duty to warn third parties as to information learned during the physician-patient relationship. Where harm is threatened to a specific target, a duty to disclose may arise. Local program counsel should be involved in any such circumstance so as to provide appropriate advance legal advice.

INFECTIOUS DISEASE CONTROL

There are a number of infectious diseases which can affect and impact athletes and the duties and responsibilities of the sports medicine staff. These can run the gamut from measles and chicken pox to herpes gladiatorum and now most seriously HIV/AIDS.[17] While there has been adequate discussion in the literature regarding most of these conditions, there has been a lack of adequate review and analysis of the HIV/AIDS problem in the sports medicine setting. Consequently, what follows is an attempt to deal with this void and to provide salient and poignant discussion.

The AIDS (Acquired Immunodeficiency Syndrome) problem has been judicially characterized as *"[T]he modern equivalent of leprosy."*[18] To be sure, this dreaded disease has created a myriad of medical, social and legal problems to date. *"[T]he public has reacted to the disease with hysteria...victims have been faced with social censure, embarrassment and discrimination in nearly every phase of their lives, including jobs, education and housing."*[19] While medicine has been searching for some cure or viable treatment for this disease, the judicial system has been struggling with the plethora of issues surrounding the syndrome. The struggle will certainly continue for some time to come. Sports programs are not "immune" from these problems.

Acquired Immunodeficiency Syndrome (AIDS) is an unusual, epidemic form of immunodeficiency that renders a person highly vulnerable to infections and a variety of illnesses. A retrovirus commonly termed Human Immunodeficiency Virus (HIV) has been shown to be the cause of AIDS (also sometimes referred to as Lymphadenopathy Associated Virus (LAV), AIDS-Associated Retrovirus (ARV) or Human T Lymphotropic Virus Type III, (HTLV-III). Persons infected with AIDS are highly susceptible to contraction of a variety of diseases and so-called "opportunistic infections" which would usually not be harmful to an uninfected person.

Although there is not absolute evidence as to all of the transmission routes for AIDS, it appears that certain groups are at high risk for infection: homosexually/bisexually active males; intravenous drug abusers; recipients of contaminated blood transfusions; hemophiliacs; children born to mothers infected with the AIDS virus; and, sexual partners of individuals from these groups. Almost all infections occur through sexual transmission, blood or blood product transfusion, use of contaminated needles or as a result of the infection of a newborn from the mother. Some recent evidence may suggest contamination of health care/laboratory workers through needle pricks, or patient blood contact as to workers with infected skin or similar occurrences. Recent reports, while subject to scientific confirmation, may also indicate the possibility of transmission by other means including transmissions through cracked skin,[20] or through other methods of transmission,[21] or even through so-called "deep" kissing.[22] Other recent reports may also indicate that contractions may be possible through dentist-patient contamination during a dental procedure.[23] The incubation period between infection and symptomatology can be many years.

One report indicates that the risk of accidental contraction of the AIDS retrovirus by those in the health-care setting is one-in-200 to one-in-250.[24] According to this report, most exposures to this possibility result from needlesticks (80%) but a full 7% can statistically result from open wound contamination while 5% can result from mucous membrane exposure. While professionals within the health-care setting certainly come into more contact with sick individuals as well as those suffering from the terminal effects of AIDS, the use of these statistical correlations in other settings may be a somewhat relevant indicator of the risk of exposure through an open wound or due to mucous membrane contact with someone who is infected.

According to some sources[25] there are three principal patient classifications for those infected with the AIDS retrovirus:

1. *HIV infected carriers* – those who are infected with the retrovirus but exhibit no obvious, outward manifestations of the disease – so-called "healthy carriers";

2. *ARC patients* – those who have reached a disease progression beyond mere infection who begin to demonstrate symptoms – often referred to as "AIDS related complex patients"; and,

3. *AIDS patients* – those who are extremely ill as a result of the infection.

Among these three groups it appears that HIV carriers and even some ARC patients are capable of carrying on employment and participating in various activities including sport.[26] In fact, it appears that those who are infected can benefit from physical activity or sport.[27]

Individuals who are merely infected with the AIDS retrovirus and even some of those suffering from ARC may be capable of participation in exercise, sport and athletic contests.[28] Given this, it appears relatively certain that some individuals participating in sport will be infected and perhaps not even be aware of their infection, given the often long period that sometimes occurs between initial exposure to the disease and infection and subsequent development of ARC or AIDS. Sometimes individuals, including health-care workers, who come into contact with HIV carriers will not know of the patient's infection or the potential for exposure and contraction of the retrovirus for some time.[29] As a partial result of such findings, guidelines for the prevention of HIV transmission in the workplace,[30] and for the handling of human blood in health-care setting[31] have been developed.

Persons infected with the AIDS retrovirus, those classified as suffering from ARC or those suffering from AIDS are considered to be or are likely to be considered as handicapped or disabled under certain federal and many state laws. Although the United States Supreme Court has not ruled that those afflicted with these conditions are deemed to be handicapped, it appears likely that such a ruling will be made based upon another decision of the court which determined that a person suffering from tuberculous was handicapped.[32] A combination of federal and state statutory laws provide various protections for those suffering from handicaps. These laws include the Rehabilitation Act, the Civil Rights Restoration Act, the Americans With Disabilities Act and the Civil Rights Act of 1964 at the federal level and similar state enactments such as Ohio Revised Code §4112.02 prohibiting certain discriminatory practices of employers and Ohio Revised Code §4112.022 prohibiting similar practices in educational institutions.

The existing statutory and regulatory schemes make it extremely likely that those suffering from relevant conditions will be deemed to be handicapped or disabled unless afforded applicable protections of law as it pertains to both employers and educational institutions. In fact, some states have taken the position that the rights of AIDS victims will be protected by law.[33] In Ohio for example, the State Civil Rights Commission has stated: _"[B]ased upon overwhelming medical and scientific evi-_

dence...

the kind of non-sexual person-to-person contact that generally occurs among workers and clients or consumers in the workplace [or in the educational setting] does not pose a risk for transmission of the AIDS virus."[34] Some states have also issued guidelines to deal with those infected with AIDS or the AIDS retrovirus. Some of these guidelines including ones issued by the state of Ohio in October of 1987 indicate: *"based on current evidence, casual person-to-person contact as would occur among school children and staff, poses no risk of transmission of HIV."* The guidelines further provide: *"children with AIDS, AIDS related complex or HIV infections should be allowed to attend school in a regular classroom setting provided that the health of the child allows participation in regular school activities. The health status should be evaluated by his/her physician."* Based upon federal and state statutory enactments and expressions such as those occurring in Ohio, it appears likely that the courts will rely upon existing medical evidence as to the risk of disease transmission and physician determination as to a student's ability to participate in given activities.

Very few courts have addressed the question of an infected student's participation in extracurricular activities. However, in the case of <u>Ray vs. School District of DeSoto County</u>,[35] it appears that some courts may be willing to restrict participation in certain sport activities such as those occurring in contact sports. The <u>Ray</u> court determined that an AIDS infected student could not be excluded from classroom enrollment, attendance and related activities and educational services and opportunities except contact sports. Under these circumstances it may be that some courts will take the position that participation in contact sports will not be permitted given the risk of possible transmission of the infection to other athletes.

The U.S. Department of Education has stated: *"With respect to a child with AIDS...medical considerations may also justify a school district placing limitations on specific activities, such as sports, in which children participate. Similarly, decisions on placement should address whether the child will conduct himself or herself in a manner that will not endanger other children."* [36] Various policies have been promulgated by some groups dealing with HIV infection and sports participation. In June of 1991, the American Academy of Pediatrics (AAP) issued a new Policy Statement entitled "Human Immunodeficiency [Acquired Immunodeficiency Syndrome (AIDS) Virus] in the Athletic Setting," *AAP News,* June, 1991, page 18. The AAP Policy Statement clearly indicates that there is a "possible" risk of transmission of the AIDS retrovirus during sports contact. Specifically, the Statement provides, among other things, as follows: *"The American Academy of Pediatrics Recommends:*

1)   Athletes infected with HIV should be allowed to participate in all competitive sports. This advice must be reconsidered if transmission is found to occur in the sports setting.

2)   A physician counseling a known HIV infected athlete in a sport involving blood exposure, such as wrestling or football, should inform him of the potential risk of contagion to others and strongly encourage him to consider another sport.

3)   The physician should respect an HIV infected athlete's right to confidentiality. This includes not disclosing this patient's infection status to the participants or the staff of athletic programs.

4)   All athletes should be made aware that the athletic program is operating under the policies in accordance with 1 and 3."

Given the Statement's indication of a possibility of infection, the question arises as to whether a sports medicine provider has a duty to communicate that possibility to his/her athletes, especially when another athlete/participant with whom the former will participate or compete is so infected – particularly for certain "high risk" sports such as wrestling, boxing or football? Assuming that the judicial system is moving toward the requirement of broader and broader provider disclosure of risks associated with given treatments or procedures, it may be that there is a medico-legal duty to provide such information to those athletes who are under the care of a sports medicine provider. While the AAP Policy Statement attempts to address these concerns, the Statement may create some confusion for providers in light of several recent judicial rulings.

A review of several of these cases may assist in this determination. The first, <u>Estate of Behringer vs. The Medical Center at Princeton</u>,[37] dealt with the duty of an HIV infected otolaryngologist and plastic surgeon to inform his patients of the potential for his transmission of infection to them during his performance of certain invasive procedures. In comparing the physician's rights to privacy with a patient's right to information from his or her physicians, the court ruled: *"If there is to be an ultimate arbiter of whether the patient is to be treated invasively by an AIDS-positive surgeon, the arbiter will be the fully informed patient. The ultimate risk to the patient is so absolute – so devastating – that it is untenable to argue against informed consent combined with the restraint on procedures which present 'any risk' to the patient."*[38] A similar result was also recently reached in a case in Pennsylvania: <u>Appeal of John Doe, M.D.</u>[39]

At about the same time as the publication of the New Jersey and Pennsylvania decisions, another decision was rendered by a California Appellate Court in the case of <u>Christian vs. Sheft, as Executor of the Rock Hudson Estate</u>.[40] In this case, the plaintiff filed an action for emotional distress and deceit against among others the Estate of Rock Hudson due to the decedent's pre-death representations that he was not then suffering from AIDS, when he in fact was so infected, during a time when he and the plaintiff engaged in high risk sex. The appellate court upheld a multi-million dollar verdict and affirmed the lower court's decision, essentially standing for the proposition that the decedent, due to the nature of the activity and the relationship between the parties, had a duty to disclose his infection.

During this same period, the Centers for Disease Control in Atlanta, Georgia, issued new guidelines for health care workers dealing with AIDS infection entitled "Recommendations for Preventing Transmission of Human Immunodeficiency Virus and Hepatitis B Virus to Patients During Exposure – Prone Invasive Procedures" which were published in the *Morbidity and Mortality Weekly Report.*[41] Among other statements contained in these recommendations, the CDC acknowledged that where there is a risk of patient infection by HIV infected health care workers (HCWs), the HCW must inform prospective patients of the HCW's infection before the performance of exposure-prone invasive procedures upon such patients. The American Medical Association (AMA) and the American Dental Association (ADA) also recently recommended that HIV infected providers either inform their patients of their conditions or refrain from the performance of such invasive procedures. A number of other prominent associations such as the American Public Health Association, the American College of Physicians and the AAP, among others, did not so recommend, apparently believing that there is no "real" risk of exposure during such activities.[42] While the risk of HIV transmission from an infected HCW during the performance of invasive medical procedures may be remote (and certainly greater than the likelihood of infection from sports contact during participation), it does not eliminate the **possibility** of infection, which has already occurred in the dental setting,[43] and which may also have already occurred in the sports setting.[44]

Given the law's apparent movement toward requiring the disclosure of mere possibilities rather than probabilities as to risks associated with given medical procedures, there certainly appears to be a conflict developing between at least some medical thought and the emerging legal considerations dealing with the issue of risk disclosure by medical providers.

When comparing the subject AAP Statement with the developing legal thought, it appears that the AAP Policy Statement may well fall short in addressing the team physician's responsibilities toward all of his/her athlete-patients when someone with whom they will come into close personal contact is HIV infected. Given the **possibility** of infection and the apparent occurrence of at least one such case of transmission in the sports setting, the question then arises as to whether the AAP Policy Statement (which provides for the counseling of an HIV infected athlete to engage in less high risk sports while informing other participants of the fact that the program **may** include someone who is HIV infected) will make the infected person's right to privacy paramount over the disclosure rights of those who face a **possibility** of infection from the infected athlete/patient. The AAP Statement appears to come down on the side of privacy contrary to what may be the emerging case law addressing this topic. While the possibilities for infection in the health care setting by infected HCWs or in the athletic setting by infected participants is very remote, the courts examining similar issues to date have not taken remoteness of potential infection into consideration. (In fact in the <u>Hudson</u> case, *supra,* testimony was provided at trial to the effect that if the plaintiff had not shown any signs of infection by time of trial – that he would not become infected as a result of his contact with Hudson – virtually eliminating any **possibility** of infection.)

If there is essentially no or only a minimal risk of the transmission of infection from an HIV infected athlete, why does the AAP Statement counsel an infected athlete to consider another, less high risk sport, than for example wrestling or football? Aside from the obvious inconsistencies in this portion of the Statement when compared to the rest of the Statement, the

Statement appears to attempt to meet the provider's disclosure responsibilities to all patient-athletes on a team by making them aware of the policy under which the program is operating (that they may be on a team with a member who is HIV infected). The question then arises as to whether such a communication is adequate in disclosing the real risk? *"A bland statement [as to risk] ...does not amount to understandable communication of any specific real risk."*[45] Is it really enough to inform athletes, particularly minors, of a program's policy in an effort to meet the provider's risk disclosure duties? If not, are the rights of potential victims of infection – not from an infected health care worker, but from another infected participant – greater than the rights of privacy of such an infected athlete? And lastly, do providers have a greater duty – perhaps a duty to warn other athletes like that which was partially addressed in the Hudson case – that will be of paramount concern?

Cases can arise in other sports medicine settings which may impose liability upon providers to third parties who were foreseeable victims of provider patients who harmed those victims due to the negligent act or omission of the providers.[46] If a failure to warn, counsel or advise participants results in foreseeable harm to other known participants, liability to those participants may follow.[47]

The complexity of the legal issues surrounding these matters, when compared and contrasted to the medical, ethical and professional concerns related to the AAP's Policy Statement as well as some emerging court decisions, seem to suggest that the Statement be reconsidered. As it now stands, it may be subject to attack from several perspectives while perhaps failing to provide adequate protection to either participants or providers.

The AIDS problem in this country has created a variety of problems and concerns. These concerns are not medical alone – rather they are a mix of a variety of complex issues involving medicine, ethics and the law. Many of these issues require a multidisciplinary approach for any thorough resolution. In addition, due to the developing nature of information about the disease, the law understandably lags behind and follows the uncovering of scientific and medical knowledge. More questions and issues are sure to arise as time goes on and new developments and discoveries come to light. Other similar statutes have also been published to date by the NCAA,[48] The Michigan Intercollegiate Athletic Association[49] as well as various high school athletic associations.[50]

Given the principal methods of retrovirus disease transmission – sexual contact with an infected individual, infection from contaminated needles or other sharps, contraction of the retrovirus from infected blood or blood products or transmission from an infected mother during birth, it appears that the athletic population consisting principally of young, sexually active individuals (some of whom are users of recreational or performance enhancing drugs) are at some risk of blood exposure, a much smaller risk to participation related exposure to HIV infected blood and an even lesser risk of contraction of infection from such infected blood.[51] At least one case of an infected drug using athlete has been documented in the medical literature,[52] and one other reported case of a collegiate wrestler becoming infected through shared needle use has been reported (the wrestler, once learning of his condition and after counseling with a sports medicine provider, decided not to continue his collegiate wrestling career).[53] One other case of actual transmission of the virus in a contact sport (soccer) has also now been reported.[54] As a result of such occurrences, one must now necessarily conclude that risk of transmission in the sports setting can occur although such a risk must be considered to be remote.

Understanding the prevalence of drug use, including steroid use in the athletic participant population, even among many high school students, it appears certain that some athlete drug users are at risk for contraction of the AIDS retrovirus or may in fact be infected.[55] Moreover, athlete contraction of the retrovirus through the skin or mucous membrane is possible.[56] (The reported infections were of three health-care workers who had direct contact of their skin with infected blood under circumstances where all three had skin lesions which may have been contaminated by the blood and one of which also had a mucous membrane exposure).

Knowing that some individuals are participating in sport, as well as athletic and recreational exercise activities who are infected with the AIDS retrovirus or are at high risk for contraction of same, three questions arise: What if anything should be done to protect others from exposure?; If anything should be done, how should such a response be implemented?; and, What can be done to lawfully develop and implement such procedures?

Obviously those athletes who are participating in a wide variety of contact sports, as well as those engaged in using performance enhancing or recreational drugs by injection are at risk of exposure to infected blood and contraction of the disease. These sports would seem to include boxing, wrestling, judo, karate, football, rugby, lacrosse, soccer, hockey, basketball, baseball and many others. Risk of contraction follows exposure to infected blood. Exposure to infected blood is a possibility of exposure to blood. Some of these listed sports may pose greater risks of blood exposure and possible contraction than others. For example, Calabrese[57] concluded: *"[B]oxing may pose some risk of transmission of blood-borne disease: when one or both boxers receive facial lacerations, there can be significant exposure of mucous membranes [or open wounds] to blood...cut or bruised wrestlers who come into close contact with other wrestlers always pose a significant health hazard."*

Although the risks of exposure in the athletic setting may not be as great as those faced by health care workers, such risks clearly exist; consequently, one must ask, do the risks necessitate mandatory preparticipation or periodic testing,[58] or some action or modification of the rules of participation or play? Given the universal precautions which have been developed heretofore for workplace and health-care workers and those contemplated by OSHA for covered employers and employees, any response should be predicated upon the concept that exposure occurs through blood contact and that all blood is potentially infected.

According to a letter article published in *Lancet,*[59] as previously reviewed herein the first sports participant contraction of HIV, the AIDS retrovirus, in a sports setting may have occurred. The letter article reported that an HIV infected soccer player collided with an opposing team participant during a contested event, resulting in bloody forehead injuries. The other player subsequently contracted an HIV infection attributed to his contact with the infected participant.

While this incident may be the first "evidence" of infection occurring in a sports setting, such risks have not heretofore been overlooked in the literature. In fact, a number of relevant articles have already been published which have recommended the adoption of appropriate policies and procedures to minimize the risks of contraction of the disease in the sports setting.[60]

In light of the predicted incidence of disease infection among sports participants, the possibility of which has now been somewhat confirmed by reason of an actual case of possible infection,[61] programs it would seem, can no longer safely escape claim and litigation related to participant contraction of the disease as a result of participation by simply claiming that such an occurrence was not foreseeable. Programs, clearly have an obligation to develop such policies or face potential claim and litigation related to a failure to do so, in light of clear scientific and now actual evidence which would seem to mandate same. Programs must begin to face this issue and deal with the development of protective policies in accordance with established recommendations or face potentially severe consequences, including the imposition of punitive damages due to willful and wanton omissions to act.[62]

Given the fact that bloody injuries do occur in soccer, although with some degree of low occurrence,[63] the bloody head collision which occurred between the two players in the cited instance which resulted in the infection of the healthy player would certainly seem to have been foreseeable. This incidence may have been avoidable in its entirety if applicable policies and procedures would have been used to govern play either through the use of protective equipment or the exclusion of the infected player from participation.[64]

While decisions to exclude individuals from play must be based upon applicable legal requirements,[65] such a choice has been made to date in at least one case (although the subsequent enactment of the Americans With Disabilities Act may call the issued decision into question).[66] In any event, the adoption of policies and procedures to deal with these potential occurrences is clearly part of the expected and owed standard of care. This may be especially true for those participating in sports when one considers the recent report of the rather quick spread of the AIDS retrovirus through the teenage and young adult population (those age groups from which most athletes come).[67]

Sports programs must come to grip with these issues and begin to address the problem. Further delay and procrastination will only complicate an already difficult situation and expose non-complying agencies to additional legal claims and potentially, punitive damages. Sports medicine physicians have a leadership role to assume in this regard. In fact, the obligation of the sports medicine physician seems clear and must be responsibly undertaken.

The principal risk of infection in sport must be considered to be through open wound and mucous membrane contamination, which in the health-care setting as discussed earlier accounts for 7% and 5% respectively of health care worker exposures. Such exposures do occur in the athletic arena and *"certainly justify re-examination of boxing rules"* and consideration by public health officials *"to exclude individuals from contact sports if they have open or weeping wounds."*[68] To see the need for precautions based upon the scientific and medical evidence to date, all one needs do is watch a boxing, wrestling, judo or karate match, where cuts, bloody noses, scrapes, open wounds, etc. are common-place. There clearly appears to be a risk of exposure and infection. Therefore a response is necessary - but how?

While some athletic commissions (boxing) have implemented universal precaution type requirements for referees and cornermen who must wear rubber gloves during matches,[69] little concern however, except for the implementation of the previously mentioned policies,[70] has been developed to date toward the protection of the athletes as opposed to support personnel. Although the Nevada Athletic Commission announced in early 1988 that it would begin mandating AIDS antibody testing for anyone who boxes in that state,[71] few other organizations have announced or adopted such policies. Some authors have contended that testing is not the answer *("Testing all athletes prior to sports participation is not only impractical but also unethical and unrealistic").*[72] A recent World Health Organization sponsored conference similarly concluded that *"There is no medical or public health justification for testing or screening athletes for HIV infection."*[73] Even the Centers for Disease Control have indicated that *"Routine serologic testing of health-care workers who do not perform invasive procedures...is not recommended...Mandatory screening as a condition for school entry is not warranted based on available data."*[74] Moreover, considering the fact that testing would have to be an ongoing, almost constant procedure to be effective and that the incidence of false positive results as well as the inability to accurately test for a period of time after initial exposure, as well as the potential for breaches of confidentiality, discrimination, etc., it may well be impractical if not impossible to engage in effective testing of athletes. However, such efforts may well be strongly challenged and have been the subject of condemnation by the preceding mentioned standards statements cited herein.[75] The resultant delays could also hamper the development and implementation of more effective methods to deal with the problem.

Based upon the scientific and medical recommendations and guidelines issued to date, and the potentially adverse legal implications associated with mandatory AIDS retrovirus testing programs, it appears that a rather vigorous approach to implementation of universal type precautions in the athletic setting would appear to be a possible solution to the problem. In fact, the development of the Occupational Safety and Health Administration (OSHA) statement on Occupational Exposure To Bloodborne Pathogens which became effective on March 6, 1992, requires the implementation of such practices at least for sports medicine personnel.[76] The approach taken by some boxing commissions for example, will help minimize exposure and possible resultant infection by support personnel from athletes and between athletes coming into contact with the same support personnel – but specific thought needs to be devoted to the protection of athletes from other athletes. Rule changes like those highlighted by Dr. Calabrese[77] may be beneficial, *e.g.,* stopping excessively bloody fights (which perhaps should be stopped for other reasons as well); requiring the wearing of protective headgears (to minimize cutting, contact with open wounds, skin contact, etc.). Other rule changes must also be considered – for example, exclusion of individuals from participation with open cuts or wounds; stopping, either temporarily or finally, contests or participation where individuals begin bleeding during participation – accompanied by adequate disinfection of the participation area as specified by the universal guidelines; requiring a change in participant clothing – perhaps to provide more protection of skin surfaces from inadvertent bleeding occurring during play[78] – allowing a change of uniforms infected with blood; requiring fresh towels for each participant so that blood stained towels are not shared; and other similar precautionary measures – all of which would treat all participants the same and which would not discriminate against any sub-group of athletes.

Applying these thoughts to a particular sport – wrestling for example – rule changes in addition to the foregoing might be considered such as the following:

A) preparticipation and pre-match inspection of wrestler's skin and other body areas for evidence of open cuts, wounds, infectious skin or other conditions which would render the athlete highly susceptible to possible infection in the event of blood spattering or which would promote bleeding;

B) preparticipation or pre-match requirements specifying that all open cuts, wounds, infections and the like be adequately covered or that the individual be excluded from participation;

C) exclusion from participation of those found to have open wounds, cuts or other adverse skin conditions which cannot be adequately covered;

D) careful preparticipation and pre-match examination of finger-nails, singlets, shoes and headgears to minimize sharp areas or objects that could cause cuts or open wounds;

E) consideration of the use of face masks for those who are frequent nose bleeders or those with severe facial skin condi-tions by which infection might be transmitted;

F) consideration of the use of different uniforms by which more skin area is covered rather than not (however, abrasive clothing for wrestlers would seem to be contraindicated for other reasons;[79]

G) strict rule making requiring coaches, trainers and others to utilize fresh protective gloves, fresh towels, fresh water bottles and other equipment for each match to minimize possible contamination between wrestlers of the same team;

H) consideration of match rules providing very strict penalties for moves which tend to precipitate bleeding *e.g.,* aggressive cross facing, head or face slapping, scratches, biting, butting, etc.

While there may be resistance by some to such rule changes or to the adoption of uniform precaution guidelines, the consequences of a failure to act can well cost an athlete not only his success during participation but his life as well - not to mention the claims and suits that will surely arise. Athletic administrators, coaches and all members of the sports medicine team have a duty not only to inform athletes of the risks inherent in participation but to take reasonable measures to protect them as well. Some state athletic associations as previously mentioned have in fact moved forward to develop such rules.

Some have rather vigorously argued that there is a very low likelihood of transmission of the AIDS retrovirus from athlete to athlete, and that the risks of contamination through open wounds or mucous membranes are minuscule, *i.e., "there is no evidence that [an infected]...individual would be a significant risk to his or her teammates or competitors."*[80] While it is true that infection from participation in athletics is not very likely, it appears equally clear that it can happen (and already may have happened). Given the fact that athletes appear to be in a potentially higher risk group than the general population for contraction of the retrovirus (due to the fact that they are young and sexually active and that some participate in intravenous drug use) it appears that some response is necessary and desirable. Mandatory testing may not be morally right or legally possible or desirable. Rule changes should be considered to minimize the chances of blood contamination in addition to vigorous and strict adoption of uniform guideline type requirements. Athletes as well as coaches, trainers and other sports medicine personnel should also be protected. Members of the sports medicine team should consider their unique position to provide information and direction based upon the available medical and scientific evidence to encourage such efforts where appropriate.

FINAL THOUGHT

A number of contemporary matters of medical importance impact the delivery of service in the sports medicine setting. These matters have a number of legal issues associated with them. Members of the sports medicine teams are uniquely situated to provide advice and counseling as well as care delivery as to some of these concerns. However, members of the sports medicine team should not become engulfed in drug testing or other inappropriate matters which may be contrary to the physician-patient/athlete relationship. Sports medicine personnel should be included in developing and implementing policies to manage infectious disease control for sports activities which may become of critical importance to the overall health of athlete/patients in the years to come.

CHAPTER 11 FOOTNOTES:

1. *See,* AAP, POLICY STATEMENT, "Screening for Drugs of Abuse in Children and Adolescents," *AAP News* 9, March, 1989.

2. *Cf.* NCAA, SPORTS MEDICINE HANDBOOK, Fifth Edition, Guidelines 2I, 27 (NCAA, Overland Park, KS 1992).

3. "Physicians License Revoked Due to Prescription of Steroids," *The Sports Medicine Standards and Malpractice Reporter* 6(2):22, 1994.

4. Webb vs. Jarvis, 533 N.E.2d 151 (Ind. App. 1 Dist. 1990).

5. *Id.* at page 153.

6. *Id.* at page 155.

7. *Citing* Duvall vs. Goldin, 139 Mich. App. 342 (1984).

8. *See, supra* footnote 4 at page 155.

9. Hobby Shops, Inc. vs. Drudy, 161 Ind. App. 699 (1974).

10. *See, supra* footnote 4 at page 155.

11. *Id.* at page 156.

12. Webb vs. Jarvis, 575 N.E.2d 992 (Indiana 1991) *analyzed in* "Steroid Prescribing Physician Not Liable," *The Sports Medicine Standards and Malpractice Reporter* 3(4):70, 1991.

13. *See,* Krejci vs. Akron Pediatric Neurology, Inc., 31 Ohio App. 3d 273 (1987).

14. Myers vs. Quesenberry, 193 Cal. App. 733 (Cal. App. 4th Dist., 1983) and Till vs. Weiss, Case No. 86-1150NM, (Macolb County Circuit Court, Michigan, March 22, 1987), *see,* PHYSICIAN'S ALERT: "Physicians May Be Held Liable For Injuries Sustained By Their Patients Where The Physician Has Been Negligent in Certifying An Individual As Under Effective Control Pursuant to State Law," *The Medical Malpractice Defense Reporter* 1(1):12-13, 1987.

15. *See,* "Physician May Have Duty to Third Party Non-Patients: Implications to Sport," *The Sports Medicine Standards and Malpractice Reporter* 5(1):12-13, 1993.

16. *See,* "A Primer for Sports Medicine Risk Management Practices – Preserving the Confidentiality of Records," *The Sports Medicine Standards and Malpractice Reporter* 5(2):20, 1993.

17. Goodman, et al., "Infectious Diseases in Competitive Sports," *JAMA* 271(11):862-867, 1994.

18. South Florida Blood Services vs. Rasmussen, 467 So.2d 798, 802 (Fla. App. 3d 1985).

19. *Id.* at page 800.

20. "Soviet hospital passes AIDS to 27 children, paper says," *The Plain Dealer,* page 5-8, (January 28, 1989).

21. *See,* "Transmission of HIV Infection From A Woman To A Man By Oral Sex - Letter," *New England Journal of Medicine* 320(4): 251, January 26, 1989.

22. *See,* "Passionate Kissing and Microlesions of the Oral Mucosa: Possible Role of AIDS Transmission-Letter," *JAMA* 261(2):244-245, January 13, 1989.

23. *See,* "Spread of AIDS Retro Virus Through General Contact?," *The Sports Medicine Standards and Malpractice Reporter* 2(4):75, 1990.

24. *American Medical News,* January 13, 1989, pages 3-19.

25. Calabrese & Kelley, "AIDS And Athletes," *The Physician and Sportsmedicine* 17(1): 127-132, January 1989 (hereinafter "Calabrese").

26. *Id.* at page 128.

27. *Id.*

28. *Id.*

29. *See,* Kelen, et. al., "Unrecognized Human Immunodeficiency Virus Infection In Emergency Department Patients," *The New England Journal of Medicine* 318:1645-1650, (1988).

30. "Recommendations For Preventing Transmission of HTLV-III/LAV In The Workplace," *MMWR* 34:681-695, (1985).

31. "Update: Human Immunodeficiency Virus Infection In Health-Care Workers Exposed To Blood Of Infected Patients," *MMWR* 36:285-289, (1987).

32. *See,* School Board of Nassau County vs. Arline, 107 S. Ct. 1123 (1987).

33. *See*, "Ohio Civil Rights Commission Press Release and Policy Statement," issued March 25, 1987.

34. *Id.* at page 2.

35. Case No. 87-88-CIV-FTM-17(C} (M)Md. Florida, August 5, 1987, *analyzed in* Drowatzky, "AIDS Victims Participation in Sports," *The Sports, Parks and Recreation Law Reporter* 2(1):1-6, June 1988.

36. U.S. Department of Education, AIDS AND THE EDUCATION OF OUR CHILDREN: A GUIDE FOR PARENTS AND TEACHERS, page 19 (January 1988 3rd printing).

37. Superior Court of New Jersey, Docket No. L88-2550, April 25, 1991.

38. *Id.*

39. Dockets 361 and 362, Pennsylvania Superior Ct., July 30, 1991, *but see,* Diaz-Reyes vs. United States, ____F. Supp. _____, (D. Puerto Rico, July 19, 1991).

40. Case No. B040290 (California Court of Appeals, Second Appellate District, Division 1, June 13, 1991).

41. 40 (RR-8) 1-9, July 12, 1991.

42. *See* Herbert, "Recent AIDS Related Litigation and Developments," *The Medical Malpractice Defense Reporter* 5(1):1-5, 1991.

43. *See,* "Doctors and AIDS," *Newsweek* 48-50, July 1, 1991.

44. See, "AIDS – A Sports Participant Killer," *The Sports Medicine Standards and Malpractice Reporter* 2(3):47-48, 1990 (commenting on Torre, et al., "Transmission of HIV-1 Infection Via Sports Injury," *Lancet* 335:1105, 1990).

45. Hiding vs. Williams, 78 So.2d 1192 (La.App. 5th Circuit, 1991).

46. *See e.g.,* Webb vs. Jarvis, 533 N.E.2d 151 (Ind.App. 1 Dist., 1990) (analyzed in "Third Party Injured by Steroid User May Sue Physician Prescriber," *The Sports Medicine Standards and Malpractice Reporter* 2(3):49-50, 1990, reversed in Webb vs. Jarvis, 575 N.E.2d 992 (Ind. 1991)).

47. *See* Drowatsky, "Tort Law, AIDS and Participation in Sports," *The Sports, Parks and Reporter* 2(4):56-59, 1989; cf. Webb vs. Jarvis, *supra* footnotes 4 and 12.

48. NCAA, SPORTS MEDICINE HANDBOOK, Fifth Edition, Guideline 2H, pages 24-25, 1992.

49. *See,* "The Michigan Intercollegiate Athletic Association Policy on Bloodborne Pathogens," *The Sports Medicine Standards and Malpractice Reporter* 5(2):23-25, 1993.

50. "High School Athletic Associations Begin to Deal with HIV/AIDS in the Sports Setting," *The Sports Medicine Standards and Malpractice Reporter* 5(2):30, 1993.

51. *See, supra* footnote 25, at page 127.

52. Sklarek, et al, "AIDS In A Bodybuilder Using Anabolic Steroids - Letter," *The New England Journal of Medicine* 311:1701 (1984).

53. ETHICAL/MEDICAL/LEGAL ISSUES WORKSHOP, July 18, 1993, sponsored by the American Medical Society for Sports Medicine, Second Annual Meeting, Sun Valley, Idaho.

54. *See,* "AIDS - A Sports Participant Killer?," *The Sports, Parks and Recreational Law Reporter* 2(3):47-48, 1990.

55. *See* Buckley, et al, "Estimated Prevalence Of Anabolic Steroid Use Among Male High School Seniors," *JAMA* 260(23):3441-3445, December 16, 1988; *see also,* Schoenburg, "Extensive Use of Anabolic Steroids In High Schools Revealed In Study," *NCAA News* page 5, December 21, 1988, (indicating that as many as a half million teenage boys may be using anabolic steroids); *see also,* Yesalis, et. al., "Self-Reported Use Of Anabolics - Androgenic Steroids By Elite Power Lifters," *The Physician and Sportmedicine* 16(12):91-100, (December 1988).

56. *Supra* footnote 40, *see also,* CDC "Update: Human Immunodeficiency Virus Infections In Health-Care Workers Exposed To Blood of Infected Patients," *MMWR* 36:285-289, (1987).

57. *See, supra* footnote 25, at page 129.

58. *See* Anderson, et al., SECOND REPLICATION OF A NATIONAL STUDY OF THE SUBSTANCE AND ABUSE HABITS OF COLLEGE STUDENT-ATHLETES, FINAL REPORT, presented to the National Collegiate Athletic Association, July 30, 1993, released to the public, September 1, 1993 (reporting that a majority of collegiate athletes believe that college athletes should be tested for the virus before being allowed to compete in athletics and that those who test positive should not be allowed to compete).

59. Torre, et al., "Transmission of HIV-1 Infection Via Sports Injury," *Lancet* 335:1105, 1990.

60. *See* Drowatzky, "Implications of AIDS in Sports: The Need for Policies and Procedures," *The Sports, Parks and Recreation Law Reporter* 3(3):41-45, 1989; Herbert, "AIDS in Sports," *The Sports, Parks and Recreation Law Reporter* 3(3):46, 1989; Herbert, "The Development of AIDS Guidelines for Sports Programs," *The Sports, Parks and Recreation Law Reporter* 3(1):12-19, 1989; Drowatzky, "Tort Law, AIDS and Participation in Sports," *The Sports, Parks and Recreation Law Reporter* 2(4):56-59, 1989. *See also,* Herbert, "New Sports Medicine Statement: A Look at The New AAP Policy Statement on AIDS in The Athletic Setting," *The Sports Medicine Standards and Malpractice Reporter* 3(4):61, 63-65, 1991.

61. *See, supra* footnote 59.

62. *Cf. see* Rabinoff, "An Examination of Four Recent Cases Against Fitness Instructors," *The Exercise Standards and Malpractice Reporter* 2(3):43-47 (1988), *analyzed in* Jacobson vs. Holiday Health Club, (Civil Action No. A 85CV 1249, Arapahoe County, Colorado, 1986).

63. *See* Fields, "Head Injuries in Soccer," *The Physician and Sportsmedicine* 17(1):69-73, 1989

64. *See also,* Letter of Carolos A. Duran, M.D., reporting a similar two person head-face bleeding incident occurring during a soccer match, *American Medical Soccer Association Newsletter,* June 11, 1990.

65. *See* Drowatzky, "AIDS Victims Participation in Sports," *The Sports, Parks and Recreation Law Reporter* 2(1):1-6, 1988.

66. *See,* Ray vs. School District, Case No. 87-88-CIV-F&M-17(c) M.D. Fla. August 5, 1987.

67. *See* Volker, "Teen Scene is Next Group of New AIDS Cases," *American Medical News,* June 16, 1989; *see also, New York Times,* "AIDS Virus Spreading Rapidly Among Teens," *The Plain Dealer* 14-A, October 8, 1989.

68. *See, supra* footnote 25, at page 129.

69. *Id.*

70. *See, supra* footnotes 36, 37, 38.

71. "Boxing: AIDS?," *JAMA* 259(11): 1613, March 18, 1988.

72. *See, supra* footnote 25 at page 130.

73. "HIV tests for athletes opposed," *American Medical News,* February 24, 1989, page 24.

74. CDC, "Summary: Recommendations for Preventing Transmission of Infection With Human T Lymphotropic Virus Type III/Lymphadenopathy-Associated Virus in the Workplace," *MMWR* 34(45): 681-685, 691-694, at 685, November 15, 1985; *see also,* CDC, "Education And Foster Care Of Children Infected With Human T Lymphotropic Virus Type III/Lymphadenopathy-Associated Virus," *MMWR* 34(34): 517-521, at page 520, August 30, 1985.

75. *But see,* reported views of a majority of college level athletes, *supra* footnote 47.

76. *See,* "The Bloodborne Pathogen Rule," *The Sports Medicine Standards and Malpractice Reporter* 4(4):59, 1992.

77. *See, supra* footnote 25.

78. *But see,* Herbert, "Will Blood Spattering Rules to Protect Against Bloodborne Pathogens Affect Play?," *The 'Sports Medicine Standards and Malpractice Reporter* 5(4):56-57, 1993.

79. *See,* "Abrasive Shorts May Contribute to Herpes Gladiatorum Among Wrestlers-Letter," *The New England Journal of Medicine* 320(9):598-599, March 2, 1989).

80. Landry, AIDS IN SPORTS, page 6 (a publication of the American Coaching Effectiveness Program, Leisure Press/Human Kinetics, Champaign, IL 1989).

12 CONCLUSION

The practice of sports medicine in the United States is becoming more complex as well as diverse, affected by a wide variety of standards of practice and greatly impacted by the operation of the legal system in specific instances. Practitioners who are well informed as to the applicable standards of care as originally developed and as modified over time are likely to be better prepared to deal with not only patient care and the provision of sports medicine services, but the reduction in possible untoward instances of patient injury, claims related thereto and potential litigation. Various techniques can be used by sports medicine health care providers to reduce their risks of claim and suit by a number of common techniques. These techniques as we have reviewed them herein include the following:

1. Utilizing personnel in proper, legally authorized and appropriate roles in carrying out services to athletes and other sports medicine patients;

2. The development of particular program policies and procedures in accordance with national standards of care but tailored to the specific activities and patient population to be served;

3. Adherence to national standards of care in the rendition of services to athletes and others utilizing sports medicine services;

4. The proper use of informed consent, assumption of risk and prospective release documents;

5. Protection of the physician-patient relationship and preservation of the confidentiality of physician-patient information, communications and documents;

6.   The appropriate use of preparticipation examinations and evaluations in accordance with current and emerging standards of care;

7.   The proper rendition of sports medicine services through appropriately authorized personnel at both practice and game activities;

8.   The development and implementation of a medically and ethically appropriate system to deal with sports medicine decisions as to the exclusion from play and re-entry to play of athletes in full accordance with the law and the athlete's paramount right to information from which such decisions must be made, while minimizing the internal conflict between team, coach, athlete/family and physician when making such determinations;

9.   The development of an appropriate and lawful system for dispensing prescription medications to athletes in the absence of team physicians;

10.   The appropriate development of a drug testing and counselling program for athletes which takes into account and preserves the physician-patient relationship with athletes;

11.   The development and implementation of appropriate procedures in accordance with Uniform Guidelines for the handling of infectious and blood-borne diseases and conditions; and,

12.   The implementation and utilization of appropriate risk management techniques for the purposes of reducing a program's on-going liability risks and securing sufficient liability insurance to protect the program and its personnel in those instances where claims and suits are filed related to patient care.

In the last analysis, there can be no absolute protection from claim and suit. However those who have sufficient and relevant information at their disposal can greatly improve their delivery of care to the patient populations which they serve, while also reducing the risks of claim and suit. It is absolutely essential that all sports medicine providers have counsel from knowledgeable legal authorities who are in a position to provide relevant, complete, personal and timely information and advice.

Despite the review of activities or potential situations as outlined in this work which have occurred to date, or which may occur in the future, providers should not be reluctant to carry on this absolutely essential and important service. Professional service in this area is necessary and vital to the patient population to be served.

LEGAL GLOSSARY

AGENCY: A concept in law creating a relationship of principal-agent, master-servant whereby the agent/servant carries out duties for the principal/master. Duties carried out within the scope of authority are attributed to the principal/master who will be responsible for the negligent performance of such duties by the agent/servant, referred to in law as **Respondeat Superior.**

ASSUMPTION OF RISK: Like contributory negligence, assumption of risk can in a proper case, be a total defense to a cause of action upon the basis of negligence. Proof of such a defense requires a showing that a person, with full knowledge and appreciation of all major risks, proceeded with the act and in so doing, assumed the risks associated with the act. Such concepts are now for the most part merged into concepts of comparative negligence.

CAUSE OF ACTION: Right to sue or institute litigation.

CONTRACT: *Syn: Agreement.* A legally effective and supportable document or understanding. Usually a promise or performance bargained for and given in exchange for a promise or performance, supported by adequate consideration (something of value).

CONTRIBUTORY NEGLIGENCE/COMPARATIVE NEGLIGENCE: Negligence of the injured party which wholly or partially caused or contributed to that person's injury, generally brought about by that person's failure to protect himself/herself. In some states, a person's contributory negligence may preclude any recovery on a cause of action predicated upon negligence or malpractice. In other states, contributory negligence may only lessen the amount of damages recovered by such a person. In a growing number of jurisdictions such negligence will often be "compared" with the other party's negligence, and damages awarded only on a proportionate basis. Such a system of damage recovery is referred to as "comparative negligence."

IMMUNITY FROM SUIT RECOVERY: Freedom from damages as a result of suit. Granted sometimes to government, charities or special groups of persons. Broad immunity has been eroded, if not almost totally abrogated, by evolving interpretations of the Constitution, and federal and state statutes due to changing socio-economic and legal factors.

New immunity laws have been granted in many states, however, protecting so-called "good samaritans," volunteers and others who come to the emergency aid of injured parties, or who volunteer their time for others. These laws such persons from successful suit by the injured party in the event of injury, **but only** where the provider did not contribute to or cause the original injury.

INFORMED CONSENT: A voluntary agreement from a legally competent person (adult and mentally fit) who **knows** and **fully** understands all major risks associated with the consent to undergo a particular procedure. In law, determined subjectively, *i.e.,* did this particular person as opposed to a so-called ordinary reasonable man, know and understand, with full knowledge and appreciation of the facts, what risks were associated with the procedure.

LOSS OF CONSORTIUM: A cause of action of a husband or wife for injury to the marital relationship with his or her spouse due to the negligence of some party causing injury to that spouse. It is a separate cause of action, but is associated with the spouse's main cause of action. In some states, a cause of action may be predicated upon a loss of consortium type claim brought by children of the injured party. In this situation, the cause of action amounts to interference with the parent/child relationship and the love and affection inherent in such situations.

MALPRACTICE: Negligence of a certain defined professional, *e.g.,* physicians, dentists, attorneys, architects, accountants (exercise specialists, trainers, other members of the sports medicine team???)

NEGLIGENCE: Failure to conform one's conduct to a generally accepted standard or duty. Standard or duty may be established by law, *e.g.,* traffic laws (everyone must stop at red light), or by facts (specialty situations such as airplane crashes or "sponge left in body" situations where proof of facts automatically and presumptively establishes, simultaneously, duty and breach thereof), or by expert opinion, professional guidelines or standards.

NEGLIGENCE AS A CAUSE OF ACTION: One's failure to exercise due care to protect another person to whom the former owed a duty or responsibility where the failure proximately caused injury to the latter person.

RELEASE: A form of contract by which one person gives up certain rights or claims in exchange for a promise or performance, such as monetary payment. Generally, in medical or quasi-medical settings releases may not be effectively given prospectively or without adequate consideration. Usually, releases are given to settle claims or lawsuits based upon such claims.

THE PRACTICE OF MEDICINE: Diagnosis of an individual's symptoms to determine what disease or ailment he is afflicted with, and then to determine, upon the basis of that information, what remedy or treatment that should be given or prescribed to treat or correct his disease. Universally defined by law, *see, e.g.,* Ohio Revised Code §4731.34: *"A person shall be regarded as practicing medicine...who examines or diagnoses for compensation of any kind, or prescribes, advises or recommends, administers or dispenses for compensation of any kind, direct or indirect, a drug or medicine, appliance mold or cast, application, operation or treatment, of whatever nature, for the care or relief of a wound,* *fracture or bodily injury, infirmity or disease...* "*Note:* Such statutes are very broadly written, all-encompassing, and are usually interpreted in like fashion by the courts.

TORT: An actionable wrong.

UNAUTHORIZED PRACTICE OF MEDICINE: The practice of medicine by an unlicensed individual. Generally a crime, usually a misdemeanor punishable by fine and/or incarceration in a penal institution for less than one year.

SAMPLE FORMS AND DOCUMENTS

Form Notation: No form or procedure should ever be adopted or initiated for sports medicine activities without individualized legal and professional assistance. The law varies from state to state and develops over time. It is dependent upon matters of fact and judgment – As a consequence, legal and other professional advice is absolutely necessary.

INFORMED CONSENT FOR EXERCISE TESTING
OF APPARENTLY HEALTHY ADULTS
(without known heart disease)

Name _____

1. *Purpose and Explanation of Test*

I hereby consent to voluntarily engage in an exercise test to determine my circulatory and respiratory fitness. I also consent to the taking of samples of my exhaled air during exercise to properly measure my oxygen consumption. I also consent, if necessary, to have a small blood sample drawn by needle from my arm for blood chemistry analysis and to the performance of lung function and body fat (skin fold pinch) tests. It is my understanding that the information obtained will help me evaluate future physical activities and sports activities in which I may engage.

Before I undergo the test, I certify to the program that I am in good health and have had a physical examination conducted by a licensed medical physician within the last _____ months. Further, I hereby represent and inform the program that I have completed the pre-test history interview presented to me by the program staff and have provided correct responses to the questions as indicated on the history form or as supplied to the interviewer. It is my understanding that I will be interviewed by a physician or other person prior to my undergoing the test who will in the course of interviewing me determine if there are any reasons which would make it undesirable or unsafe for me to take the test. Consequently, I understand that it is important that I provide complete and accurate responses to the interviewer and recognize that my failure to do so could lead to possible unnecessary injury to myself during the test.

The test which I will undergo will be performed on a motor driven treadmill or bicycle ergometer with the amount of effort gradually increasing. As I understand it, this increase in effort will continue until I feel and verbally report to the operator any symptoms such as fatigue, shortness of breath or chest discomfort which may appear. It is my understanding, and I have been clearly advised, that it is my right to request that a test be stopped at any point if I feel unusual discomfort or fatigue. I have been advised that I should immediately upon experiencing any such symptoms or if I so choose, inform the operator that I wish to stop the test at that or any other point. My wishes in this regard shall be absolutely carried out.

It is further my understanding that prior to beginning the test, I will be connected by electrodes and cables to an electrocardiographic recorder which will enable the program personnel to monitor my cardiac (heart) activity. During the test itself, it is my understanding that a trained observer will monitor my responses continuously and take frequent readings of blood pressure, the electrocardiogram, and my expressed feelings of effort. I realize that a true determination of my exercise capacity depends on progressing the test to the point of my fatigue.

Once the test has been completed, but before I am released from the test area, I will be given special instructions about showering and recognition of certain symptoms which may appear within the first 24 hours after the test. I agree to follow these instructions and promptly contact the program personnel or medical providers if such symptoms develop.

2. Risks

It is my understanding, and I have been informed, that there exists the possibility of adverse changes during the actual test. I have been informed that these changes could include abnormal blood pressure, fainting, stroke, disorders of heart rhythm, and very rare instances of stroke, heart attack or even death. Every effort I have been told, will be made to minimize these occurrences by preliminary examination and by precautions and observations taken during the test. I have also been informed that emergency equipment and personnel are readily available to deal with these unusual situations should they occur. I understand that there is a risk of injury, stroke, heart attack or even death as a result of my performance of this test but knowing those risks, it is my desire to proceed to take the test as herein indicated.

3. Benefits to be Expected and Alternatives Available to the Exercise Testing Procedure

The results of this test may or may not benefit me. Potential benefits relate mainly to my personal motives for taking the test, *i.e.,* knowing my exercise capacity in relation to the general population, understanding my fitness for certain sports and recreational activities, planning my physical conditioning program or evaluating the effects of my recent physical activity habits. Although my fitness might also be evaluated by alternative means, *e.g.,* a bench step test or an outdoor running test, such tests do not provide as accurate a fitness assessment as the treadmill or bike test nor do those options allow equally effective monitoring of my responses.

4. *Confidentiality and Use of Information*

I have been informed that the information which is obtained in this exercise test will be treated as privileged and confidential and will consequently not be released or revealed to any person without my express written consent. I do however agree to the use of any information for research or statistical purposes, so long as same does not provide facts which could lead to the identification of my person. Any other information obtained however, will be used only by the program staff to evaluate my exercise status or needs.

5. *Inquiries and Freedom of Consent*

I have been given an opportunity to ask questions as to the procedure. Generally these requests which have been noted by the testing staff and their responses are as follows:

_____

_____

_____

_____

I further understand that there are also other remote risks that may be associated with this procedure.

I acknowledge that I have read this document in its entirety or that it has been read to me if I have been unable to read same.

I consent to the rendition of all services and procedures as explained herein by all program personnel.

Date_____

Patient's Signature

_____

Witness' Signature

_____

Test Supervisor's Signature

Alternative Form:
INFORMED CONSENT FOR
EXERCISE TESTING PROCEDURES
OF APPARENTLY HEALTHY ADULTS

Name _____

1. *Purpose and Explanation of Test*

It is my understanding that I will undergo a test to be performed on a motor driven treadmill or bicycle ergometer with the amount of effort gradually increasing. As I understand it, this increase in effort will continue until I feel and verbally report to the operator any symptoms such as fatigue, shortness of breath or chest discomfort which may appear or until the test is completed or otherwise terminated. It is my understanding and I have been clearly advised that it is my right to request that a test be stopped at any point if I feel unusual discomfort or fatigue. I have been advised that I should immediately upon experiencing any such symptoms or if I so choose, inform the operator that I wish to stop the test at that or any other point. My stated wishes in this regard shall be carried out. **IF CORRECT AND YOU AGREE AND UNDERSTAND, INITIAL HERE** _____.

It is further my understanding that prior to beginning the test, I will be connected by electrodes and cables to an electrocardiographic recorder which will enable the program personnel to monitor my cardiac (heart) activity. During the test itself, it is my understanding that a trained observer will monitor my responses continuously and take frequent readings of blood pressure, the electrocardiogram and my expressed feelings of effort. I realize that a true determination of my exercise capacity depends on progressing the test to a point of my fatigue. Once the test has been completed, but before I am released from the test area, I will be given special instructions about showering and recognition of certain symptoms which may appear within the first 24 hours after the test. I agree to follow these instructions and promptly contact the program personnel or medical providers if such symptoms develop. **IF CORRECT AND YOU AGREE AND UNDERSTAND, INITIAL HERE** _____.

Before I undergo the test, I certify to the program that I am in good health and have had a physical examination conducted by a licensed medical physician within the last _____ months. Further, I hereby represent and inform the program that I have accurately completed the pre-test history interview presented to me by the program staff and have provided correct responses to the questions as indicated on the history form or as supplied to the interviewer. It is my understanding that I will be interviewed by a physician or other person prior to my undergoing the test who will, in the course of interviewing me, determine if there are any reasons which would make it undesirable or unsafe for me to take the test. Consequently, I understand that it is important that I provide complete and accurate responses to the interviewer and recognize that my failure to do so could lead to possible unnecessary injury to myself during the test. **IF CORRECT, AND YOU AGREE, INITIAL HERE _____.**

2. *Risks*

It is my understanding and I have been informed that there exists the possibility of adverse changes during the actual test. I have been informed that these changes could include abnormal blood pressure, fainting, disorders of heart rhythm, and very rare instances of heart attack or even death. I have also been informed that aside from the foregoing other risks exist. These risks include, but are not necessarily limited to the possibility of stroke, or other cerebrovascular incident or occurrence, mental, physiological, motor, visual or hearing injuries, deficiencies, difficulties or disturbances, partial or total paralysis, slips, falls, or other unintended loss of balance or bodily movement related to the exercise treadmill (or bicycle ergometer) which may cause muscular, neurological, orthopedic or other bodily injury as well as a variety of other possible occurrences, any one of which could conceivably, however remotely, cause bodily injury, impairment, disability or death. Any procedure such as this one carries with it some risk however unlikely or remote. THERE ARE ALSO OTHER RISKS OF INJURY, IMPAIRMENT, DISABILITY, DISFIGUREMENT, AND EVEN DEATH. **I ACKNOWLEDGE AND AGREE TO ASSUME ALL RISKS. IF YOU UNDERSTAND AND AGREE, INITIAL HERE _____.**

Every effort I have been told, will be made to minimize these occurrences by preliminary examination and by precautions and observations taken during the test. I have also been informed that emergency equipment and personnel are readily available to deal with these unusual situations should they occur.

Knowing and understanding all risks, it is my desire to proceed to take the test as herein described. **IF CORRECT, AND YOU AGREE AND UNDERSTAND, INITIAL HERE _____.**

3. *Benefits to be Expected and Alternatives Available to the Exercise Testing Procedure*

I understand and have been told that the results of this test may or may not benefit me. Potential benefits relate mainly to my personal motives for taking the test., *i.e.,* knowing my exercise capacity in relation to the general population, understanding my fitness for certain sports and recreational activities, planning my physical conditioning program or evaluating the effects of my recent physical activity habits. Although my fitness might also be evaluated by alternative means, *e.g.,* a bench step test or an outdoor running test, such tests do not provide as accurate a fitness assessment as the treadmill or bike test nor do those options allow equally effective monitoring of my responses. **IF YOU UNDERSTAND, INITIAL HERE _____.**

4. *Consent*

I hereby consent to voluntarily engage in an exercise test to determine my circulatory and respiratory fitness. I also consent to the taking of samples of my exhaled air during exercise to properly measure my oxygen consumption. I also consent, if necessary, to have a small blood sample drawn by needle from my arm for blood chemistry analysis and to the performance of lung function and body fat (skinfold pinch) tests. It is my understanding that the information obtained will help me evaluate future physical fitness and sports activities in which I may engage. **IF CORRECT AND YOU AGREE, INITIAL HERE _____.**

5. *Confidentiality and Use of Information*

I have been informed that the information which is obtained in this exercise test will be treated as privileged and confidential and will consequently not be released or revealed to any person without my express written consent. I do however agree, to the use of any information for research or statistical purposes, so long as same does not provide facts which could lead to the identification of my person. Any other information obtained however, will be used only by the program staff to evaluate my exercise status or needs. **IF YOU AGREE, INITIAL HERE _____.**

6. *Inquires and Freedom of Consent*

I have been given an opportunity to ask questions as to the procedures. Generally these requests which have been noted by the testing staff and their responses are as follows:

**IF THIS NOTATION IS COMPLETE AND CORRECT,
INITIAL HERE _____.**

I acknowledge that I have read this document in its entirety or that it has been read to me if I have been unable to read same.

I consent to the rendition of all services and procedures as explained herein by all program personnel.

Date: _____

_____
Witness' Signature

_____
Participant's Signature

_____
Witness' Signature

_____
Spouse's Consent

_____
Test Supervisor's Signature

INFORMED CONSENT FOR PARTICIPATION
IN AN EXERCISE PROGRAM
FOR APPARENTLY HEALTHY ADULTS
(without known or suspected heart disease)

Name_____

1. *Purpose and Explanation of Procedure*

I hereby consent to voluntarily engage in an acceptable plan of exercise conditioning. I also give consent to be placed in program activities which are recommended to me for improvement of my general health and well-being. These may include dietary counseling, stress reduction, and health education activities. The levels of exercise which I will perform will be based upon my cardiorespiratory (heart and lungs) fitness as determined through my recent laboratory graded exercise evaluation. I will be given exact instructions regarding the amount and kind of exercise I should do. I agree to participate three times per week in the formal program sessions. Professionally trained personnel will provide leadership to direct my activities, monitor my performance, and otherwise evaluate my effort. Depending upon my health status, I may or may not be required to have my blood pressure and heart rate evaluated during these sessions to regulate my exercise within desired limits. I understand that I am expected to attend every session and to follow staff instructions with regard to exercise, diet, stress management, and smoking cessation. If I am taking prescribed medications, I have already so informed the program staff and further agree to so inform them promptly of any changes which my doctor or I have made with regard to use of these. I will be given the opportunity for periodic assessment with laboratory evaluations at 6 months after the start of my program. Should I remain in the program thereafter, additional evaluations will generally be given at 12 month intervals. The program may change the foregoing schedule of evaluations, if this is considered desirable for health reasons.

I have been informed that during my participation in exercise, I will be asked to complete the physical activities unless symptoms such as fatigue, shortness of breath, chest discomfort or similar occurrences appear. At that point, I have been advised it is my complete right to decrease or stop exercise and that it is my obligation to inform the program personnel of my symptoms. I hereby state that I have been so advised and agree to inform the program personnel of my symptoms, should any develop.

I understand that during the performance of exercise, a trained observer will periodically monitor my performance and, perhaps measure my pulse, blood pressure or assess my feelings of effort for the purposes of monitoring my progress. I also understand that the observer may reduce or stop my exercise program, when any of these findings so indicate that this should be done for my safety and benefit.

2. *Risks*

It is my understanding, and I have been informed, that there exists the remote possibility during exercise of adverse changes including abnormal blood pressure, fainting, disorders of heart rhythm, and very rare instances of stroke, heart attack or even death. Every effort I have been told, will be made to minimize these occurrences by proper staff assessment of my condition before each exercise session, staff supervision during exercise and by my own careful control of exercise efforts. I have also been informed that emergency equipment and personnel are readily available to deal with unusual situations should these occur. I understand that there is a risk of injury, stroke, heart attack or even death as a result of my exercise, but knowing those risks, it is my desire to participate as herein indicated.

3. *Benefits to be Expected and Alternatives Available to Exercise*

I understand that this program may or may not benefit my physical fitness or general health. I recognize that involvement in the exercise sessions will allow me to learn proper ways to perform conditioning exercises, use fitness equipment and regulate physical effort. These experiences should benefit me by indicating how my physical limitations may affect my ability to perform various physical activities. I further understand that if I closely follow the program instructions, that I will likely improve my exercise capacity after a period of 3-6 months.

4. *Confidentiality and Use of Information*

I have been informed that the information which is obtained in this exercise program will be treated as privileged and confidential and will consequently not be released or revealed to any person without my express written consent. I do however agree to the use of any information which is not personally identifiable with me for research and statistical purposes so long as same does not identify my person or provide facts which could lead to my identification. Any other information obtained however, will be used only by the program staff in the course of prescribing exercise for me and evaluating my progress in the program.

5. *Inquiries and Freedom of Consent*

I have been given an opportunity to ask certain questions as to the procedures of this program. Generally these requests which have been noted by the interviewing staff member and his/her responses are as follows:

_____

_____

I further understand that there are also other remote risks that may be associated with this program.

I acknowledge that I have read this document in its entirety or that it has been read to me if I have been unable to read same.

I consent to the rendition of all services and procedures as explained herein by all program personnel.

Date:_____   _____
                      Participant's Signature

_____
Witness' Signature

_____
Test Supervisor's Signature

ALTERNATIVE CLAUSES TO BE ADDED IF APPROPRIATE TO INFORMED CONSENT FORMS OR PROGRAM ADMISSION FORMS

1) *Anxious Patient - Additional Spousal Consent*

I have been informed by _____, that a full disclosure of all known risks associated with the procedure to be performed by my spouse has not been given to my spouse because in the professional opinion and judgment of _____such a disclosure would have adverse consequences to my spouse and would expose my spouse to an increased risk while undergoing the procedure due to his/her anxiety and nervousness as to the procedure itself and the risks involved with treatment procedures. Consequently, I have been informed by _____of the following risks which were not disclosed to my spouse:

_____
_____
_____

It is my agreement and consent that despite these risks, and that lack of full communication of same to my spouse that the procedure be carried out as to my spouse inasmuch as _____has explained to me that the following benefits may be derived from the procedure: _____

_____
_____
_____

I agree with the assessment of _____, that further explanation as to the details of the test would undoubtedly cause increased anxiety and stress in my spouse and as a consequence thereof, I believe that no further disclosure should be made to my spouse and that the test procedure should be performed as previously described.

2) *Prospective Release Claims*

In consideration of my admission to this program, I do hereby agree to assume all risks of injury or death to myself while using the program's facilities and equipment. I represent that I am completely aware of all risks and hazards inherent in my participation in the program. I agree that the program and personnel shall not be liable for any dangers arising from personal injury or death to myself even if such injuries or death shall be caused by the negligence of the program of any of its agents. I agree to and do hereby release the program and all of its personnel and agents, successors and assigns from any and all damages, demands, claims, causes of action, present or future, disclosed or undisclosed, anticipated or unanticipated, caused by or resulting from the negligence of the program or any of its employees or agents or otherwise and arising out of my use or attempted use of any of the progam's facilities or equipment.

This agreement shall be binding upon the undersigned and my heirs, executors, and administrators.

3) *Severability Clause for Use With Prospective Release Form Containing Exculpatory Language*

In the event that any court should conclude that any portion of this document is unenforceable or void, such a determination shall not affect the remaining provisions of the document which shall survive such a declaration.

4) *Release of Information Clause*

I agree to allow the program to take my photograph or photographs either while I am at rest or while exercising or performing any activity with the program. I further agree to allow the program to use any of my photographs for publicity purposes to advertise the program. I also agree to the use of any likeness of myself in connection therewith and to the disclosure of my name, address, age and other personal information in connection therewith.

5) *Additional Language for Informed Consents for Patients In Those Jurisdictions Where Children May Have a Separate Cause of Action for Loss of Parental Consortium*

I (We), the undersigned participant (and spouse of the participant) do hereby agree to indemnify and hold the program and its personnel absolutely harmless from any and all claims, causes of actions, or damages which may be sought or assessed against the program or its personnel by reason of any claim or demand or suit brought by my estate or by my (our) heirs or children as a result of any claimed injuries to me or as the result of any claimed interference with the relationship of parent and child. I (We) agree to indemnify the program and its personnel against all costs, fees, including attorney fees, damages and expenses of any kind by reason of any claims or suits brought or threatened as aforesaid.

INFORMED CONSENT/PARTICIPANT'S SPOUSE

Date_____

    I, the undersigned spouse of _____, do hereby voluntarily agree and consent to my spouse's participation in an exercise testing/training program conducted by the personnel of _____. It is my understanding that this procedure shall be designed to test and study my spouse's physical condition for the following purposes:

_____

_____

_____

    I have been fully and completely informed by program personnel as to the possibilities of physical risk to my spouse inherent in the testing procedure and the exercise program which risks have been explained to me as follows:

_____

_____

_____

    I have been given an opportunity to ask questions regarding the procedures to be utilized in the course of the exercise test and/or exercise program. I hereby affirm and ratify that all questions have been answered to my satisfaction and that all the information as to this matter which I desire to receive prior to my execution of this consent as to my spouse's participation in the program has been communicated to me. I further represent that I have read my spouse's informed consent and completely understand same.

Witness:

_____

Spouse's Signature

_____

Witness' Signature

Date:_____

AGREEMENT AND RELEASE OF LIABILITY

1. In consideration of gaining membership or being allowed to participate in the activities and programs of _____ and to use its facilities, equipment and machinery in addition to the payment of any fee or charge, I do hereby waive, release and forever discharge _____ and its officers, agents, employees, representatives, executors, and all others from any and all responsibilities or liability for injuries or damages resulting from my participation in any activities or my use of equipment or machinery in the above mentioned facilities or arising out of my participation in any activities at said facility. I do also hereby release all of those mentioned and any others acting upon their behalf from any responsibility or liability for any injury or damage to myself, including those caused by the negligent act or omission of any of those mentioned or others acting on their behalf or in any way arising out of or connected with my participation in any activities of _____ or the use of any equipment at _____. **(Please initial _____).**

2. I understand and am aware that strength, flexibility and aerobic exercise, including the use of equipment is a potentially hazardous activity. I also understand that fitness activities involve a risk of injury and even death, and that I am voluntarily participating in these activities and using equipment and machinery with knowledge of the dangers involved. I hereby agree to expressly assume and accept any and all risks of injury or death.
    (Please initial _____).

3. I do hereby further declare myself to be physically sound and suffering from no condition, impairment, disease, infirmity or other illness that would prevent my participation in any of the activities and programs of _____ or use of equipment or machinery except as hereinafter stated. I do hereby acknowledge that I have been informed of the need for a physician's approval for my participation in an exercise/fitness activity or in the use of exercise equipment and machinery. I also acknowledge that it has been recommended that I have a yearly or more frequent physical examination and consultation with my physician as to physical activity, exercise and use of exercise and training equipment so that I might have recommendations concerning these fitness activities and equipment use. I acknowledge that I have either had

a physical examination and have been given my physician's permission to participate, or that I have decided to participate in activity and/or use of equipment and machinery without the approval of my physician and do hereby assume all responsibility for my participation and activities, and utilization of equipment and machinery in my activities.

_____   _____

Date   Signature

MEDICAL APPROVAL

_____ has medical approval to

participate in fitness programs and in the use of _____

_____ equipment and machinery at

_____. The following restrictions

apply (if none, so state):

_____

_____

_____

_____

_____

Physician's Signature

_____

Physician's Name

_____

Address

_____

_____

Date

EMERGENCY MEDICAL
AUTHORIZATION IDENTIFICATION

I, (We), the undersigned, am(are) the father and mother of
_____, minor(s).

CONSENT

We hereby give consent, in the event I/We cannot be contacted within a reasonable time, for: (1) the administration of any treatment deemed necessary for our children by Dr. _____, or any of his associates, the preferred physician, or Dr. _____ _____, or any of his associates, the preferred dentist, or in the event the appropriate preferred practitioner is not available, by another licensed, qualified physician or dentist; and (2) the transfer of any of our children to _____ Hospital, the preferred hospital, or any hospital reasonably accessible.

MAJOR SURGERY

This authorization does not cover non-emergency major surgery unless the medical opinions of two other licensed physicians or dentists concurring in the necessity for such surgery are obtained prior to the performance of such surgery and unless all reasonable attempts to contact us have been unsuccessful, defining such period for non-emergency surgery as 24 hours.

MEDICAL DATA

The following is needed by any hospital or practitioner not having access to our children's medical history:

Allergies: _____

Medication Being Taken: _____

Physical Impairments: _____

Other pertinent facts to which physician should be alerted:

_____

Medical Insurance Coverage: _____

We, the undersigned parents, also do by these premises appoint and constitute _____ and _____ and/or _____ as temporary custodians of our children above mentioned, for the period of _____, 19____, THROUGH AND INCLUDING _____, 19____, and do hereby authorize them to obtain any x-ray examination, anesthesia, medical or surgical diagnosis or treatment, and hospital care to be rendered to our children in our absence, under the general or special supervision, and on the advice of a licensed physician, surgeon, anesthesiologist, dentist or other qualified personnel acting under their supervision

WITNESSES:

_____   _____

_____   _____

STATE OF _____
                    SS:
_____ COUNTY

Before me, a Notary Public in and for said County and State, personally appeared the above-named _____ and _____, who acknowledged that they did sign the foregoing instrument and that the same is their free act and deed.

IN TESTIMONY WHEREOF, I have hereunto set my hand to this, and affixed my official seal, at _____, _____, this _____ day of _____, 19___.

_____
Notary Public

ATHLETIC CLUB REGISTRATION

Athlete's Full Name: _____

Addess: _____

Age: _____ Weight: _____ Phone No.: _____

School: _____ Grade Next Sept.: _____

Father's Full Name: _____

Address: _____

City: _____ State: _____ Zip: _____

Mother's Full Name: _____

Address: _____

City: _____ State: _____ Zip: _____

Do Parents Carry Hospitalization? _____ YES _____ NO

THIS CLUB DOES NOT CARRY MEDICAL INSURANCE FOR PARTICI-PANTS. THE PARTICIPANT'S PARENTS AND/OR LEGAL GUARDIAN ASSUME ALL RESPONSIBILITY FOR SAID INSURANCE

CONSENT TO PARTICIPATE, RELEASE, WAIVER OF LIABILITY AND INDEMNITY AGREEMENT

In consideration of your acceptance of the undersigned athlete into the athletic program, we the undersigned, with the intent to be legally bound, do for ourselves, our heirs, executors, administrators and all others claiming by or through us, or as a result of any claim related to the athlete's participation in the\club's activities or programs, do hereby state that we the undersigned consent to the participant's participation in the activities and that we are aware of **all** risks, hazards and uncertainties connected with participation in the programs and activities of the Club, and do hereby waive, release and discharge the Club, and all of its officers, directors, officials, coaches, employees, volunteers, umpires and any other individuals acting for or on behalf of the Club, from any and all claims while participating in, traveling to, or from or competing in any of the activities or functions of the Club or those it attends. It is the undersigned's specific intent to release, acquit and forever discharge the Club all of its officers, directors, officials, coaches, employees, volunteers, umpires and any other individuals acting for or on behalf of the Club, from all claims, demands, actions, causes of action, and for all liability for injury, damage or loss of whatsoever kind, nature or description that may arise or be sustained by the participant which is due in any way or connected in any way with the participants participation in the Club or any of its functions or activities. It is further our specific intent that this release apply to any injury, damage or claims arising from any act or omission of the Club or any of the individuals released hereby including any injury, damage or claim arising from any negligent act or negligent omission of such organization or individuals.

The participant and the undersigned hereby assume full responsibility for all risk of bodily injury, death or property damage due to the negligent or other conduct of those parties released hereby or otherwise, as a result of any activities connected in any way with the Club. The undersigned on behalf of the participant and for themselves, and all of their heirs, executors and administrators and all others, do hereby further covenant not to sue the Club or any of the individuals released hereby in the event of any injury or damage of any kind or description whatsoever and should any such suit or claim be instituted at any time, including any claim, demand or suit by the minor participant either before he reaches the age of majority or thereafter, the undersigned do hereby further agree to indemnify and hold the Club, and all of those individuals released hereby, completely and absolutely harmless from all expenses, demands, claims, fees, and costs of whatever description or nature which may arise as the result of any such claims being instituted at any time including all costs, fees and expenses involved in defending or investigating any and all claims, demands or causes of action whatsoever that may hereafter be asserted or brought by the participant or anyone on his or her behalf for the purpose of enforcing any claim for damages on account of any injuries or damages sustained during participation in any of the activities of the Club.

EMERGENCY MEDICAL AUTHORIZATION

We, the undersigned, do hereby consent and authorize any duly authorized doctor, emergency medical technician, hospital or other medical facility to treat or attempt to treat the participant for any injuries received by said participant while he participates in any activity of the Club, or while traveling to or from or competing in any Club activity. We further authorize any licensed physician to perform any procedure which he or she deems advisable in attempting to treat or relieve any injuries or any related unhealthy conditions in said participant that may be encountered during any necessary procedure or operation. We further consent to the administration of any anesthesia as deemed advisable by any licensed physician, and do hereby further authorize any x-ray examination, medical or surgical diagnosis or treatment, and hospital care to be rendered to the participant in our absence under the general or special supervision and on the advice of a licensed physician, surgeon, anesthesiologist, dentist or other qualified personnel acting under their supervision.

We, the undersigned, realize and appreciate that there is a possibility of complication and unforeseen consequence in any medical treatment, and we assume any such risk on behalf of ourselves and the participant as stated herein. We acknowledge that there has been no warranty made as to the results of any such treatment or diagnostic procedure.

Each of the undersigned expressly acknowledge and agree that they have read and understood the terms of this form, including the CONSENT TO PARTICIPATE, RELEASE, WAIVER OF LIABILITY AND INDEMNITY AGREEMENT coupled with the EMERGENCY MEDICAL AUTHORIZATION and further state that no oral representations, statements or inducements apart from the foregoing written provisions have been made.

WE HAVE READ, UNDERSTOOD AND VOLUNTARILY SIGNED THIS RELEASE.

_____   _____
Parent or Guardian   Parent or Guardian

_____   _____
Athlete-Participant   Date

EXPRESS ASSUMPTION OF RISK
FOR MY PARTICIPATION IN
ATHLETICS AND RELEASE OF LIABILITY

We, the undersigned, hereby expressly and affirmatively state that we wish for the undersigned athlete to participate in school sponsored athletic events, including practice and game participation in various athletic contests, including *e.g.,* football. We realize that the undersigned athlete's participation in these activities involves risk of injury including but not limited to any injuries which may arise from participation, including reinjury or aggravation to an injury which was recently suffered by the undersigned athlete consisting of a_____. We understand that his/her participation in practice, conditioning, exercise and other activities, including game participation, involves further risk of injury including serious and disabling injuries which may arise due to his/her participation in these activities. We further understand, recognize and agree that the team physicians who have treated him/her have not released him/her to participate. We the undersigned specifically request that the individual athlete be allowed to participate in all athletic activities including conditioning, participation in practice, and actual game competition in athletics including *e.g.,* football, knowing and understanding that there are substantial and serious risks associated with his/her participation, especially in light of his/her recent injury which has not healed or progressed to the point that his/her physicians have agreed to release him/her for participation. We acknowledge and understand that the risks of injury and aggravation of injury and other risks may adversely affect his/her present and future state of health, present and future achievements and opportunities in athletics and otherwise, and present and future vocational and employment opportunities.

Knowing and understanding all of the risks including those mentioned herein, which we realize are not all inclusive, it is our desire that the undersigned athlete proceed to participate in all athletic events sponsored by the Board of Education despite the risks and possibilities of injury.

In consideration of the undersigned athlete being allowed to participate under these circumstances, in the activities and programs of the Board of Education, we, the undersigned, do hereby expressly waive, release and forever discharge the Board of Education, and all of its principals, officers and agents including coaches, employees, physicians, trainers and other individuals involved in rendering any service whatsoever to said program and their respective successors and assigns, heirs, executors and administrators, from and against any and all responsibility for any injuries or damages resulting from his/her participation in any activities sponsored by or carried on by the above-mentioned parties who are hereby released. We, the undersigned, do hereby release all of those mentioned and any others acting upon their behalf from any and all responsibility for any injury or damage to him/her including those caused by any negligent act or omission which arises out of or is in any way connected with his/her participation in any of the activities of the said Board of Education.

In the event that the undersigned athlete ever attempts to disaffirm or set aside this agreement, or institute any claim or suit against the parties hereby released, the undersigned parents shall indemnify, defend and hold those parties released hereby absolutely harmless from and against any and all such claims, suits, causes of action, demands, damages, monies, costs, fees, expenses, attorney fees and judgments which may be sought or obtained by said athlete against the parties hereby released.

We do hereby voluntarily sign this assumption of risk agreement and release of liability this _____ day of _____, 19____. We have had an opportunity to ask questions and fully understand and appreciate the legal effect of signing this document. It is our specific understanding that by signing this document we will be giving up our right to hold any party hereby released responsible for any liability for any cause for any present, past or future harm to the undersigned athlete including any such harm caused by any negligent act or omission.

We, the undersigned, are all of full age, sound mind and memory and taking no medication or other substance that would impair our ability to read and understand this document. Furthermore, we indicate that we have read and understand this document and agree to proceed as stated. This agreement shall be binding upon the individuals and their respective heirs, executors, administrators and assigns.

Signed in the presence of:

_____   _____
                                        Athlete

_____   _____
                                        Parent

                                        _____
                                        Parent

STATE OF _____, _____ COUNTY, SS:

_____ being first duly sworn, deposes and states that he is the father of _____ and that he did sign the forgoing instrument and that the same is his free act and deed.

   IN WITNESS WHEREOF, I have hereunto set my hand and affixed my official seal at _____, _____, this _____ day of _____, 19_____.

                                        _____
                                        Notary Public

STATE OF _____, _____ COUNTY, SS:

_____ being first duly sworn, deposes and states that she is the mother of _____ and that she did sign the forgoing instrument and that the same is her free act and deed.

   IN WITNESS WHEREOF, I have hereunto set my hand and affixed my official seal at _____, _____, this _____ day of _____, 19_____.

                                        _____
                                        Notary Public

STATE OF _____, _____ COUNTY, SS:

_____ being first duly sworn, deposes and states that he/she did sign the forgoing instrument and that the same is his/her free act and deed.

IN WITNESS WHEREOF, I have hereunto set my hand and affixed my official seal at _____, _____, this _____ day of _____, 19_____.

_____
Notary Public

SELECTED REFERENCES

BOOKS:

AACVPR, GUIDELINES FOR CARDIAC REHABILITATION PROGRAMS (Human Kinetics, Champaign, IL 1991).

AAP, RECOMMENDATIONS FOR PARTICIPATION IN COMPETITIVE SPORTS (American Academy of Pediatrics, Elk Grove, IL 1988).

AAP, SCHOOL HEALTH: A GUIDE FOR HEALTH PROFESSIONALS (American Academy of Pediatrics, Elk Grove, IL 1987).

AAP, SPORTS MEDICINE: HEALTH CARE FOR YOUTH ATHLETES (American Academy of Pediatrics, Elk Grove, IL 1983).

Abbott, A., Medicolegal considerations in professional services, pp. 257-272. In: Hall, L., C. Meyer, and H. Hellerstein, CARDIAC REHABILITATION: EXERCISE TESTING AND PRESCRIPTION (S.P. Medical-Scientific Books, Jamaica, NY 1984).

ACC, BETHESDA CONFERENCE REPORT, 16th BETHESDA CONFERENCE: CARDIOVASCULAR ABNORMALTIES IN THE ATHLETE: RECOMMENDATIONS REGARDING ELIGIBILITY FOR COMPETITION (American College of Cardiovascular, Bethesda, MD 1984, also in *JACC* 6(6):1186-1231, December 1985).

ACSM, GUIDELINES FOR EXERCISE TESTING AND EXERCISE PRESCRIPTION, 3rd Ed. (Lea & Febiger, Philadelphia, PA 1986).

ACSM, POSITION PAPERS OF THE AMERICAN COLLEGE OF SPORTS MEDICINE (American College of Sports Medicine, Indianapolis, IN 1979).

ACSM, RESOURCE MANUAL FOR GUIDELINES FOR EXERCISE TESTING AND PRESCRIPTION (Lea & Febiger, Philadelphia, PA 1988).

AHA, The Committee on Exercise, EXERCISE TESTING AND TRAINING OF APPARENTLY HEALTHY INDIVIDUALS: A HANDBOOK FOR PHYSICIANS (Dallas, TX 1972).

AHA, The Committee of Exercise, EXERCISE TESTING AND TRAINING OF INDIVIDUALS WITH HEART DISEASE OR AT HIGH RISK FOR ITS DEVELOPMENT: A HANDBOOK FOR PHYSICIANS (Dallas, TX 1975).

AHA, THE EXERCISE STANDARDS BOOK (reprinted from *Circulation* 59:421 A, 1979; *Circulation* 59:849 A, 1979; *Circulation* 59:1084 A, 1979; *Circulation* 62:699 A, 1980 (Dallas, TX 1980).

AHA, RECREATIONAL AND OCCUPATIONAL RECOMMENDATIONS FOR YOUNG PATIENTS WITH HEART DISEASE (American Heart Association (Dallas, TX 1986).

AHA, The Subcommittee on Emergency Cardiac Care, McIntyre, J., and J. Lewis (Eds), TEXTBOOK OF ADVANCED CARDIAC LIFE SUPPORT, (2nd Ed., Dallas, TX 1983).

AMA, A GUIDE FOR MEDICAL EVALUATION OF CANDIDATES FOR SCHOOL SPORTS (American Medical Association, Chicago, IL 1966, revised 1972).

AMA, LEGAL IMPLICATIONS OF PRACTICE PARAMETERS (American Medical Association, Chicago, IL 1990).

AMA, MEDICAL EVALUATION OF THE ATHLETE...A GUIDE (American Medical Association, Chicago, IL 1976).

Appenzeller, H., ATHLETICS AND THE LAW (The Michie Corporation, Charlottesville, VA 1975).

Appenzeller, H., FROM THE GYM TO THE JURY (The Michie Corporation, Charlottesville, VA 1971).

Appenzeller, H., SPORTS & LAW (The Michie Corporation, Charlottesville, VA 1985).

Appenzeller, H. and T. Appenzeller, SPORTS AND THE COURTS (The Michie Corporation, Charlottesville, VA 1980).

Baley, J. and D. Matthews, LAW AND LIABILITY IN ATHLETICS, PHYSICAL EDUCATION AND RECREATION (Wm. C. Brown, Dubuque, IA 1988).

Clement, A., LAW IN SPORT AND PHYSICAL ACTIVITY (Benchmark Press, Indianapolis, IN 1988).

Ebel, H., N. Sol, D. Bailey, and S. Schecter (Eds), PRESIDENTIAL SPORTS AWARD FITNESS MANUAL (FitCom Corp., Havertown, PA 1983).

"Exercise Danger: 30 Exercises to Avoid Plus 100 Safer and More Effective Alternatives" (Wellness Australia, 1989 reprint).

Falvo, D., "Informed Consent" pp 193-214, In: EFFECTIVE PATIENT EDUCATION: A GUIDE TO INCREASED COMPLIANCE (Aspen Systems Corp., Rockville, MD 1985).

Froelicher, V., EXERCISE TESTING & TRAINING (Year Book Medical Publishers, Inc., Chicago, IL 1983).

Golding, L., C. Myers, and W. Sinning (Eds), THE Y'S WAY TO PHYSICAL FITNESS (revised): A GUIDEBOOK FOR INSTRUCTORS (Program Resources Office for the National Board of YMCA of the U.S.A., Rosemont, IL 1982).

Herbert, D. and W. Herbert, "Medical-Legal Issues" In: ACSM, GUIDELINES FOR THE TEAM PHYSICIAN (Lea & Febiger, Malvern, PA 1991).

Herbert, W. and D. Herbert, "Legal Considerations" In: Blair, S., Painter, P., Pate, R., Smith, L. and Taylor, C. (Eds), RESOURCE MANUAL FOR GUIDELINES FOR EXERCISE TESTING AND PRESCRIPTION (Lea & Febiger, Philadelphia, PA 1988).

Herbert, D. and W. Herbert, LEGAL ASPECTS OF PREVENTIVE AND REHABILITATIVE EXERCISE PROGRAMS: THIRD EDITION (PRC Publishing, Inc., Canton, OH 1993).

Kaiser, R., LIABILITY AND LAW IN RECREATION, PARKS AND SPORTS (Prentice-Hall, Englewood Cliffs, NJ 1986).

Landry, AIDS IN SPORTS (Leisure Press/Human Kinetics, Champaign, IL 1989).

Mueller, F. and R. Schindler, ANNUAL SURVEY OF FOOTBALL INJURY RESEARCH 1931-1987 (American Football Coaches Association, et al., 1988).

NATA, CODE OF PROFESSIONAL PRACTICE (National Athletic Trainers Association, Inc., Greenville, NC 1983).

NATA, STANDARDS OF PRACTICE (National Athletic Trainers Association, Inc., Greenville, NC 1986).

NIRSA, STANDARDS FOR COLLEGIATE RECREATIONAL SPORTS (National Intramural-Recreational Sports Association, Corvallis, OR 1988).

NOCSAE, MANUAL (National Operating Committee on Standards For Athletic Equipment (NOCSAE) Kansas City, MO 1987).

Nygard, G. and T. Boone, COACHES GUIDE TO SPORT LAW (Human Kinetics, Champaign, IL 1985).

Pollock, M., J. Wilmore and S. Fox, EXERCISE IN HEALTH AND DISEASE: EVALUATION AND PRESCRIPTION FOR PREVENTION AND REHABILITATION (W.B. Saunders Co., Philadelphia, PA 1984).

Riffer, J., SPORTS AND RECREATIONAL INJURIES (McGraw-Hill, Colorado Springs, CO 1985).

Sagall, E., and R. Gumatay, "Exercise Testing, Exercise Training Programs, and The Law," pp. 233-239. In: N.K. Wenger (Ed), EXERCISE AND THE HEART (F.A. Davis, Philadelphia, PA 1978).

Sagall, E., "Legal Implications of Cardiac Rehabilitation Programs," pp 640-649. In: Pollock, M., and D. Schmidt (Eds), HEART DISEASE AND REHABILITATION (Houghton-Mifflin, Boston, MA 1979).

Siegel, G., "The Law and Cardiac Rehabilitation," pp 387-391, In: Naughton, J., H. Hellerstein, and I Mohler (Eds), EXERCISE TESTING AND EXERCISE TRAINING IN CORONARY HEART DISEASE (Academic Press, New York, NY 1973).

U.S. Department of Education, AIDS AND THE EDUCATION OF OUR CHILDREN: A GUIDE FOR PARENTS AND TEACHERS (3rd printing, January, 1988).

Van der Smissen, B., LEGAL LIABILITY AND RISK MANAGEMENT FOR PUBLIC AND PRIVATE ENTITIES (Anderson Publishing Company, Cincinnati, OH 1990).

Weistart, J. and C. Lowell, THE LAW OF SPORTS (The Bobbs-Merrill Company, Inc., Indianpolis, IN 1979).

Wilson, P., P. Fardy, and V. Froelicher, CARDIAC REHABILITATION, ADULT FITNESS AND EXERCISE TESTING (Lea & Febiger, Philadelphia, PA 1981).

PERIODICALS:

"AIDS - A Sports Participant Killer?," *The Sports Medicine Standards and Malpractice Reporter* 2(3):47-48, 1990.

AAP, Policy Statement - "Bicycle Helmets," *AAP News* 12 December, 1989.

AAP, Policy Statement - "Screening for Drugs of Abuse in Children and Adolescents," *AAP News* 9, March, 1989.

Abbott, "Financially Successful Cardiac Rehab Programs: Problems and Solutions," *The Exercise Standards and Malpractice Reporter* 2(6):81-86, 1988.

"Accident-Proofing Your Weight Room," *Athletic Business* 52-55, July 1988.

AMA, Committee on Exercise and Physical Fitness, "Evaluation For Exercise Participation: The Apparently Healthy Individual," *JAMA* 219:900-901, 1972.

AMA, Council on Scientific Affairs, "Indications and Contraindications for Exercise Testing (A Council Report)," *JAMA* 246:1015-1018, 1981.

AMA, "Standards and Guidelines for Cardiopulmonary Resuscitation (CPR) and Emergency Cardiac Care (ECC)," *JAMA* 244:453-509, 1980.

Angsten, "Dance Fitness Standards: To Screen or Not to Screen Participants?," *The Exercise Standards and Malpractice Reporter* 1(1):8-10, 1987.

Angsten, "Overview of Dance Exercise Injury Studies, From Bad to Better: An Industry Improves," *The Exercise Standards and Malpractice Reporter* 2(1):10, 1989.

Angsten, "An Overview of the Standards of Practice for Dance Exercise and Aerobics," *The Exercise Standards and Malpractice Reporter: Lawyer's Edition* 1(2):17-22, 1987.

Angsten, "An Overview of the Standards of Practice for Dance Exercise and Aerobics, Part II: The Use of Expert Witnesses and Standards of Practice in Court," *The Exercise Standards and Malpractice Reporter: Lawyer's Edition* 1(3):36-38, 1987.

Angsten, "Prescription of Activity for Aerobic Dance," *The Exercise Standards and Malpractice Reporter* 2(4):49-51, March, 1989.

Ball, "Playing By The Rules: Roles and Responsibilities of Sportcare Professionals," *Sportcare and Fitness* 40-42, March/April 1989.

Banja, "Informed Consent: Historical Development and Relevance To Exercise and Cardiac Rehabilitation Programs," *The Exercise Standards and Malpractice Reporter* 3(4):53-60, 1989.

Barnes, "Beloved Outlaws - Trainers Look at Liability," *The Physician and Sportsmedicine* 121-129, September 1978.

Benda, "Precamp Physical Exams: Their Value May Be Greater Than You Think," *The Physician and Sportsmedicine* 17(5):167-169, May 1988.

"Bracing Those Knees: How Effective?," *JAMA* 263(2):201, January 12, 1990.

Braden, "Preparticipation Screening for Sudden Cardiac Death in High School and College Athletes," *The Physician and Sportsmedicine* 16(10):128-141, October, 1988.

Brent, "Risk Management in Home Heath Care: Focus on Patient Care Liability," *Loyola University Law Journal* 20:775-795, 1989.

Calabrese & Kelley, "AIDS And Athletes," *The Physician and Sportsmedicine* 17(1):127-132, January, 1989.

Casenote, "Shifting Risks: Washington Blocks Student Athlete Releases," *Gonzaga L. Rev.* 25:259-372, 1989-90.

"Catastrophic Injury: Team Physicians Speak," *The Physician and Sportsmedicine* 16(9):47, September 1988.

Clement, "A Selected Checklist of Risk Management Concerns in Recreational/Sport/Exercise Programs," *The Sports, Parks and Recreation Law Reporter* 1(2):32-34, 1987.

Comodeca, "Constitutional Rights and Participation in Interscholastic Athletics: The Courtroom As The new Playing Field," *The Sports Medicine Standards and Malpractice Reporter* 3(3):47-51, 1991.

Comodeca, "Acknowledgment of Risk Forms: The Best Defense for Sports Medicine Practitioners," *The Sports Medicine Standards and Malpractice Reporter* 4(4):49, 51-54, 1992.

Cooper and Willig, "Nonphysicians for coronary care delivery: are they legal?," *American Journal of Cardiology* 28:363-365, 1971.

Cumming, "Counterpoint: Supervision of Exercise Tests," *ACSM News* 8:6-8, 1973.

DeBusk, "Exercise Test Supervision: Time For a Reassessment," *The Exercise Standards and Malpractice Reporter* 2(5):65-71, 1988.

Deutsch, "Patching Up An Image," *Sports Inc.* 42-43, August 22, 1988.

Deutsch, "Reconditioning A Career," *Sports Inc.* 46-47, February 8, 1988.

Deutsch, "The Fast Flooding of Sports Medicine," *Sports Inc.* 14-20, March 7, 1988.

Deutsch "Rx: Becoming A Team Doctor," *Sports Inc.* 44, January 25, 1988.

Dougherty, "Risk Management in Sports Medicine Programs," *The Sports Medicine Standards and Malpractice Reporter* 1(3):47, 50-54, 1989.

Drowatzky, "AIDS Victims Participation In Sports," *The Sports, Parks and Recreation Law Reporter* 2(1):1-6, 1988.

Drowatzky, "Implications of AIDS in Sports: The Need For Policies and Procedures," *The Sports, Parks and Recreation Law Reporter* 3(3):41-45, 1989.

Drowatzky, "Tort Law, AIDS and Participation in Sports," *The Sports, Parks and Recreation Law Reporter* 2(4):56-59, 1989.

Duda, "Qualifying Care, Patient Rapport, and Sports Medicine Lawsuits," *The Physician and Sportsmedicine* 13(8):165-167, August 1985.

DuRant, et al. "The Pre-Participation Examination of Athletes," *A.G.D.C.* 657-661, 1987.

Dyment, "New Guidelines For Sports Participation," *The Physician and Sportsmedicine* 16(5):45-46, May, 1988.

Edelman, "The Case of <u>Tart v. McGann</u>: Legal Implications Associated with Exercise Stress Testing," *The Exercise Standards and Malpractice Reporter* 1(2):21-26, 1987.

Ehrlick, "Release Signed By Minor Gymnast Deemed to be Unenforceable," *The Sports, Parks and Recreation Law Reporter* 2(2):30-31, 1988.

Eichner, "Sickle Cell Trait and Risks of Exercise-Induced Death," *The Physician and Sportsmedicine* 15(12):41-43, December, 1987.

Evans, "The NCAA Drug Program: Out of Bounds But Still in Play," *Journal of Law & Education* 19(2):161-191, Spring 1990.

Faulkner, "Viewpoint: Screening For and Supervision of Graded Exercise Tests," *ACSM News* 8:6-7, 1973

Feinstein, et al., "The National Survey of Pre-participation Physical Examination Requirements," *The Physician and Sportsmedicine* 16(5):51-59, May 1988.

Feld, Sports Medicine Forum: "Improving Emergency Care," *The Physician and Sportsmedicine* 16(11):44, November, 1988.

Fimrite, "The Battle of His Life," *Sports Illustrated* 67(8):72-80, August 24, 1987.

Franklin, "Exertion - Induced Cardio-Vascular Complications: Is Vigorous Exercise Worth The Risk?," *The Exercise Standards and Malpractice Reporter* 2(3): 33-41, 1988.

Gallup, "Death on the Court: A look at the tragic death of NBA star Reggie Lewis," *The Sports Medicine Standards and Malpractice Reporter* 6(1):12, 1994.

Gerson, "No Pain, No Gain - What's Wrong With Some Exercise Leadership," *The Exercise Standards and Malpractice Reporter* 1(4):52-55, 1987.

Goldberg, "Injury Patterns in Youth Sports," *The Physician and Sportsmedicine* 17(3):175-186, 1989.

Golding, "An Examination of the Standards of Practice of the Young Mens Christian Association (YMCA)," *The Exercise Standards and Malpractice Reporter: Lawyer's Edition* 1(3):29-37, 1987.

Golding, "Standards of Competency For Dance Exercise Instructors," *The Exercise Standards and Malpractice Reporter* 1(3):37-41, 1987.

Graham, "Dodging The Malpractice Bullet," *The Physician and Sportsmedicine* 13(8):168-174, August 1985.

Groves, "Football Heros," *American Medical News* 29-33, January 13, 1989.

Groves, "Pro Football: Do Players Play With Their Health?," *The Physician and Sportsmedicine* 17(1):168-177, January 1989.

Guarriello, "Nursing malpractice litigation: toward better patient care," *Trial* 18:78-82, 1982.

Hawkins, "Sports Medicine Record Keeping: The Key to Effective Communication and Documentation," *The Sports Medicine Standards and Malpractice Reporter* 1(2):31-35, 1989.

Hawkins, "The Legal Status of Athletic Trainers," *The Sports, Parks and Recreation Law Reporter* 2(1):6-9, 1988.

Hawkins, "The Role of Written Wellness Assessments in Exercise Programming," *The Exercise Standards and Malpractice Reporter* 3(1):8-11, 1989.

Herbert, "Avoiding Equipment Injuries and Claims," *Fitness Management* 36, August 1985.

Herbert, "A Profile of the American College of Sports Medicine," *The Exercise Standards and Malpractice Reporter: Lawyer's Edition* 1(2):13-17, 1987.

Herbert, "The Use of Prospective Releases Containing Exculpatory Language in Exercise and Fitness Programs," *The Exercise Standards and Malpractice Reporter* 1(5):75-78, 1987.

Herbert, "Who Will Judge Your Professional Conduct in Court?," *The Exercise Standards and Malpractice Reporter* 1(1):14-16, 1987.

Herbert, "Is There a Duty to Warn Those Within a Zone of Danger During Recreational Exercise Activities?," *The Exercise Standards and Malpractice Reporter* 1(3):39-40, 1987.

Herbert, "The Application of Informed Consent Principles to Exercise Stress Testing Procedures," *The Exercise Standards and Malpractice Reporter: Lawyer's Edition* 1(3):43-44, 1987.

Herbert, "Is There a Legally Mandated Duty to Screen Exercise Participants Prior to Exercise?," *The Exercise Standards and Malpractice Reporter* 1(2):22-23, 1987.

Herbert, "Legal Aspects of Fitness Management," *Fitness Management* 28, 49, Nov/Dec 1987.

Herbert, "The Use of Prospective Releases Containing Exculpatory Language in a Medical Setting...," *The Exercise Standards and Malpractice Reporter* 1(5):75-78, 1987.

Herbert, "Provide Services or Just Facilities? The Legal Concerns are Different," *Fitness Management* 45, January 1988.

Herbert, "Are Nutritionists Engaged in the Unauthorized Practice of Medicine?," *The Exercise Standards and Malpractice Reporter* 2(5):76-78, 1988.

Herbert, "Coach and Administrator Responsibility for Mismatches and Injuries Due to Fatigue - An Examination of Recent Trends," *The Sports, Parks and Recreation Law Reporter* 2(3):33-38, December 1988.

Herbert, "Equipment Injury Trends," *The Exercise Standards and Malpractice Reporter* 2(4):57-58, 1988.

Herbert, "Frequent Claims and Suits in Equipment Related Injuries," *Fitness Management* 22, July, 1988.

Herbert, "Is Physician Supervision of Exercise Stress Testing Required?," *The Exercise Standards and Malpractice Reporter* 2(1):6-7, 1988.

Herbert, "Know Your Legal Responsibilities in Administering Stress Testing," *Fitness Management* 16, 67, July/August, 1988.

Herbert, "Legal Aspects of Fitness Premises Liability," *Fitness Management* 17-19, September, 1988.

Herbert, "Legal Aspects of Water Based Activities," *Fitness Management* 37, March 1988.

Herbert, "Legal Aspects of Sports Medicine Programs," *Fitness Management* 14, May/June 1988.

Herbert, "Managing the Risk of Dance Exercise Programs," *Fitness Management* 45, 51, April 1988.

Herbert, "Risk Disclosure in The Informed Consent Process: Judging the Adequacy of Disclosure in Light of the Patient's Need for Information, An Emerging Trend," *The Exercise Standards and Malpractice Reporter* 2(4):56-57, 1988.

Herbert, "Should Athletic Trainers Be Held To The Standard of Care of Physicians," *The Sports, Parks and Recreation Law Reporter* 1(4):56-58, 1988.

Herbert, "AIDS in Sports," *The Sports, Parks and Recreation Law Reporter* 3(3):46, 1989.

Herbert, "Protection From Claim And Suit in Fitness Activities for Kids," *Fitness Management* 5(3):15-16, March 1989.

Herbert, "A Runner's Death: Suit Against Race 'Sponsor' Results in Defense Verdict," *The Exercise Standards and Malpractice Reporter* 3(1):27-28, 1989.

Herbert, "Appropriate Use of Wellness Appraisals," *Fitness Management* 23, September 1989.

Herbert, "Dispensing Prescription Medications to Athletes: Pitfalls and Potential Problems," *The Sports Medicine Standards and Malpractice Reporter* 1(4):67, 69-73, 1989.

Herbert, "Exercise Equipment Injury Trends," *The Exercise Standards and Malpractice Reporter* 3(1):25-27, 1989.

Herbert, "Keeping Up With the Changing Standard of Care," *The Exercise Standards and Malpractice Reporter* 3(3):37-43, 1989.

Herbert, "The Development of AIDS Guidelines for Sports Programs," *The Sports, Parks and Recreation Law Reporter* 3(1):12-19, 1989.

Herbert, "Prospective Releases Must Conform to Law," *Fitness Management* 24, July 1989.

Herbert, "Legal Implications in Health Screening Use," *Fitness Management* 19, December 1989.

Herbert, "The Use of Prospective Releases in Exercise Facilities: An Update," *The Exercise Standards and Malpractice Reporter* 3(2):32-35, 1989.

Herbert, "Legal Aspects of Nutritional Advice," *Fitness Management* 19-39, February 1989.

Herbert, "Medical-Legal Concerns and Risk Management Suggestions For Medical Directors of Exercise and Rehabilitation and Maintenance Programs," *The Exercise Standards and Malpractice Reporter* 3(3):44-48, 1989.

Herbert, "Dieting Advice Can Lead to Litigation," *Fitness Management* 42, January 1990.

Herbert, "Express Assumption of Risk and Decisions to Exclude From Play - The Sports Medicine Dilemma," *The Sports Medicine Standards and Malpractice Reporter* 2(1):1, 3-7, 1990.

Herbert, "Is There a Need to Screen Participants Before Recreational Activity?," *The Sports Medicine Standards and Malpractice Reporter* 2(1):11-12, 1990.

Herbert, "Liability Associated With Dieting Advice and Publications," *The Exercise Standards and Malpractice Reporter* 4(1):9, 1990.

Herbert, "Personal Fitness Trainers' Higher Duty of Care," *Fitness Management* 23, July 1990.

Herbert, "The Death of Hank Gathers: An Examination of the Legal Issues," *The Sports Medicine Standards and Malpractice Reporter* 2(3):45-47, 1990.

Herbert, "The Death of Hank Gathers: Implications to The Standard of Care for Pre-participation Screening?," *The Sports Medicine Standards and Malpractice Reporter* 2(3):41-45, 1990.

Herbert, "Coach/Administrator Interference With Medical Care For Athletes," *The Sports Medicine Standards and Malpractice Reporter* 3(1):1, 3-5, 1991.

Herbert, "The Use of Warning/Instructional Signs in Activity Areas," *The Sports Medicine Standards and Malpractice Reporter* 3(1):5-6, 1991.

Herbert, "Conspiracy to Withhold Information Case Against Professional Hockey Team and Physician Dismissed: The Case of Martin vs. Casagrande," *The Sports Medicine Standards and Malpractice Reporter* 3(1):8-9, 1991.

Herbert, "New Sample Informed Consent Forms From The AHA, AACVPR and The ACSM," *The Sports Medicine Standards and Malpractice Reporter* 3(2):21, 23-25, 1991.

Herbert, "A Critical Review of Emergency Response in Sports Medicine," *The Sports Medicine Standards and Malpractice Reporter* 3(2):32-33, 1991.

Herbert, "New Sports Medicine Standards: A Look at the New AAP Policy Statement on AIDS in the Athletic Setting," *The Sports Medicine Standards and Malpractice Reporter* 3(4):61, 63-65, 1991.

Herbert, "Supervision of Children," *The Sports Medicine Standards and Malpractice Reporter* 3(4):69, 1991.

Herbert, "A Look at Potential Damages in Sports Medicine Malpractice Cases," *The Sports Medicine Standards and Malpractice Reporter* 4(1):1, 3, 1992.

Herbert, "Fitness Examination Results in Malpractice Action," *The Sports Medicine Standards and Malpractice Reporter* 4(1):5, 1992.

Herbert, "Self Referrals in Sports Medicine," *The Sports Medicine Standards and Malpractice Reporter* 4(2):17, 19-21, 1992.

Herbert, "An Examination of Weight Training For Children," *The Sports Medicine Standards and Malpractice Reporter* 4(2):22, 1992.

Herbert, "Stress Test Results in Death and Million Dollar Verdict," *The Sports Medicine Standards and Malpractice Reporter* 4(3):33, 36, 1992.

Herbert, "An Examination of the New ACSM Standards and Guidelines for Health/Fitness Facilities," *The Sports Medicine Standards and Malpractice Reporter* 4(3):42-43, 1992.

Herbert, "Just Who Is A Sports Medicine Practitioner?," *The Sports Medicine Standards and Malpractice Reporter* 4(4):56-57, 1992.

Herbert, "New ACSM Standards For Health Clubs Come Under Attack," *The Sports Medicine Standards and Malpractice Reporter* 4(4):60, 1992.

Herbert, "HIV/AIDS and Athletic Participation – The Year in Review," *The Sports Medicine Standards and Malpractice Reporter* 5(1):1, 4, 1993.

Herbert, "NCAA Drug Distribution Study For University Athletic Programs," *The Sports Medicine Standards and Malpractice Reporter* 5(1):5-6, 1993.

Herbert, "Another Basketball Star Dies," *The Sports Medicine Standards and Malpractice Reporter* 5(2):17, 19-20, 1993.

Herbert, "Exercise Tests Are Not Inherently Dangerous," *The Sports Medicine Standards and Malpractice Reporter* 5(3):33, 36-37, 1993.

Herbert, "Developing Policies and Procedures for Sports Medicine Programs," *The Sports Medicine Standards and Malpractice Reporter* 5(3):43, 1993.

Herbert, "New Standards of Practice and Professional Concerns: Debate over provider standards is not new," *The Sports Medicine Standards and Malpractice Reporter* 5(4):49, 52-53, 1993.

Herbert, "Will Blood Spattering Rules to Protect Against Bloodborne Pathogens Affect Play?," *The Sports Medicine Standards and Malpractice Reporter* 5(4):56-57, 1993.

"Herpes Gladitorium at a High School Wrestling Camp - Minnesota," *MMWR* 39(5):69-71, February 9, 1990.

"Herpes Gladitorium Pins Wisconsin Wrestlers," *The Physician and Sportsmedicine* 17(3):50, 255, March 1989.

"Highly Regarded Study Supports Knee Braces," *The Physician and Sportsmedicine*12):19-20, December 1989.

Howe, "Primary Care Sports Medicine: A Part Timer's Perspective," *The Physician and Sportsmedicine* 16(1):103-114, January 1988.

Hyman & Feiger, "Legal Aspects of Health and Fitness Clubs: A Healthy and Dangerous Industry," *The Colorado Lawyer* 1787-1794, October 1986.

Herbert & Herbert, "A Window of Legal Vulnerability?," *Optimal Health* 1(4):22-25, March/April, 1985.

Herbert & Herbert, "Equipment Deficiencies and Improper Instruction," *Fitness Management* 12-19, Jan. 1989.

Herbert & Herbert, "Frequent Claims and Suits in Equipment Related Injuries," *Fitness Management* 22, 1988.

Herbert & Herbert, "Legal Implications of Wellness and Health Promotion Programs," *Fitness in Business* 210-215, 1988.

Herbert & Herbert, "Reducing Your Potential Liabilities Through Risk Management Services," *Fitness Management* 31-32, 83, 1988.

Herbert & Herbert, "The Legal Aspects of Exercise Leadership in Fitness Programs," *Aerobics & Fitness* 4(1):52-54, 1986.

Herbert & Herbert, "Waivers and Releases," *American Fitness* 38-39, September 1987.

Herbert & Herbert, "Exercise Testing in Adults: Legal and Procedural Considerations for the Physical Educator and Exercise Specialist," *JOPHER* 17-19, June, 1975.

Herbert, Herbert & Berger, "A Trial Lawyer's Guide to the Legal Implications of Recreational, Preventive and Rehabilitative Exercise Program Standards of Care," *American Journal of Trial Advocacy* 11(3):433-452, 1988.

Howell, "Primary Care Sports Medicine: A Part Timer's Perspective," *The Physician and Sportsmedicine* 16(1):103-114, 1988.

Hyman & Feiger, "Legal Aspects of Health & Fitness Clubs: A Healthy and Dangerous Industry," *Colorado Lawyer* 15:1787-1794 (1986).

Johnson, "Some Sports-Medicine Specialists May Not Give Special, or Safe Care," *The Wall Street Journal,* Tuesday, November 12, 1985, p. 6.

Jones, et al., "Sudden Death in Sickle-Cell Trait," *The New England Journal of Medicine* 282:323-5, 1970.

Kark, et al., "Sickle-Cell Trait As A Risk Factor For Sudden Death in Physical Training," *The New England Journal of Medicine* 317(13):781-787, September 24, 1987.

Kimiecik, "Who Needs Coaches' Education? - Us Coaches Do," *The Physician and Sportsmedicine* 16(11):124-136, November 1988.

King, "The Duty and Standard of Care For Team Physicians," *Houston Law Review* 18(4):657-705, May 1981.

Kenney, "Considerations for Preventive and Rehabilitative Exercise Programs During Periods of High Heat and Humidity," *The Exercise Standards and Malpractice Reporter* 3(1):1-7, 1989.

Koeberle, "Personal Fitness Liability: A Trainer's Guide to Legal Fitness," *The Exercise Standards and Malpractice Reporter* 3(5):74-79, 1989.

Koeberle, ONE-TO-ONE: "Liability in the Home," *IDEA Today* 40-43, April 1990.

Kupcho, "What Is Risk Management?," *The Exercise Standards and Malpractice Reporter* 1(2):26-27, 1987.

Laster-Bradley, "Legal Aspects of Drug Distribution in Athletic Training Rooms," *The Sports Medicine Standards and Malpractice Reporter* 5(1):6-9, 1993.

Leslie, War and Peace With Hypocrates - A Modern Dilemma Facing Sports Medicine," *The Sports Medicine Standards and Malpractice Reporter* 2(2):21, 24-28, 1990.

Loeffler, "On Being A Team Physician," *Sports Medicine Digest* 9(2):1-3, February 1987.

Lubell, "Does Steroid Abuse Cause - or Exercise Violence?," *The Physician and Sportsmedicine* 17(2):176-185, February 1989.

Lubell, "Insurance, Liability, and the American Way of Sports," *The Physician and Sportsmedicine* 15(9):192-200, September, 1987.

Lubell, "Potentially Dangerous Exercises: Are They Harmful to All?," *The Physician and Sportsmedicine* 17(1):187-192, 1989.

Lubell, "Questioning the Athlete's Right to Sue," *The Physician and Sportsmedicine* 17(3):240-244, March 1989.

Macri, "The Negative Effect of the Legal System on Sports Medicine," *The Sports Medicine Standards and Malpractice Reporter* 6(1):1, 4-5, 1994.

Manahan, "Sickle Cell Trait - A Risk For Sudden Death During Physical Activity?," *The Physician and Sportsmedicine* 15(12):143-145, December 1987.

Marks, "Is Your Fitness Instructor's Certification Legally Defensible," *The Exercise Standards and Malpractice Reporter* 2(4): 53-56, 1988.

McKeag, "Criteria For Return to Participation," *The Sports Medicine Standards and Malpractice Reporter* 2(4):61, 65-69, 1990.

Merk, "Youth Athletics: A Guide to Safe Participation," *The Sports Medicine Standards and Malpractice Reporter* 6(1):6-11, 1994.

Mitten, "Practitioners' Duties to Advise and to Warn: Legal issues concerning HIV-positive athletes," *The Sports Medicine Standards and Malpractice Reporter* 6(1):13-15, 1994.

Mitten, "Team Physicians and Competitive Athletes: Allocating Legal Responsibility for Athletic Injuries," *The Sports Medicine Standards and Malpractice Reporter* 3(1):1, 3-5, 1991.

Monahan, "Sickle-Cell Trait: A Risk For Sudden Death During Physicial Activity?," *The Physician and Sportsmedicine* 15(12):143-145, December, 1987.

Mueller, et al., "Catatrophic Spine Injuries in Football," *The Physician and Sportsmedicine* 17(10):51-53, October 1989.

Munnings "A Team Physician At Work," *The Physician and Sportsmedicine* 16(1):177-179, January 1988.

Munnings, "The Death of Hank Gathers: A Legacy of Confusion," *The Physician and Sportsmedicine* 18(5):97-102, May 1990.

Nichols, et al., "A Historical Perspective of Injuries in Professional Football: Twenty Six Years of Game-Related Events," *JAMA* 260(7):939-944, August 19, 1988.

Rabinoff, "An Examination of Four Recent Cases Against Fitness Instructors," *The Exercise Standards and Malpractice Reporter* 2(3):43-47, 1988.

Rabinoff, "Weight Room Litigation: What's it All About?," *The Sports Medicine Standards and Malpractice Reporter* 5(4):53-55, 1993.

Richie, "Medical-Legal Implications of Dance Exercise Prescription and Leadership: The Risk of Injury," *The Exercise Standards and Malpractice Reporter* 2(2):17-23, 1988.

Richie, "Medical-Legal Implications of Dance Exercise Leadership: The Aerobic Dance Floor Surface," *The Exercise Standards and Malpractice Reporter* 2(6):87-88, 1988.

Richie, "Medical-Legal Implications of Dance Exercise Leadership: The Role of Footwear," *The Exercise Standards and Malpractice Reporter* 3(4):60-62, 1989.

Robertson, "Hank Gather's Case Challenges The Role of Team Physicians," *Medical Malpractice Law & Strategy* 7(7):3, May 1990.

Rochmis and Blackburn, "Exercise Tests: A Survey of Procedures, Safety and Litigation Exerience in Approximately 170,000 Tests," *JAMA* 217(8):1061-1066, 1971.

Roos, "Are Physician Credentials in Sports Medicine Needed Now?," *The Physician and Sportsmedicine* 14(3):262-270, March 1986.

Roy, et al., "Body Checking in Pee Wee Hockey," *The Physician and Sportsmedicine* 17(3):119-126, 1989.

Rupp, "Ethics in Sports Medicine Research: The Role of The Institutional Review Board," *The Sports Medicine Standards and Malpractice Reporter* 3(3):41, 44-46, 1991.

Rushing, "Legal Liability Associated With The Spread of Herpes Gladiatorum," *The Sports Medicine Standards and Malpractice Reporter* 4(3):37-39, 1992.

Russell, "Legal and Athical Conflicts Arising From the Team Physician's Dual Obligation to the Athlete and Management," *JOSM* 25-26, December 1987.

Ryan, "Establishing The Identity of Sports Medicine Physicians," *The Physician and Sportsmedicine*16(8):31, August 1988.

Samples, "Mind Over Muscle: Returning the Injured Athlete To Play," *The Physician and Sportsmedicine*15(10):172-180, October 1987.

Samples, "The Team Physician: No Offered Job Description," *The Physician and Sportsmedicine*16(1):169-175, January 1988.

"Sharing A Water Bottle: A Dangerous Practice?," *The Physician and Sportsmedicine*16(7):29-30, July 1988.

"Steroids and Human Growth Hormone," *JAMA* 259(11):1703-1705, March 18, 1988.

Strauss, EDITORS NOTES: "Learning About Risk The Hard Way," *The Physician and Sportsmedicine* 18(5):3, May 1990.

Strauss, "Sports Physicians: Caught Between Health and the Pursuit of Happiness," *The Physician and Sportsmedicine*18(5):26, May 1990.

Todaro, "Sports Medicine Malpractice," *Trial* 34-38, May 1985.

Tucker, et al., "Medical Coverage of High School Football in New York State," *The Physician and Sportsmedicine*16(a):120-130, September 1988.

Thomas & Cantwell, "Sudden Death During Basketball Games," *The Physician and Sportsmedicine*18(5):75-78, May 1990.

Thompson, "Clinical Laboratory Improvement Amendments of 1988," *The Sports Medicine Standards and Malpractice Reporter* 4(4):55-56, 1992.

"Wrestling Headgear Prevents Ear Damage," *The Physician and Sportsmedicine*17(10):29, October, 1989.

INDEX